MW00795231

WOMEN'S STUDIES QUARTERLY
VOLUME 46   NUMBERS 1 & 2   SPRING/SUMMER 2018

An educational project of the Feminist Press at the City University of New York, the College of Staten Island, City University of New York, and LaGuardia Community College, City University of New York, with support from the Center for the Study of Women and Society at the Graduate Center, City University of New York

EDITORS
Natalie Havlin, LaGuardia Community College, City University of New York
Jillian M. Báez, College of Staten Island, City University of New York

FICTION/NONFICTION/PROSE EDITOR
Rosalie Morales Kearns

POETRY EDITOR
Patricia Smith

EDITORIAL ASSISTANTS
Elena Cohen
Lindsey Eckenroth
Melina Moore

EDITORS EMERITAE
Matt Brim 2014–2017 ▪ Cynthia Chris 2014–2017
Amy Herzog 2011–2014 ▪ Joe Rollins 2011–2014
Victoria Pitts-Taylor 2008–2011 ▪ Talia Schaffer 2008–2011
Cindi Katz 2004–2008 ▪ Nancy K. Miller 2004–2008
Diane Hope 2000–2004 ▪ Janet Zandy 1995–2000
Nancy Porter 1982–1992 ▪ Florence Howe 1972–1982; 1993–1994

The Feminist Press at the City University of New York

EXECUTIVE DIRECTOR
Jamia Wilson

ART DIRECTOR
Drew Stevens

EDITOR
Lauren Rosemary Hook

SENIOR GRAPHIC DESIGNER
Suki Boynton

ASSOCIATE EDITOR
Alyea Canada

SALES & MARKETING MANAGER
Jisu Kim

WSQ: Women's Studies Quarterly, a peer-reviewed, theme-based journal, is published in the summer and winter by the Feminist Press at the City University of New York.

COVER ART
Decolonize Pussy Power Ed. 7.20 by Favianna Rodríguez

WEBSITE
feministpress.org/wsq

EDITORIAL CORRESPONDENCE
WSQ: Women's Studies Quarterly, The Feminist Press at the City University of New York, The Graduate Center, 365 Fifth Avenue, Suite 5406, New York, NY 10016; wsqeditorial@gmail.com.

PRINT SUBSCRIPTIONS
Subscribers in the United States: Individuals—$60 for 1 year; $150 for 3 years. Institutions—$85 for 1 year; $225 for 3 years. Subscribers outside the United States: Add $40 per year for delivery. To subscribe or change an address, contact *WSQ* Customer Service, The Feminist Press at the City University of New York, The Graduate Center, 365 Fifth Avenue, Suite 5406, New York, NY 10016; 212-817-7915; info@feministpress.org.

FORTHCOMING ISSUES
Protest, Elena L. Cohen, The Graduate Center, City University of New York, Melissa
    M. Forbis, Stony Brook University, State University of New York, Deepti Misri,
    University of Colorado Boulder, and Saadia Toor, College of Staten Island, City
    University of New York
Asian Diasporas, Lili Shi, Kingsborough Community College, City University of
    New York and Yadira Perez Hazel, University of Melbourne

RIGHTS & PERMISSIONS
Fred Courtright, The Permissions Company, 570-839-7477; permdude@eclipse.net.

SUBMISSION INFORMATION
For the most up-to-date guidelines, calls for papers, and information concerning forthcoming issues, write to wsqeditorial@gmail.com or visit feministpress.org/wsq.

ADVERTISING
For information on display-ad sizes, rates, exchanges, and schedules, please write to *WSQ* Marketing, The Feminist Press at the City University of New York,
The Graduate Center, 365 Fifth Avenue, Suite 5406, New York, NY 10016; 212-817-7918; sales@feministpress.org.

ELECTRONIC ACCESS AND SUBSCRIPTIONS
Access to electronic databases containing backlist issues of *WSQ* may be purchased through JSTOR at www.jstor.org. Access to electronic databases containing current issues of *WSQ* may be purchased through Project MUSE at muse.jhu.edu, muse@muse.jhu.edu; and ProQuest at www.il.proquest.com, info@il.proquest.com. Individual electronic subscriptions for *WSQ* may also be purchased through Project MUSE.

ISSN: 0732-1562   ISBN: 978-1-936932-20-7 $25.00

Emily Wilbourne, Queens College and the Graduate Center, City University of
   New York
Karen Winkler, Psychotherapist
Elizabeth Wissinger, Borough of Manhattan Community College and the Graduate
   Center, City University of New York

Ex officio:
Hester Eisenstein, Acting Director, Program in Women's and Gender Studies, Center for
   Study of Women and Society, The Graduate Center, City University of New York

Contents

9   **Note from the Board**
Elena Glasberg and Elizabeth Wissinger

13   **Introduction: Revisiting Beauty**
Natalie Havlin and Jillian M. Báez

PART I. **PERFORMING BEAUTY**

29   **Big, *Bakla*, and Beautiful: Transformations on a Manila Pageant Stage**
Emmanuel David and Christian Joy P. Cruz

46   **Mapping Beauty, Fashion, and Femininity: Recent Contributions by Blain Roberts, Marcia Ochoa, and Vanita Reddy**
Manuel G. Avilés-Santiago

PART II. **THE POLITICS OF STYLE**

53   **Style Politics and Self-Fashioning in Mamie Garvin Fields's *Lemon Swamp and Other Places***
Erica L. Ball

70   **Dying to Be Beautiful: (Re)Membering the Women of Juárez, the Commodification of Death, and the Nonuniversal Standards of Beauty**
Bernadine Hernández

88   **Fashioning Identity Work: The Perils, Politics, and Pleasures of Aesthetic Labor**
David A. Sanchez-Aguilera

94 **Picture Perfect: Lessons in the War for Self-Love**
Jodi M. Savage

PART III. **MEDIATING BEAUTY**

105 **Remnants of Venus: Signifying Black Beauty and Sexuality**
Janell Hobson

121 **Putting a "Good Face on the Nation": Beauty, Memes, and the
Gendered Rebranding of Global *Colombianidad***
María Elena Cepeda

139 **Beauty as an "act of political warfare":
Feminist Makeup Tutorials and Masquerades on YouTube**
Michele White

157 **A Fair Face**
Monica Macansantos

PART IV. **RETHINKING BEAUTY IDEALS AND PRACTICES**

167 **Toward a Phenomenological Analysis of Historicized Beauty Practices**
Allison Vandenberg

181 **The Soccer Tournament as Beauty Pageant: Eugenic Logics in
Brazilian Women's *Futebol Feminino***
Cara Snyder

199 **Controlling Beauty Ideals: Caribbean Women, Thick Bodies,
and White Supremacist Discourse**
Kamille Gentles-Peart

215 **Subject/Object/Body: Recent Perspectives on Beauty and
Aesthetics in Gender Studies**
Freda Fair

221 **A Brief History of Beauty**
Nina Sharma

PART V. **"AN UNSHAMED CLAIM TO BEAUTY IN THE FACE OF INVISIBILITY":**
         REVISITING SINS INVALID

227 **Ten Principles of Disability Justice**
     Patricia Berne, David Langstaff, and Aurora Levins Morales,
     on behalf of Sins Invalid

231 **Reclaiming and Honoring: Sins Invalid's Cultivation of Crip Beauty**
     Shayda Kafai

237 **Disability Justice and Beauty as a Liberatory Practice**
     Mordecai Cohen Ettinger

241 **"Beauty Always Recognizes Itself": A Roundtable on Sins Invalid**
     Patricia Berne, Jamal T. Lewis, Stacey Milbern, Malcolm Shanks,
     Alok Vaid-Menon, and Alice Wong

PART VI. **POETIC WORK**

255 **Now I will crack my sternum**
     Kristi Carter

256 **Congratulations:**
     Kristi Carter

259 **To Come Undone**
     Tanya Grae

261 **If Barbie Had a Brain**
     Tanya Grae

262 **On Demand**
     Linda Flaherty Haltmaier

263 **Processing Imperfections Over Lunch**
     Linda Flaherty Haltmaier

265 **From Underwater**
     Sarah Janczak

266 **After the Illness Came I Went**
     Sarah Janczak

268 **Congenitus**
Sarah Janczak

270 **I've Lost My Looks**
Elizabeth Johnston

272 **Big Fat Truth**
Elizabeth Johnston

274 **Snake Oil**
Donna J. Gelagotis Lee

PART VII. **ALERTS AND PROVOCATIONS**

279 **On Beauty and Protest**
Vanessa Pérez-Rosario

Note from the Board

Elena Glasberg and Elizabeth Wissinger

Beauty is a killer. It hurts. That is the consensus of the authors collected here. It hurts to be beautiful. And it hurts even more not to be beautiful. This conundrum may explain why the conversation around beauty keeps lingering: the more you critique beauty, the more its mask, its allure, becomes real. If beauty is the hazy cultural fantasy that has real consequences, insisting on its materiality and on the materiality of the female body might kill beauty—before it gets you. But do the authors in this issue want to kill beauty, really? No. Because, for them, beauty is a real, and necessary, enemy.

Beauty is a cultural ideal suited for humanities; a measurable (if highly contested) standard in evolutionary science; an ideal enforced in the fashion industries both strictly and playfully. It is a métier of self-fashioning, and a currency in business and social and familial reproduction. Such a pervasive, if unequally valued, topic across the disciplines might have produced a range of critical and intellectual results. Yet, more than in any recent issue of *WSQ*, the assumptions, concerns, and approaches of these authors cohere and zone in on a very specific target.

Here and now, beauty is the face of white supremacy, so intimately tied to whiteness that, as many of the articles demonstrate, to even counter this ideal and replace it with a specific modifier, such as Black Is Beautiful, seems perversely to strengthen the very exclusions that produced the need for critique. The longing and anger that beauty instigates is palpable and understandable, given the Global North's powerfully relentless racism and sexism, currently voiced in spasmodic outbursts from the highest office of power in the United States. Whether a submissive, sexy, or stilettoed professional gal, the conservative point of view holds women to a standard of

WSQ: Women's Studies Quarterly 46: 1 & 2 (Spring/Summer 2018) © 2018 by Elena Glasberg and Elizabeth Wissinger. All rights reserved.

whiteness, traditional femininity, and conscious display. During Donald J. Trump's presidential campaign, his obsession with appearances played out in his derisive comparison of his wife to that of fellow presidential candidate Ted Cruz. Pitting a regular woman against a supermodel in a beauty contest? Of course the model will win. These games are played with full knowledge of the symbols they invoke. Consider how Ivanka's lean lines in her white pantsuit still sting a year after Inauguration Day. Co-opting its historic feminist meaning for her own ends, it was a clear rebuke to Hillary's stodginess, as if to say *this* is how it's done, ladies.

In this political moment, it goes without saying that beauty is not only raced but also hyperfeminized—think of Melania and Ivanka's fembot proportions sheathed in a granite veneer as the insanely skewed "standard." Most insistently, this collection reflects a beauty conversation within feminism as a women-to-women transmission. Perhaps, given its current and historical connections to femininity, beauty as a topic opens itself up to an anti-woman bias that, it appears, runs through the feminist community as deeply as it does in the greater world. No matter the historical and complexities of populations, beauty disproportionately continues to shape and burden the category and sign of woman.

Is beauty a plot? Is its goal to exclude an enormous outcast group— basically everyone on earth except for normative-bodied, cis, heterosexual, young, thin, healthy, employed women of vaguely European descent—a group that seems to be precisely delineated but really means the white women in our immediate orbits? Many of the essays collected here lean toward assuming beauty as a standard, specifically a white, heterosexist standard deployed (even designed) to promote the power of the few over an ugly, nonwhite, majority world.

These articles document a struggle against this assumed white, hyperfeminine ideal from a range of subject positions. Yet, excoriating beauty paradoxically risks promoting its foundational lie: there just is not enough beauty to go around, that it is a finite resource, an allocation distributed strictly along racial lines from mother to daughter and through advertising and other institutions, even when run by nonwhites. One of the implications of beauty standards, if not beauty itself, is to tamp down diversity, or to disallow multiple or even unimagined beauties. And yet, this special issue's almost universally indignant and suspicious response to beauty may be the beginning of another kind of beauty emergent beyond the political horizon.

But in the meantime, it might be possible to ruin beauty, or at least spoil its power to ruin us. We see glimmers of this in the accounts of those who admit their failure in the face of cruel beauty, as in Emmanuel David and Christian Joy P. Cruz's ethnography of the contestants in Bilbiling Pilipinas, who with remorseless humor perform their unfitness in mock beauty contests for appreciative audiences around Manila, or the creators of YouTube makeup tutorials, written about by Michele White, who expose the tacit rules behind the production of feminine beauty in campy countertutorials that are all the more incisive for not entirely dismissing genuine advice: you can learn to choose a more flattering foundation even while being encouraged to "crush capitalism." Rather than obeying the conscripts of gender politics, making up your face becomes an art of the takedown, an act of "political warfare." A slash of red lipstick is a source of pleasure, defiance, and cunning. Refashioning for resilience rather than retooling for acceptance is offered as a more effective means of reconfiguring the sexist, white-supremacist, beauty complex that so many of these essays engage. Is fighting for inclusion within a static ideal just as powerful as renegotiating that ideal by sending it up, to laugh at its role in inflicting shame and pain? Can rhinestones, sequins, and wit defang the beast in beauty? When there's power in knowing your own body, to name it and claim it, there is also power to name your own terms rather than be externally defined.

The consistency of the response to beauty's assault across time and discipline hints at the surprising depth of the problem (the beast). Speaking truth to beauty is often an ugly business. It requires just the kind of seriousness and persistence demonstrated in this issue of WSQ. This political-critical work, so grinding and single-minded and yet so necessary, is figured in Tanya Grae's poem calling up the ultimate icon of all that is not right with beauty: Barbie. It turns out Barbie, the obvious, even exhausted plastic idol we love to hate and hate ourselves for loving (and hating), has a brain somewhere above her famously smooth torso and impossibly proportioned limbs. Severed from her body, her head does the thinking for us:

She knows

about the curb, where your things tend
to end & wants you to know

doll patience is painted.

In this poem, rather than replace Barbie with a more suitable, holistic beauty that might empower women, or even kill her outright, instead the castoff persists and perseveres from the curb that feminism kicked her to. Her goal, however, is not to be re-membered or resurrected and made whole again or to be made more representative of a range of real women, but through her ever-vigilant mask to outlast even her own history of being the face of oppression.

Barbie's "doll patience" is a double haunting of the castoffs of a beauty complex already figured as excess. It will be the ugly and rejected, the ill and the challenged, the nonconformists and parodists who might lead the way out from under beauty's coercions, who along with the feminist social critique gathered in this special issue, outlast and even transform beauty into, to borrow from Mordecai Cohen Ettinger's title, "a liberatory practice."

Elena Glasberg
Expository Writing Program
New York University

Elizabeth Wissinger
Professor of Fashion Studies
Graduate School and University Center
Master's Program in Liberal Studies
Professor of Sociology
Borough of Manhattan
     Community College
City University of New York

Introduction: Revisiting Beauty

Natalie Havlin and Jillian M. Báez

As Central America's smallest, but most densely populated country, El Salvador sits at the edge of the Pacific Ocean. In some ways, El Salvador is a progressive nation following its civil war (1979–1992), spurred by military repression and income equality. For example, despite its small geographic size and poverty, El Salvador is internationally known for refusing to accept Monsanto's genetically modified seeds (Malkin 2014). Monsanto, a large and powerful corporation based in the United States, holds a monopoly over seeds sold to farmers throughout the globe. However, El Salvador is also the most violent nation in the Western hemisphere (Data Team 2017) fueled by political corruption, economic depression (partly due to changing the currency to the U.S. dollar in 2001), and patriarchal and homophobic norms governing post–civil war Salvadoran society. While the violence of Salvadoran gangs—largely comprised of disenfranchised and undocumented youth growing up in U.S. cities who are frequently deported to El Salvador—are often reported in U.S. news outlets, non-gang-related violence is less known outside of El Salvador. For example, trans people face the most violence in El Salvador than in any other nation in the world (Renteria 2017). Trans women are most often attacked because of their appearance and whether or not they pass for cis women. Beauty practices are at the heart of this type of violence because one's life is dependent on conforming to local, hyperfeminine beauty ideals.

We open *Beauty* with this specific case as a reminder that beauty is not a frivolous concept nor practice. In many corners of the world, if and how one chooses to challenge beauty regimes cannot only lead to marginal-

WSQ: Women's Studies Quarterly 46: 1 & 2 (Spring/Summer 2018)

ization but also sometimes violence. As such, this issue emphasizes the
materiality of beauty.

The politics of beauty have been heavily debated within feminist studies and LGBTQ studies. While some feminists critiqued beauty as an extension of patriarchal gender regimes, other feminists reconceptualized
beauty as a form of play and identity expression (Church Gibson 2013). At
the same time, women of color feminists, particularly black and Chicana
feminists, such as bell hooks and Amalia Mesa-Bains (2006), and María
Elena Cepeda (2008), acknowledge the significance of beauty—not only
as personal adornment but also as a mode of survival. Moving away from
white second wave feminists who dismissed beauty as mere compliance
with patriarchal expectations, some women of color feminists embraced
beauty as a site of agency. In response, LGBTQ studies and critical disability studies critique heteronormative beauty regimes and explore the po-
tentials of non-gender-normative stylizations and more inclusive modes
of recognition. This issue of *WSQ* places new interventions in gender and
sexuality studies in conversation with these debates.

The pieces in this issue take a critical and transgressive approach to
gendered and sexualized conceptions of beauty. What is gendered beauty?
How can we know that something is beautiful? Is the pursuit of beauty
a fruitful endeavor in gender and sexuality studies? How is beauty being
redefined, especially in light of race, disability, class, gender, sexuality, and
economics? How are dominant beauty regimes steeped in racism, gender
binaries, sexism, able-bodiedness, homophobia, colonialism, and capitalism? How do marginalized communities engage in beauty practices as
forms of survival and resistance? How does beauty undergird countercultural movements? What is the relationship between beauty and aesthetics?

Early germinal feminist scholarship dismisses beauty as a form of patriarchal subjugation. For example, in her classic text *The Beauty Myth* (1990),
Naomi Wolf calls attention to the unrealistic beauty standards expected of
women in our male-dominated society. In *Unbearable Weight: Feminism,
Western Culture, and the Body* (1993), Susan Bordo builds on Wolf's critique and links popular culture representations of beauty to female pathology, particularly eating disorders. Bordo also notes that women's beauty
regimes are not only sexist, but also largely Eurocentric. Black feminists
also note the Eurocentrism in dominant beauty regimes, but at the same
time note that beauty politics are complicated in Black communities. For
example, Maxine Leeds Craig in her book *Ain't I a Beauty Queen? Black*

Women, Beauty, and the Politics of Race (2002) and Shirley Tate in her book *Black Beauty: Aesthetics, Stylization, Politics* (2009) illustrate the importance of affirming beauty among Black women given the white supremacy in the dominant culture. In *Fresh Lipstick: Redressing Fashion and Feminism* (2006) Linda Scott challenges Wolf's and Bordo's assumptions by providing a historical account of the ways that stylization have been important for women as a form of personal expression. In doing so, Scott decouples beauty and objectification in mainstream feminist ideals.

Recent scholarship in queer, feminist, and critical disability studies has resituated the problem and production of beauty in relation to tastemaking, the global political economy, the stylistics of social space, colonial and racial violence, and the politics of personal stylization (Altiney 2013; Connell 2013; Griffiths 2013; McWilliams 2013; Meszaros 2017; Ochoa 2008). Recent creative aesthetic interventions such as the performance project Sins Invalid, organized with a mission to make "an unashamed claim to beauty in the face of invisibility," and the anthology *Beauty Is a Verb: The New Poetry of Disability* (2011) also critically engage the continuing influence of beauty in late-capitalist commodifications of the body by seeking to reimagine and re-vision modes and forms of recognition inclusive of diverse capacities, corporealities, genders, sexualities, and desires.

Considering this scholarship and artistic production on beauty as it pertains to women's, gender, and sexuality studies, we sought scholarship and creative work that explore new theories of beauty to help us understand the production, performances, practices, and critiques of beauty today. This issue also pushes scholars toward examining the tensions in how women's studies, gender studies, and LGBTQ studies view beauty. How do these areas of intellectual inquiry overlap and diverge? The pieces in this volume cut across these fields and demonstrate a multiplicity in approaches to understanding the significance of beauty in popular culture, art, fashion, social media, and daily life.

Nonnormative expressions of beauty are a common strategy marginalized groups use to counter white, Eurocentric, patriarchal, and homophobic norms. Several of the pieces in this issue demonstrate that the ubiquitous woman-as-nation trope is embodied by both cisgender and trans women. The essays by Emmanuel David and Christian Joy P. Cruz, and María Elena Cepeda alongside Manuel G. Avilés-Santiago's book review, focus on the performance of the woman-as-nation trope in beauty

pageants across the globe. Janell Hobson explores the current recircula-
tion of the Hottentot Venus evident in coverage of celebrities like Nicki
Minaj; Michele White examines countercultural feminist makeup tutorials on YouTube; and Monica Macansantos explores some of these same
issues in her fictional piece on the performance of beauty.

Beauty as Liberation: Contested Histories and Rethinking Beauty Ideals

As this issue engages current articulations of beauty by trans and women
of color feminists, we also consider how activating and redefining beauty as a mode of liberation and decolonization were vital to past everyday
survival practices and social movements. As Erica L. Ball demonstrates in
"Style Politics and Self-Fashioning in Mamie Garvin Fields's *Lemon Swamp
and Other Places*," early-twentieth-century African American women such
as Mamie Garvin Fields strategically deployed Black middle-class fashion and domestic arts in the 1920s through the 1940s to practice self-
determination. Puerto Rican, Mexican, Chicana, and Chinese migrant
women in the United States and the Caribbean during the 1920s and
1930s joined African American women in participating in and creating
beauty cultures that both engaged and diverged from New Woman aesthetics to advance self and community empowerment (Vera-Rojas 2010;
Ruiz 2008; Patterson 2010). Indigenous women in the 1920s and 1930s,
such as Sioux writer Zitkála-Ša, countered hegemonic racial discourses
casting Native women as exotic "beauties" by asserting Indigenous survival as an act of beauty against the violence of displacement and cultural
description brought on by settler colonialism (Kelsey 2008). Jewish immigrant writer Anzia Yezierska also portrayed working immigrant women,
often employed in the New York City garment industry, as staking a "claim
to a bit of beauty" for themselves as central to advancing a collective struggle for justice in the 1920s (1920, 228; Cardon 2016).

The claiming and celebrating of beauty by women of color and immigrant women in the United States called into question white femininity as
the mainstream touchstone of beauty and aesthetics. Yet many of the practices and discourses of beauty advanced by women of color and immigrant
women articulated gender binaries and heteronormativity with these liberatory racial and class-based deployments of beauty. In the post–World
War II era, Black Is Beautiful, one of the most well-known deployments
of beauty as a political liberatory aesthetic, served as a touchstone for

1970s and 1980s Black political aesthetics that symbolically emphasize militancy and an affirmation of Black culture (Davis 1994; hooks 1995; Ongiri 2009; Camp 2015). During the same era, Chicano/a movement activists adapted the slogan to assert Brown Is Beautiful, confronting Eurocentric aesthetics and linking an affirmation of Indigenous and mestizo culture to the broader political movement for Chicano power (Blackwell 2011). As Chicana artist Marcella Lucero-Trujillo explains, since the 1970s, Chicana artists and activists recuperating Indigenous culture is central to Chicanas and Chicanos' "quest for identity and affirmation that brown is beautiful" (1997, 621).

While the Black Is Beautiful campaign challenged stereotypes and encouraged Black communities to create and embrace new approaches to beauty, Black feminist scholars and writers also noted the limits of Black Is Beautiful in terms of challenging norms and hierarchies. Toni Morrison's novel *The Bluest Eye* (1970) and Audre Lorde's poem "Naturally" (1970), for example, explored the tensions of beauty within Black communities. In Lorde's poem, the speaker reasons: "Since Naturally Black is Naturally Beautiful / I must be proud / And, naturally, Black and / Beautiful /who always was a trifle / yellow / and plain, though proud / Before" (1970). Margo Natalie Crawford reads Lorde's poem as a skeptical consideration of "light-skinned blackness, becoming a badge of shame in the 'Black Is Beautiful' lens that fought against the fetishism of light-skinned blackness" (2006, 155). Lorde's skepticism in "Naturally" also extends to the function of Black Is Beautiful as not addressing the economic exploitation of Black communities. The speaker concludes: "But I've bought my can of / Natural Hair Spray- / made and marketed in Watts- / still thinking more / Proud Beautiful Black Women / could better make and use / Black bread." (Lorde 1970). As the closing lines critique the commodification of Black Is Beautiful in the form of "Natural Hair Spray" produced by Black workers in Watts and marketed to politically conscious consumers, the speaker emphasizes that economic self-determination would better benefit "Proud Beautiful Black Women."

In the decade following Lorde's critique of Black Is Beautiful as producing beauty hierarchies and aligning potentially radical aesthetics with capitalist market imperatives, Black feminist theorist Patricia Hill Collins further clarified the nexus of self-empowerment aesthetics and U.S. hegemonic discourse that Black women often navigate in the now classic "Mammies, Matriarchs, and Other Controlling Images" (1990).

Contributors Kamille Gentles-Peart and Cara Snyder build on Hill Collins's methodology and analysis of "controlling images" to advance new considerations of the particularities and mediated performances of anti-Black beauty norms in the Caribbean and Brazil.

While Gentles-Peart and Snyder critically analyze the anti-Black logics of beauty ideals in relation to everyday experiences of racial capitalism, Allison Vandenberg's essay in this issue argues that the visceral and affective dimensions of beauty practices have contributed to disrupting U.S.-hegemonic, feminine beauty standards. Further foregrounding embodiment as practice as a point of entry to understanding gender and beauty, Freda L. Fair's review of recent scholarship by Uri McMillian (2015), Sherri Irvin (2016), and Meeta Rani Jha (2016) identifies the interanimating production of the "Subject/Object/Body" as critical to advancing feminist and gender studies challenges to neoliberal beauty politics performed by women of color in the United States and globally. Nina Sharma's creative prose meditation, "A Brief History of Beauty," and Jodi M. Savage's memoir, "Picture Perfect: Lessons in the War for Self-Love," complement Vandenberg's and Fair's attention to embodiment by bringing to life the affective contours of beauty as shaped by struggles for self-determination with respect to the disciplining impact of gender normativity and U.S. racial logics.

Beauty Transgressing Boundaries and Performing Justice

Examining beauty at the scale of gendered embodiment also requires attention to the social and material structures shaping experience and the realm of aesthetic and political possibility. Inherently relational, beauty as metaphor, aesthetic, and product emerges from nexus of land, capital and consumption, nation-building, ideological currents, colonialisms and imperialisms, natural resources, and built environment. Feminist labor research on the conditions and structures of the beauty industry have detailed the exploitation and violence that women and other workers experience in factories, part-time piece work, the beauty service economy and surrounding communities (Jones 2010; Hatcher and Nguyen Tu 2017). In this issue, Bernadine Hernández offers a new study of the further commodification of the death of women of Juárez, Mexico—an industrial export-processing zone and site of an ongoing femicide of thousands of women and girls since 1993—by the collaboration of Los Angeles fashion house Rodarte and MAC Cosmetics, owned by Estée Lauder. Likewise, in a review of recent scholarship by Minh-Ha T. Pham (2015) on the labor of Asian bloggers and garment workers and Reina Lewis (2015) on Muslim women's fashion culture, David A. Sanchez-Aguilera encourages readers of this issue to consider the labor of aesthetic and taste work as a negotiation of transnational capital flows and power in addition to the religious, racialized, classed, and gendered identity production.

In the current North American context, the recent mainstream exposure and explicit circulation of anti-Native, anti-Black, and anti-immigrant aesthetics of hate and white supremacy provides a reminder that feminist theorizations of beauty need to attend to what Chicana feminist writer Elizabeth "Betita" Martínez described as the "three major pillars of U.S. nationhood: genocide, enslavement, and imperialist expansion" (1998, 43). The legacies and continued operation of violence and repression through racial capitalism and heteropatriarchy—from the heightened U.S. and Mexico border policing, the militarized repression of the Black Lives Matter movement and the Indigenous-led resistance to the Dakota Access Pipeline at Standing Rock, the Trump administration's travel and refugee ban targeting Muslim immigrants, the continued targeting and murder of trans women, and the public resurgence of organized white supremacist and fascist groups—produce the spatial and material terrain shaping beauty markets, work, ideologies, and aesthetics.

Simultaneously, the ongoing normativization of hate aesthetics in the form of white-supremacist beauty ideals and the violent displacement of peoples from land and resources, continues to be met with resistance. Indigenous feminists have reclaimed and continue to advance definitions of beauty that contest settler colonialism and reassert transformative sovereignties. In her play *Princess Pocahontas and the Blue Spots* (1991), for example, Monique Mojica parodies the trope of the beauty pageant, staging a five-hundred-year-long "Miss North American Indian Beauty Pageant," to expose the violence of colonialism and patriarchy for Indigenous women. Like Mojica, Leslie Marmon Silko (1996) emphasizes the interlocking oppression of colonialisms and social hierarchies in thinking through beauty as a signifier of "social status" in Western culture. In contrast to "the definitions of beauty in contemporary Western culture," she learned from her experiences with her grandmother that in the old-time Pueblo world, beauty was manifested in behavior and in one's relationships with other living beings. Beauty was as much a feeling of harmony as it was a visual, aural, or sensual effect. The whole person had to be beautiful, not just the face or the body; faces and bodies could not be separated from hearts and souls (1996, 65).

This ideal does not limit beauty to the body, but it is treated in a more holistic fashion. More recently, this beauty ideal is expressed in YouTube channels by young Native American women, such as Seukteoma, luxielane, and NativeBeauty. These vloggers offer content that challenges the commodification of Indigenous aesthetics and colonial beauty standards through chatty makeup tutorials and discussions of Native American identity politics.

Paralleling, and at times intersecting with, Indigenous and Native feminist art and theory to situate beauty as a mode of resistance and sovereignty, immigrant-rights activists have also deployed beauty to imagine a world without social or material borders. Favianna Rodríguez's image *Migration Is Beautiful* visually participates in reimagining migrant community networks through utilizing the butterfly as a metaphor of hope and movement (fig. 1). Created in a collaborative process while Rodríguez served as executive director of CultureStr/ke, the "butterfly image and tagline" serves to "reimagine borders as permeable rather than militarized, reinvigorating a metaphor that many migrants have looked to for generations" (CultureStr/ke, n.d.). After creating an offset poster of the image, Rodríguez launched the Migration Is Beautiful campaign to inspire people

FIG. 1. Favianna Rodríguez, *Migration Is Beautiful*, 2012 © Favianna Rodríguez.

in Arizona protesting anti-immigrant legislation outside the Democratic National Convention in 2012.

Rodríguez worked on *Migration Is Beautiful* with Julio Salgado, a prominent artist and activist in the immigrant rights movement. Both Rodríguez's and Salgado's artwork promotes an intersectional understanding of migration whereby undocumented immigrants are triply oppressed by their citizenship status, gender, and sexual orientation. In particular, Salgado's artwork for the UndocuQueer project with the Undocumented Queer Youth Collective and the Queer Undocumented Immigrant Project (QUIP) brought necessary attention to the plight of undocumented LGBTQ immigrants. Rodríguez's art redefines beauty as a practice and recognition of the work of maintaining and building communities disrupting spatial and national borders.

The crucial work of reclaiming and envisioning beauty for liberation and justice has also been the focus of the political education and performance collective Sins Invalid, the focus of the "Classics Revisited" section of this issue. Founded in 2005 by and for disabled queer and gender-variant artists of color, Sins Invalid enacts an "unshamed claim to beauty" through workshops and performances featuring storytelling, dancing, singing, movement, poetry, dialogues, and aesthetic interventions. As Alexis Shotwell has noted, "Sins Invalid offer[s] a coproduced experience of beauty and sexiness that pushes at and replaces the limited forms of beauty and collective life dictated under current conditions" (2012, 1009). After more than ten years of performances and the recent publication of *Skin, Tooth, and Bone: The Basis of Movement Is Our People, A Disability Justice Primer* (2016), Sins Invalid continues to challenge feminist and queer politics to embrace and recognize the desire experienced by people with disabilities as central to the process of dismantling interlocking structures of ableism, gender binaries and normativities, racism, colonialism, capitalism, and heteropatriarchy. We open the "Classics Revisited" section by reprinting Sins Invalid's "Ten Principles of Disability Justice," written by Patricia Berne with the support of Aurora Levins Morales and David Langstaff, and on the behalf of Sins Invalid, as well as illustrations and graphic designs by Sins Invalid collaborator Micah Bazant that offer a radical creative praxis for recognizing and enacting the beauty of collective change. Essays by Shayda Kafai and Mordecai Cohen Ettinger discuss the influence and interventions of Sins Invalid for feminist and queer studies and theory. Richard Downing's photographs of Sins Invalid performances capture brief moments of two performances from 2011.

We close the section with a consideration of the implications of Sins Invalid's vision of beauty and justice for feminist and queer politics today with a roundtable featuring Sins Invalid cofounder Patricia Berne, disability justice activists Stacey Milbern and Alice Wong, filmmaker Jamal T. Lewis, racial justice organizer Malcolm Shanks, and performance artist Alok Vaid-Menon. Together the essays, art, photographs, and roundtable offer a renewed provocation to feminist and queer scholars and activists to explore beauty as a radical interdependent practice of collective liberation to create "a world in which every body and mind is known as beautiful" (Sins Invalid 2016).

Following Sins Invalid's invitation to reclaim beauty by unraveling hegemonic normativities and imagining new modes of liberation through art, we close the final sections of this issue with poetry. In the poetry, beauty surfaces through embodied pleasure and desire while simultaneously indexing an ongoing struggle against the everyday interpellation of gendered and racialized ideals of able-bodied, youthful, and sized feminine performance. From the new research, revisitation of Sins Invalid's influential work, and creative prose and poetry in this issue, it is our hope that *WSQ: Beauty* provokes new considerations of beauty as a critical entry point to understanding not only the material and ideological structures of violence and inequity produced through the matrix of hetero-cis-patriarchy and racial capitalism but also the radical potential for mobilizing beauty to imagine and create new liberatory practices.

Acknowledgments

Like all *WSQ* issues, *Beauty* was a collaborative effort. A very special thank you goes to *WSQ*'s editorial assistants past and present Lindsey Eckenroth, Elena Cohen, and Melina Moore for their careful attention to the many details of this issue. We also appreciate the tremendous support we received from the Feminist Press, especially from Jamia Wilson, Lauren Hook, Alyea Canada, Suki Boynton, and Drew Stevens. Research assistant Lauren Neglia's assistance with transcription and permissions was very helpful later in the process. We thank *WSQ*'s creative editors, Rosalie Morales Kearns for editing the prose and fiction and Patricia Smith for curating the poetry.

This issue would not have been possible without the enthusiasm expressed by the previous *WSQ* editors, Cynthia Chris and Matt Brim.

Cynthia and Matt were integral in the early stages of conceptualizing the issue. Likewise, *WSQ's* editorial and advisory boards were eager for this issue and provided invaluable feedback throughout various stages of production. We especially thank Rosamond King for soliciting the "Alerts and Provocations" section and Elena Glasberg and Elizabeth Wissinger for writing the Note from the Board.

We are very grateful to have had the opportunity of working with various artists on this issue. We thank Favianna Rodríguez for generously allowing us to reprint her art. Likewise, Micah Bazant and Richard Downing kindly allowed us to reprint art and photography created in collaboration with Sins Invalid. We also thank Sins Invalid members and collaborators, particularly Patricia Berne, for working closely with us on the "Classics Revisited" section. We especially thank Patricia for allowing us to reprint "Ten Principles of Disability Justice" and coordinating the roundtable response with such dedicated thinkers, artists, and activists. We thank the peer reviewers for their time and expertise. We also extend our appreciation to all of the contributors in this issue. Finally, we would like to recognize the generosity of the Office of the Provost Gary Reichard, the Dean of Humanities and Social Sciences Nan Sussman at the College of Staten Island, and the Office of the Provost Paul Arcario at LaGuardia Community College.

Natalie Havlin is associate professor of English at LaGuardia Community College at the City University of New York. Her research focuses on feminist theories of coalition and Latina/o cultural production with special attention to the aesthetics and affective economies of liberation movements. She can be reached at nhavlin@lagcc.cuny.edu.

Jillian M. Báez is assistant professor in the Department of Media Culture at the College of Staten Island at the City University of New York. She is the author of *In Search of Belonging: Latinas, Media, and Citizenship*. She can be reached at jillian.baez@csi.cuny.edu.

Works Cited

Altiney, Rustem Ertug. 2013. "From a Daughter of the Republic to a Femme Fatale: The Life and Times of Turkey's First Professional Fashion Model, Lale Belkıs." *WSQ* 41 (1/2): 113–30.

Blackwell, Maylei. 2011. *¡Chicana Power! Contested Histories of Feminism in the Chicano Movement*. Austin: University of Texas Press.

Camp, Stephanie. M. H. 2015. "Black Is Beautiful: An American History." *Journal of Southern History* 81 (3): 675–90.

Cardon, Lauren S. 2016. *Fashion and Fiction: Self-Transformation in Twentieth-Century American Literature.* Charlottesville: University of Virginia Press.

Cepeda, María Elena. 2008. "Survival Aesthetics: U.S. Latinas and the Negotiation of Popular Media." In *Latina/o Communication Studies Today*, edited by Angharad N. Valdivia, 237–56. New York: Peter Lang.

Church Gibson, Pamela. 2013. "'To Care for Her Beauty, to Dress Up, Is a Kind of Work': Simone de Beauvoir, Fashion, and Feminism." *WSQ* 41 (1/2): 197–201.

Connell, Catherine. 2013. "Fashionable Resistance: Queer 'Fa(t)shion' Blogging as Counterdiscourse." *WSQ* 41 (1/2): 209–24.

Crawford, Margo Natalie. 2006. "Natural Black Beauty and Black Drag." In *New Thoughts on the Black Arts Movement*, edited by Lisa Gail Collins and Margo Natalie Crawford, 155–72. New Brunswick, NJ: Rutgers University Press.

CultureStr/ke. n.d. "Migration Is Beautiful." Accessed November 27, 2017. http://www.culturestrike.org/project/migration-is-beautiful.

Data Team. 2017. "The World's Most Dangerous Cities." *Economist*, March 31. https://www.economist.com/blogs/graphicdetail/2017/03/daily-chart-23.

Davis, Angela Y. 1994. "Afro Images: Politics, Fashion, and Nostalgia." *Critical Inquiry* 21 (1): 37–45.

Griffiths, Jennifer. 2013. "Erotically Engaged: Olga Carolina Rama's Politically Defiant Bodies." *WSQ* 41 (3/4): 79–94.

Hatcher, Jessamyn, and Thuy Linh Nguyen Tu. 2017. "'Make What You Love': Homework, the Handmade, and the Precarity of the Maker Movement." *WSQ* 45 (3/4): 271–86.

hooks, bell. 1995. *Killing Rage: Ending Racism*. New York: Henry Holt & Company.

hooks, bell, and Amalia Mesa-Bains. 2006. *Homegrown: Engaged Cultural Criticism*. Boston: South End Press.

Jones, Geoffrey. 2010. *Beauty Imagined: A History of the Global Beauty Industry*. Oxford: Oxford University Press.

Kelsey, Penelope Myrtle. 2008. *Tribal Theory in Native American Literature: Dakota and Haudenosaunee Writing and Indigenous Worldviews*. Lincoln: University of Nebraska Press.

Lucero-Trujillo, Marcella. 1997. "The Dilemma of the Modern Chicana Artist and Critic." In *The Woman That I Am: The Literature and Culture of Contemporary Women of Color*, edited by D. Soyini Madison, 619–26. New York: St. Martin's Griffin.

Lorde, Audre. 1970. "Naturally." In *The Black Woman: An Anthology*, edited by
　　Toni Cade Bambara, 18. New York: New American Library.

Malkin, Elisabeth. 2014. "El Salvador Ends Dispute with U.S. Over Seeds." *New
　　York Times*, July 4. https://www.nytimes.com/2014/07/04/business/
　　international/el-salvador-ends-dispute-with-us-over-seeds.html?mtrref=
　　www.google.com&gwh=722F7B6B5AD3C9697F0EE8BFDB1F5A46&
　　gwt=pay.

Martínez, Elizabeth "Betita". 1998. *De Colores Means All of Us: Latina Views for a
　　Multi-Colored Century*. Boston: South End Press.

McWilliams, Sally E. 2013. "'People Don't Attack You If You Dress Fancy':
　　Consuming Femininity in Contemporary China." *WSQ* 41 (1/2): 162–81.

Meszaros, Julia. 2017. "American Men and Romance Tourism: Searching for
　　Traditional Trophy Wives as Status Symbols of Masculinity." *WSQ* 45
　　(1/2): 225–42.

Ochoa, Marcia. 2008. "Perverse Citizenship: Divas, Marginality, and
　　Participation in '*Loca*-Lization.'" *WSQ* 36 (3/4): 146–69.

Ongiri, Amy Abugo. 2009. *Spectacular Blackness: The Cultural Politics of the
　　Black Power Movement and the Search for a Black Aesthetic*. Charlottesville:
　　University of Virginia Press.

Patterson, Martha H. 2010. *Beyond the Gibson Girl: Reimagining the American
　　New Woman, 1895–1915*. Urbana: University of Illinois Press.

Renteria, Nelson. 2017. "Transgender Murders in El Salvador Leave Community
　　in Fear." *Huffington Post*, March 28. https://www.huffingtonpost.com/
　　entry/el-salvador-transgender-murders_us_58dac266e4b01ca7b4278e8a.

Ruiz, Vikki L. 2008. *From Out of the Shadows: Mexican Women in Twentieth-
　　Century America*. Oxford: Oxford University Press.

Shotwell, Alexis. 2012. "Open Normativities: Gender, Disability, and Collective
　　Political Change." *Signs: Journal of Women in Culture and Society* 37 (4):
　　989–1016.

Silko, Leslie Marmon. 1996. *Yellow Woman and a Beauty of the Spirit: Essays on
　　Native American Life Today*. Touchstone: New York.

Vera-Rojas, María Teresa. 2010. "Polémicas, feministas, puertorriqueñas y
　　desconcidas: Clotilde Betances Jaeger, María Mas Pozo y sus charlas
　　femeninas." *Centro Journal* 22 (2): 5–33.

Yezierska, Anzia. 1920. *Hungry Hearts*. New York: Houghton Mifflin Company.

PART I. **PERFORMING BEAUTY**

Big, *Bakla*, and Beautiful:
Transformations on a Manila Pageant Stage

Emmanuel David and Christian Joy P. Cruz

Abstract: This article explores the cultural politics of beauty among fat *bakla* subjects in the urban Philippines. Drawing on firsthand observations, we provide a descriptive account of a beauty pageant for plus-size queer and gender nonconforming contestants. We argue that these subjects, by putting their bodies and subordinate statuses on display, have constructed a fat bakla counterpublic. In the first section, we provide an ethnographic description of the pageant setting. In the following sections, we examine the themes that emerged from candidate performances, particularly those that reveal the intertwined nature of gender, class, sexuality, race, and fat bodies. Finally, we examine how participants used the pageant as a platform for advocacy, constructing a counterpublic for a wide range of identities and embodiments. **Keywords:** *bakla*, beauty pageants, fat studies, counterpublics, advocacy, Philippines

Candidate Fourteen: I am proud to be a Filipino. A pleasant evening to each and everyone, standing before your very eyes is an eighteen-year-old stunner.... At bago ko po lisanin ang apat na sulok ng entabladong ito o rather anim na sulok ng entabladong ito.... Nais ko pong sabihin sa inyo o iwanan sa inyo ang mga katagang "Nakikiusap po ako sa mga taong naluklok ngayon sa Senado, gayun din po sa gobyerno na sana po'y ibaba, ibaba, ibaba ..." (Before I leave the four corners of this stage or rather six corners of this stage.... I would like to tell you or to leave you with this saying, "I am pleading to our elected senators and also to the government that they bring down, bring down, bring down ...")

Audience, in unison: "Ang alin?" (Bring down what?)

Candidate Fourteen: "Ang presyo ng taba (The price of fats). *Thank you and good evening!"*[1]

—*Contestant introduction at the Bilbiling Pilipinas pageant*

WSQ: Women's Studies Quarterly 46: 1 & 2 (Spring/Summer 2018) © 2018 by Emmanuel David and Christian Joy P. Cruz. All rights reserved.

FIG. 1. Candidate Fourteen in the national costume competition at the Bilbiling Pilipinas beauty pageant. Photograph by Emmanuel David.

With tens across the board, Candidate Fourteen received the only perfect score during the entire Bilbiling Pilipinas competition, a plus-size beauty pageant held in an urban poor neighborhood in metropolitan Manila, Philippines. Her speech was a humorous take on a popular chant among urban poor and working-class protesters calling for lower gas prices (*ibaba, ibaba ang presyo ng langis*), and her call to bring down the price of fats linked the economic struggles of the poor audience with the struggles of being fat and *bakla*.[2] While her thematization of "fat" as a social, political, and economic issue was compelling, it was not the only reason she earned a perfect score. She also appeared onstage in what might have been the evening's most extravagant costume. Her oversized, carnivalesque back piece made entirely of *abaniko* (handheld fans made from dried leaves and stems) took up almost the entire stage. It was so tall and cumbersome that she entered and exited the stage from the side with assistance from event organizers, while other contestants easily made their way onstage under a small bright-green awning.

Big was the event's overarching theme, as evidenced by the pageant title Bilbiling Pilipinas: Miss Gay Queensize Edition, which comes from the Filipino word *bilbil*, a term referring to the folds of skin or flab on the abdomen—a close translation in English is love handles. Bilbiling Pilipinas was written in glittery silver on a black cloth banner hung across the stage, accompanied by a hand-drawn logo depicting a silhouette of a full-figured anthropomorphic pig holding a scepter and wearing a bikini and a crown. The pageant recruitment flyers circulated on social media announced, "Open to all transexuals, gays & bisexuals who are healthy, chubby & huggable."[3] Organizers described it as the first pageant of its kind.

On a sweltering hot evening, we were seated at the foot of the stage as two of the five judges responsible for scoring the contestants.[4] The organizers had invited us, a queer Filipino American scholar from the United States and a member of a prominent advocacy organization for Filipina transsexual women, to judge. We were joined by a floor director from a local television station, an elected youth leader representative for the *barangay* (city district), and a representative of the barangay council. Twenty-four contestants were vying for the title, sash, and cash award.

Something quite profound was unfolding before our eyes. Reflecting on footage we recorded with a small digital camera, the pageant appears to have an enduring significance as part of a long tradition of queer beauty pageants and cultural performances in the Philippines and its diaspora (Cannell 1999; Diaz 2016; Johnson 1997; Manalansan 2003). But it was more than that. We realized that by flashing flabby brown skin onstage, contestants were involved in a renegotiation of global beauty ideals, displaying their oversized bodies to carve out what Michael Warner terms a "counterpublic" (2005) in which fat brown gender nonconforming bodies could be celebrated as beautiful. For Warner, counterpublics are in tension with a larger, dominant public; that is, "a counterpublic maintains at some level, conscious or not, an awareness of its subordinate status" (119). For these pageant contestants, identities were not simply formed elsewhere and brought onstage ready-made; rather "participation in such a public is one of the ways by which its members' identities are formed and transformed." Embodying the subordinate statuses of both fat and bakla, Bilbiling Pilipinas contestants were likely aware of the hierarchies and stigma of participating in this counterpublic setting, "One enters at one's own risk" (121). But doing so collectively, we argue, enabled them to carve out new worlds and transform their subordinate status into something else, something beautiful.

On a global scale, beauty pageants reveal the "entanglement of gender, contests, and power" (Cohen, Wilk, and Stoeltje 1996, 11; Banet-Weiser 1999). As contradictory sites of power and resistance, pageants are empirical locations where intersectional identities and institutional forces collide with powerful beauty ideologies. In recent years, scholars have begun "taking beauty contests seriously," looking at their power structures and productions of difference and challenging notions that pageants are trivial and unworthy of serious scholarly investigation (Cohen, Wilk, and Stoeltje 1996, 5). For example, Maxine Leeds Craig (2002) documents the limited gains made by black women seeking to integrate white pageants in the 1960s and tracks important shifts from integrationist strategies to the emergence of "parallel institutions," separate black beauty contests that celebrate black women's beauty, challenging white supremacy as well as the valorization of lighter skin. Scholars have also documented numerous sites where marginalized groups use pageant stages and beauty cultures to craft national identities and normalize nonnormative bodies (Beauboeuf-Lafontant 2003; De Casanova 2004; Patterson-Faye 2016), for example, beauty pageants and transnational beauty markets that take up issues of deaf subjectivities (Burch 2006); fat bodies (Calleja 2012; Chalkin 2015); transgender femininities (Ochoa 2014); and women as symbols of the nation (Balogun 2012; Radhakrishnan 2005).

Extending these literatures, this article explores the cultural politics of beauty among fat bakla subjects in the urban Philippines. Drawing on our firsthand observations—as contest judges and members of the audience—we provide a description of this cultural scene to highlight intersections between disparate but related literatures, including transgender studies, fat studies, transnational feminism, and queer studies in the Global South. In the first section, we provide a brief ethnographic description of the pageant, focusing on the structure and organization of the segments and on descriptions of the candidates. We then examine themes that arose from candidate performances, particularly those revealing the intertwined nature of gender, class, sexuality, race, and fat bodies. We see these intersections in the paradoxes and moral economies of fatness, the sexualization of food consumption, and the racialization of fat. In the final section, we return to the concept of the fat/bakla counterpublic and examine how participants used the pageant stage as a platform for advocacy and a space for transformation. Here, we examine speech and modes of address at the intersection of gender, class, sexuality, race, and fatness, and we demonstrate how candidates advocated for diverse identities and embodiments.

Bilbiling Pilipinas

On a Sunday night in October 2012, the Bilbiling Pilipinas pageant took place in an impoverished neighborhood in metropolitan Manila, one with around eight thousand residents (National Statistics Office 2012). The venue was an open-air basketball court upon which a temporary stage had been constructed, creating an elevated T-ramp with six large pieces of plywood. A long piece of white cloth was draped across the stage front, with a large bow gathered at the center. Stage right there was a small portable screen for projecting the titles of the pageant segments. Spotlights stood on each side of the stage, and a single microphone was placed at the center. The basketball court also functioned as a public plaza, opening up to the local chapel, a series of *sari-sari* stores, and residential housing where clothes were drying in windows.

We arrived by taxi at the edge of the neighborhood at 9:00 p.m. and were led by organizers through a maze of alleyways and dense residential housing; the area is described by some observers as "informal settlements," a polite term for slums or squatter areas. Along the way we stepped over open-air canals filled with trash, debris, and raw sewage. When we arrived at the plaza, a large crowd had already assembled, increasing in size over the next few hours and eventually reaching about five hundred spectators. We were led to a small table directly in front of the stage where our names had been printed on bright yellow placards. A set of scorecards with large numbers was on the table, bound together by a metal ring. As we took our seats in plastic chairs, the crowd—comprised of the young and old, women and men, queer and straight—pressed against our backs and throughout the pageant, several children would rest their hands on our shoulders.

The pageant started with a ritual quite common in this largely Catholic country—a group prayer, led by a neighborhood girl who said, "*Kayo po sana Lord yung gumabay throughout this competition Lord and sana po magbigay ito ng kasiyahan sa lahat ng mga tao na nandito*" (Please guide us through the competition and may it bring joy to all present today). Then the crowd sang the national anthem.

The contest began with a short introduction by the emcee, a thin bakla stand-up comedian who warmed up the crowd. The emcee noted that this was a pageant for "*ating nagsisiksikang mga kandidata*" (heavy candidates), and then said, "*Of course ang ating mga contestants ngayong gabi ay twenty-four so kakayanin kaya ng entablado natin ang kanilang mga timbang?*" (Of course we have twenty-four contestants tonight, will the stage be able to bear all their weight?) Then came a short speech from the organizer, who sought to create a pageant for candidates with "bodies like me," and the pageant opened with the national costume competition in which the candidates individually walked across the stage to high-energy dance music, first to the right, then to the left, and ending at center stage in front of the microphone. Their introductions were in Filipino, English, or Taglish (a mix of Tagalog and English), and included their name and a few brief memorized quotations, sometimes in other languages, such as Ilocano. Next came the evening gown and swimsuit rounds used to choose the top ten finalists who would then compete in the question and answer segment. With twenty-four contestants, the pageant ran behind schedule and organizers decided to cut the talent competition. As organizers calculated the scores between segments, dance troupes comprised of teenage boys danced to K-pop, hip-hop, and pop songs. These boys, dressed in masculine attire, used the occasion to signal small departures from masculine expectations and thus were part of the counterpublic; for example, one troupe performed in entirely gender-appropriate attire offset by a flash of bright red lipstick. The pageant lasted six hours, even after cutting the talent competition, and the show finished after three in the morning, with large numbers of the crowd still in attendance.

The candidates ranged in age from sixteen to twenty-five years old, and most came from metropolitan Manila areas such as Quezon City, Pasig, Pasay, Marikina, and Manila (specifically mentioned was Tondo, the biggest and most populated area of Manila).[5] Of those who mentioned their education, two were college graduates and eight were currently enrolled in college courses. They were competing for a sash, a stuffed toy pig, and comparatively high cash prizes for a nonprofessional, barangay-level pageant in the Manila area: fourth runner-up, Philippine pesos (PHP) 1,000 ($24); third runner-up, PHP 1,500 ($36); second runner-up, PHP 2,000 ($48); first runner up, PHP 3,000 ($72); and first place, PHP 5,000 ($120). By comparison, at another Miss Gay pageant we attended two weeks earlier, the cash prizes were only 500, 500, 1000, 2000, 3000 PHP. With the daily minimum wage for Metro Manila ranging from PHP 409 to PHP 446 (about $10) (National Wages and Productivity Commission 2017), winning the title meant receiving a cash prize comparable to several weeks of minimum wage.

Paradoxes of Fatness

While the monetary prizes were considered to be relatively high, this fat-centered event did not confer the same status or prestige as other gay or transgender pageants held regularly in the Philippines, such as Miss Gay Philippines, Manila's Five Prettiest, Queen Philippines, or Miss Amazing Philippines. Yet the fact that dozens of contestants spent hours putting their fat bodies on public display, even at the risk of harsh critique, suggests that there exists a complex relation between beauty, visibility, and socioeconomic considerations. Because participation was, first and foremost, a form of labor aimed at potential earnings, we begin by foregrounding a class analysis of the pageant.

Many contestants were part of so-called "beauty pageant clans," self-organized social networks that adopt the surnames of elite families in the Philippines. Clan membership allows for beauty professionalization and the cultivation of skills and performance techniques on the pageant circuit, as well as access to resources and mentorship in the informal pageant economy sustained. Material resources, like makeup and gowns, are often shared among members, and should a contestant win, monetary prizes are divided among the contestant, manager, makeup artists, and anyone else who labored for the winner. The emcee, too, was there to earn; we were told she received around PHP 2,500 (about $60) for her time introducing the candidates, engaging with the audience, and performing between segments.

Our class analysis of the pageant must go beyond simply identifying the types of labor performed and also look at the ways in which fat embodiment symbolizes socioeconomic hierarchies in the Philippines. Situating the aesthetic meanings of fat in a local context requires looking at what some scholars describe as the paradox of fatness in Philippine popular culture. Maria Rhodora G. Ancheta observes that "in the Philippines, as in many other Asian countries, fatness is usually associated with wealth, status, and well-being, in the same guise as thinness, or emaciation, is equated with poverty" (2009, 28). Building on Ancheta's interpretation, Gabriela Lee writes, "Culturally speaking, the fat Filipino body is a contradiction in terms: to be fat is to have wealth, and to be fat is to be selfish, gluttonous" (2016, 64).

Put simply, the fat body in the Philippines is often seen as a symbolic and material embodiment of social inequalities.[6] In a class-divided society in which economic precarity, chronic hunger, and food scarcity are made visible through the emaciated bodies of Manila's urban poor, the very presence of fat bodies onstage created an uncomfortable moral friction, an antisocial affront that suggests certain moral failures on the part of individuals who consume too much without regard for those in the community suffering economically. Yet this affront occurs in the same bodies of those who are marginalized because of their minority genders and sexualities. These contestants, then, responded in ways that sought to recoup the moral dignities tied to sexual and gender identity and expression, but also to negotiate what might be characterized as an already wayward body in Philippine culture that many may understand as an embodiment of antisociality. Because of this moral economy of fatness—being perceived as well fed, occupying space in ways that might be read as excessive—contestants needed to publicly negotiate these meanings onstage. Thus, we now turn to the ways some contestants made accounts for their big bodies as they intersect with bakla subjectivities.

An Appetite for Fat: Sexualizing Bodies, Food, and Consumption

Queer and feminist scholars have begun examining the links between sex and size and food and fat (Probyn 1999; Whitesel 2014), especially as food consumption and eating habits are linked to moral evaluations of fat bodies and identities (Gimlin 2002). Many of the pageant contestants took up these links in powerful and creative ways, resignifying stigmatized identities and practices in an effort to neutralize negative meanings and associations. Some contestants did this by sexualizing food and eating, others told narratives that likened themselves to food, imagining themselves as sexy bodies desirable for consumption. In each of the cases, the contestants negotiated notions of body, food, and sexuality in the context of a fat bakla counterpublic and almost always couched these remarks in humor to nullify a potentially hostile, anti-fat climate.

For example, after giving her vital statistics, "36-24-36 equals 186 per kilo," Candidate Two introduced herself in ways that likened her body to fresh produce, "*Fresh na fresh* (very fresh) *with no preservatives*"—perhaps prompted by the recruitment materials calling for "healthy, chubby & huggable" contestants. Another candidate, who assumed the name and likeness of Sharon Cuneta, a Filipina actress and singer who struggled publicly with weight issues, gave the following introductions: "*Hayaan ninyo po akong mag-iwan sa inyo ng pick-up line sa inyong lahat, 'Gusto ko pag bumili ako ng cake, ako ang maghihiwa . . .'*" (Let me leave you all a pick up line, "When I buy a cake, I would like to be the one to cut/slice it . . ."). The audience shouted in unison, "*Bakit?*" (Why?), to which she replied, "*Para matikman ninyo ang aking hiwa. Salamat po!*" (So that you can taste my cut/slice. Thank you!). In this exchange, the contestant used food humor and sexual innuendo to establish rapport with the audience and judges, thus setting this beauty pageant apart from those that are intended to be serious and respectable.

In a third example, Candidate Twenty-Three—who went by the name Maria Cristina Briganta Alya Quintana Maria Ezperanza Pinky Monteverde—delivered these remarks that thematize orality and sexual appetite, "*Ang sabi nga po nila, ang mga bakla daw sawang sawa sumubo ng ulo, ang sabi naman daw ng mga Abu Sayaf, sila rin daw sawang-sawa mamugot ng ulo*" (What people say is that, the bakla is already satiated with giving head, while what the Abu Sayyaf says, is that they are already fed up with dismembering/maiming heads). The joke relies on the audience making a connection between stereotypes of the bakla subjects' lust for oral sex and the desires of a terrorist group in the southern Philippines known for kidnapping and beheading foreigners. The candidate's extremely long name, composed of numerous Spanish first names and surnames, evokes the higher socioeconomic class of the former Spanish colonizers, thus adding to the queer performance of inauthenticity that made the entire performance even more captivating for the urban poor audience.

Finally, even the appetites of the audience members were referenced in the collective sexualizing of food, fat, and appetite. During the swimsuit competition, contestants were brought onstage, eight at a time, to engage collectively in the "quarter turn," in which the candidates lined up and turned around to give the audience a 360-degree view of their bodies. "*O di ba . . . nakakagutom na pangitain*" (Oh, you see . . . a sight that will make you hungry), the emcee announced gleefully.

Racializing Fat

In addition to challenging hegemonic pageant cultures by making crass connections between food, appetite, and sexuality, the contestants also negotiated global beauty conventions by linking fat, bakla, and racialized subjectivities. Most of the participants appeared in light-skinned makeup, powdering their faces to appear fair. For instance, one contestant adopted the persona of Paris Hilton, appearing on stage with light makeup and blond hair. These engagements with hierarchies of skin tones evoke the phenomenon that Maxine Leeds Craig describes in her study as "pigmentocracy," or the favoring of light-skinned black people (2002,

46). Moreover, we could describe this as a form of "colorism," a term Evelyn Nakano Glenn uses to describe the "preference for and privileging of lighter skin and discrimination against those with darker skin," something she argues is a "persisting frontier of intergroup and intragroup relations in the twenty-first century" (2008, 281).

In contrast to global beauty ideologies that privilege white Western subjects (Haubegger 1994), a small handful of contestants made efforts to celebrate brown as beautiful. Like the black contestants who adopted the "Black Is Beautiful" mantra during U.S. black power movements (Craig 2002), these contestants made their brown skin the focus of attention. For example, Candidate Four approached the microphone, introduced herself by name and said, "*Mataba man o maitim, may kagandahang din namang taglay na masasabi kong tunay at sariling akin. Salamat po*" (I may be fat or dark-skinned, but still I have beauty that is true and all mine. Thank you). Other contestants engaged with racialization through their bodily aesthetics rather than words; they chose makeup that matched their complexion or made their skin appear darker. At least three candidates appeared in dark makeup and the attire of the indigenous communities in the northern Philippines, known for being untouched by Spanish influence, thus combining fat embodiment with brownness and indigeneity.

Platforms for Advocacy: Fat Is Beautiful

A beauty pageant is never *just* a pageant. In addition to being a location where participants entertained and earned wages in the informal economy, the Bilbiling Pilipinas stage also provided contestants with the opportunity to portray themselves and their bodies positively, as being big, brown, bakla, and beautiful. Their verbal and visual messages constituted powerful forms of address aimed at advancing the interests and goals of fat and/or bakla individuals and communities. We saw this fat/bakla world-making communicated in two ways: first through words and verbal messages and second through stage presence and nonverbal cues. In these ways, contestants were not unlike the women participants Debra L. Gimlin studied, in the U.S.-based National Association to Advance Fat Acceptance's (NAAFA) Fat Feminist Caucus. NAAFA is an organization that stresses that "personal and political 'empowerment' is possible through a shared understanding of each other's experiences and the bond of shared oppression" (2002, 125).

Verbal messages comprise the first way these contestants engaged in practices that helped construct a fat bakla counterpublic. As Kathleen LeBesco has pointed out, "Language may be used to carry out the revolution that replaces the spoiled identity of fatness—an identity so powerful that even fat people roundly abhor their own bodies—with a more inhabitable subject position" (2001, 76). The candidates we observed spoke passionately about making the world better for fat and bakla subjects; they used humor not only to make the show entertaining but also to offer social and political messages that redefined fat as positive.

Here is an example from Candidate One, who opened the evening with a short vignette presenting the pageant as a platform for collective meaning:

> *Bago po ako sumali sa patimpalak na ito, nagtext po ang aking nanay and the text goes like this, "Anak huwag ka na sumali sa patimpalak na iyan, mababastos ka lang." Agad-agad po akong nag reply sa aking nanay, "Inay ang patimpalak po na ito ay sumisimbulo sa aming pagkatao, ang patimpalak na ito ay ipinapakita na dapat kaming mahalin, respetuhin, igalang bilang homosexual dahil walang masama sa mata ng Diyos at sa mata ng madla kung alam mong wala kang ginagawang kahiyahiya."*

> (Before I joined this contest, my mother sent me a text message and the text goes like this, "Child, please do not join that contest, you will just be disrespected." I immediately replied to her, "Mom, this contest symbolizes our personality, this contest will show that we need to be loved, respected as a homosexual because nothing is bad in the eyes of God and [in] the eyes of people if you know that you did nothing shameful.")

Candidate One countered the idea that her participation would simply be a spectacle, and she sought to redeem a stigmatized sexual subject position by making social and moral claims to dignity and respect. Candidate Twelve said something similar: "*Nagpapaalala sa ating lahat na kailan man ang pagiging baklang mataba ay hindi naging masama sa mata ng Diyos at sa mata ng taong madla, liban na lamang kung kami mismo ang gagawa ng sarili naming ikasasama*" (Being a fat bakla is not bad in the eyes of God and in the eyes of people, not unless we ourselves do something bad). Unlike Candidate One, who didn't utter the words *mataba* or fat, Candidate Twelve made direct links between morality, fat, and bakla subjectivities. Nonetheless, the entire pageant context suggested that the "we" included the whole slate of fat bakla contestants as deserving of love and respect.

On this evening, numerous candidates sought to redeem fat and bakla as valued characteristics, both at the individual and group levels. Candidate Eighteen, for example, stressed the importance of one's character rather than appearance, saying in English, "Never judge a person by his looks, neither by his sexuality because in this age of individuality, what is more important is a man's character and how he can handle himself in the society." Candidate Eleven offered a similar vision, "To be, become what you are and to be capable of what you are becoming, it is a secret of a happy life, for every living thing has its own talent, perseverance, and wit, so don't be afraid, just be yourself." A related theme was the social construction of beauty standards. Rather than adhering to narrow definitions of beauty, Candidate Twenty-Six made appeals that resonate with fat activists' size-acceptance discourses (Connell 2013), "Beauty comes in different shapes, forms, and sizes. Tonight we celebrate human diversity and gender equality."

Researchers who have observed other beauty pageants and talent shows for fat people argue that these events allow participants the cultural space to proclaim "fatness as a valid, valued identity and/or aspect of embodiment" (Chalkin 2015, 90). Following this scholarship, as well as the work of Courtney J. Patterson-Faye (2016)—who theorizes sexiness at the intersections of fatness and blackness—we see fat bakla visibility onstage not only as valid and valued but also as undeniably sexy. The candidates posed and turned onstage, *rumampa* (sashayed) onstage to the pop tunes of Right Said Fred's "I'm Too Sexy" and "Sexy and I Know It" by LMFAO. One candidate appeared in a bikini bottom with flower-shaped nipple pasties, another sported a long knee-length khaki overcoat, did a twirl, and dropped the coat to reveal a blue-and-gold two-piece. At one point the emcee exclaimed, "*So alam niyo na, yan na ang usong katawan ngayon. Ang tawag sa ganyang katawan ay voluptuous, from the root word 'vola'*" (So now you know, in terms of bodies, that's the fad nowadays. You can call that body voluptuous, from the root word 'vola' [in Filipino, *bola* is ball]).

In her book *Fashioning Fat: Inside Plus-Size Modeling*, Amanda M. Czerniawski argues that scholars in the field of fat studies have made calls for a "reclamation of one's embodiment as a form of resistance against the cultural stigma of fat" (2015, 20). This reclamation, Czerniawski continues, reinscribes fat embodiment and imbues fatness with more positive meanings. This separation of stigma from the fat body is often achieved through the "physical performance of fat," that is, the "performance, itself, reveals and redefines fat" (2015, 20). This all illustrates a central feature of counterpublics: transformation. As Warner writes, "In a counterpublic setting, such display often has the aim of transformation. Styles of embodiment are learned and cultivated, and the effects of shame and disgust that surround them can be tested, in some cases revalued" (2005, 62).

This revaluation of bodies and identities at Bilbiling Pilipinas took many forms. The pageant's national costume segment allowed contestants to demonstrate their creativity by posing on stage with campy, over-the-top costumes combined with witty remarks to show their poise, confidence, and intelligence. The evening gown competition allowed them to display their big bodies in elegant, floor-length gowns adorned with rhinestones and sequins, challenging fatness as carnivalesque or grotesque and showing how it can be glamorous. And the swimsuit segment, publicly exposing skin that in most other contexts remained covered, allowed them to be sexy.

Conclusion

This article focused on the cultural dimensions of a fat bakla beauty pageant in the urban Philippines. It examined how pageant organizers and contestants carved out spaces to make fat gender nonconforming bodies visible and negotiate their paradoxical meanings in public by reinterpreting fat stigma through words and bodily actions that thematized fat—negotiating its class association with wealth and status (i.e., well-fed)—and resignified its meaning through the process of making it visible. Contestants sexualized food and eating practices, thereby taking an activity that is frequently used to signify moral failure, and thus moral responsibility for fatness (Gimlin 2002), and reinvesting it with new meanings. In addition, several contestants made direct connections between fat bakla bodies and racial and ethnic subjectivities, but they did not do so in uniform ways. Some highlighted lightness, while others proclaimed that being fat and *maitim* (being dark) is beautiful.

While the Bilbiling Pilipinas pageant created the context for the resistant renegotiation of fat as a sociopolitical cause, we acknowledge the limitations of these settings for bringing about sustained, long-term, and systemic change in society. We recognize that these subjects, however creative they may be, were only able to create a counterpublic under certain conditions and conventions. Similarly, because we were focused on candidates, we have not given sustained attention to audience participation in or reception of these messages. Thus, we cannot tell if the event resonated with their lives. Nonetheless, we have demonstrated some of the small, but not insignificant ways the contestants engaged in resistant practices to imbue fatness with positive meaning. And while the prospects of sustained social change may be limited, the contestants all challenged conventional beauty standards and they did so collectively. As Gimlin notes, many of her study participants who engaged in "body work" were "working together to find common solutions to a shared problem" (2002, 108). So when the lights went down, when the music stopped playing, when the contestants went home for the evening, we wondered about whether the construction of an alternative culture could be sustained beyond the stage.

Back on the main road, as we waited for a taxi at 3:00 a.m., two motorized pedicabs approached us from behind and turned the corner. Headed home was a small group of fat bakla contestants with their supporters, along with their bags and oversized costumes hanging precariously from the outside of the vehicle. We waved goodbye and hands emerged from the pedicabs to give us perfect pageant waves. Looking back at the pageant now, the contestants may have been in competition with one another, but they also used the evening to create and sustain group bonds by interacting in a primarily fat, brown, and bakla arena where they could celebrate themselves—and each other—as beautiful.

Emmanuel David is assistant professor of women and gender studies at University of Colorado Boulder. His work has appeared in *Gender & Society*, *GLQ*, *Radical History Review*, and *TSQ*. He can be reached at emmanuel.david@colorado.edu.

Christian Joy P. Cruz is university researcher at the University of the Philippines Population Institute. Her areas of specialization include fertility, gender and sexuality, adolescent studies, population projections, and population aging. She can be reached at christian_joy.cruz@up.edu.ph.

Notes

1. Unless otherwise noted, all translations by Christian Joy P. Cruz.
2. *Bakla* refers to a vibrant group of people in the Philippines who were assigned male at birth, but whose gender identities/expressions and/or sexual orientations do not conform to conventional gender norms or heteronormative society. Bakla is not just a term for sexual orientation, it also denotes sexual identity, gender identities, and feminine gender expressions (Alegre 2013; Atadero, Umbac, and Cruz 2014; Cruz, Saballe, and Alegre 2015; Diaz 2015; Manalansan 2003). For many Filipinos, bakla is consid-

ered a derogatory term; however, in recent years it has begun to take on a more positive meaning (Manalansan 2015). We use bakla here because of how frequently it was expressed in the pageant, though we realize that it exists in tension with other terms such as homosexual, gay, bisexual, transgender, and transsexual. On the transnational flows of these terms, see Fajardo 2011.

3. To our knowledge, there was no minimum weight requirement. However, another case provides insight into requirements for big pageant contestants. An application for the 2016 Queensize of the South Pageant states that contestants must weigh at least two hundred pounds.

4. No judging criteria were given; rather it was assumed that we knew how to evaluate candidates.

5. Metropolitan Manila, composed of sixteen cities and a municipality, is home to nearly twelve million residents.

6. We thank the anonymous reviewers for raising these issues.

Works Cited

Alegre, Bryan R. 2013. "Toward a Better Understanding of Hormone and Silicone Injection Use and Self-Perception of Transgender Women in the Philippines and Hong Kong." PhD Dissertation, University of Santo Tomas, Manila.

Ancheta, Maria Rhodora G. 2009. "Fat in the Philippines: The 'Freakish' Body and Its Inscription in Philippine Humour." In *Crossing Cultural Boundaries: Taboo, Bodies and Identities*, edited by Lili Hernández and Sabine Krajewski, 26–38. Newcastle, UK: Cambridge Scholars Publishing.

Atadero, Oscar E., Sylvia Angelique Umbac, and Christian Joy P. Cruz. 2014. "Kwentong Bebot: Lived Experiences of Lesbians, Bisexual and Transgender Women in the Philippines." In *Violence: Through the Lens of Lesbians, Bisexual Women and Transgender People in Asia*, 161–94. New York: The International Gay and Lesbian Human Rights Commission.

Balogun, Oluwakemi M. 2012. "Cultural and Cosmopolitan: Idealized Femininity and Embodied Nationalism in Nigerian Beauty Pageants." *Gender & Society* 26 (3): 357–81.

Banet-Weiser, Sarah. 1999. *The Most Beautiful Girl in the World: Beauty Pageants and National Identity*. Berkeley: University of California Press.

Beauboeuf-Lafontant, Tamara. 2003. "Strong and Large Black Women? Exploring Relationships between Deviant Womanhood and Weight." *Gender & Society* 17 (1): 111–21.

Burch, Susan. 2006. "'Beautiful, though Deaf': The Deaf American Beauty Pageant." In *Women and Deafness: Double Visions*, edited by Brenda Jo

Brueggemann and Susan Burch, 242–61. Washington, DC: Gallaudet University Press.

Calleja, Niña. 2012. "'Bilbiling Mandaluyong': Fat is Beautiful." *Philippine Daily Inquirer*, February 12. http://newsinfo.inquirer.net/151867/ 'bilbiling-mandaluyong'-fat-is-beautiful.

Cannell, Fenella. 1999. "Beauty and the Idea of 'America.'" In *Power and Intimacy in the Christian Philippines*, 203–26. Cambridge: Cambridge University Press.

Chalkin, Vikki. 2015. "All Hail the Fierce Fat Femmes." In *Fat Sex: New Directions in Theory and Activism*, edited by Helen Hester and Caroline Walters, 85–98. New York: Routledge.

Cohen, Colleen Ballerino, Richard Wilk, and Beverly Stoeltje, eds. 1996. *Beauty Queens on the Global Stage: Gender, Contests, and Power.* New York: Routledge.

Connell, Catherine. 2013. "Fashionable Resistance: Queer 'Fa(t)shion' Blogging as Counterdiscourse." *WSQ* 41 (1/2): 209–24.

Craig, Maxine Leeds. 2002. *Ain't I a Beauty Queen? Black Women, Beauty, and the Politics of Race.* New York: Oxford University Press.

Cruz, Christian Joy P., Charlese Saballe, and Brenda Alegre. 2015. "The Social Experiences of Trans People in the Philippines." In *Transrespect versus Transphobia: The Social Experiences of Trans and Gender-Diverse People in Colombia, India, the Philippines, Serbia, Thailand, Tonga, Turkey and Venezuela*, edited by Carsten Balzer/Carla LaGata and Jan Simon Hutta, 36–43. Berlin, Germany: Transgender Europe (TGEU), transrespect.org/ wp-content/uploads/2015/08/TvT-PS-Vol9-2015.pdf.

Czerniawski, Amanda M. 2015. *Fashioning Fat: Inside Plus-Size Modeling.* New York: New York University Press.

De Casanova, Erynn Masi. 2004. "'No Ugly Women': Concepts of Race and Beauty among Adolescent Women in Ecuador." *Gender & Society* 18 (3): 287–308.

Diaz, Robert. 2015. "The Limits of *Bakla* and Gay: Feminist Readings of *My Husband's Lover*, Vice Ganda, and Charice Pempengco." *Signs: Journal of Women in Culture and Society* 40 (3): 721–45.

———. 2016. "Queer Unsettlements: Diasporic Filipinos in Canada's World Pride." *Journal of Asian American Studies* 19 (3): 327–50.

Fajardo, Kale Bantigue. 2011. *Filipino Crosscurrents: Oceanographies of Seafaring, Masculinities, and Globalization.* Minneapolis: University of Minnesota Press.

Gimlin, Debra L. 2002. *Body Work: Beauty and Self-Image in American Culture.* Berkeley: University of California Press.

Glenn, Evelyn Nakano. 2008. "Yearning for Lightness: Transnational Circuits in the Marketing and Consumption of Skin Lighteners." *Gender & Society* 22 (3): 281–302.

Haubegger, Christy. 1994. "I'm Not Fat, I'm Latina." *Essence*, December 8.

Johnson, Mark. 1997. *Beauty and Power: Transgendering and Cultural Transformation in the Southern Philippines*. Oxford: Berg.

LeBesco, Kathleen. 2001. "Queering Fat Bodies/Politics." In *Bodies Out of Bounds: Fatness and Transgression*, edited by Jana Evans Braziel and Kathleen LeBesco, 74–87. Berkeley: University of California Press.

Lee, Gabriela. 2016. "The Word of the Body: Depictions of Positive Body Image in Philippine Young Adult Literature." *Philippine Humanities Review* 18 (1): 59–75.

Manalansan IV, Martin F. 2003. *Global Divas: Filipino Gay Men in the Diaspora*. Durham, NC: Duke University Press.

———. 2015. "Bakla (Philippines)." In *The International Encyclopedia of Human Sexuality*, edited by Patricia Whelehan and Anne Bolin, 113–14. Hoboken, NJ: John Wiley & Sons.

National Statistics Office of the Philippines. 2012. 2010 Census of Population and Housing.

National Wages and Productivity Commission, Department of Labor and Employment. 2017. Summary of Daily Minimum Wage Rates Per Wage Order, By Region Non-Agriculture (1989–2017). Last updated November 10, 2017. http://www.nwpc.dole.gov.ph/pages/statistics/stat-wage-rates-1989-present-non-agri.html.

Ochoa, Marcia. 2014. *Queen for a Day: Transformistas, Beauty Queens, and the Performance of Femininity in Venezuela*. Durham, NC: Duke University Press.

Patterson-Faye, Courtney J. 2016. "'I Like the Way You Move': Theorizing Fat, Black, and Sexy." *Sexualities* 19 (8): 926–44.

Probyn, Elspeth. 1999. "An Ethos with a Bite: Queer Appetites from Sex to Food." *Sexualities* 2 (4): 421–31.

Radhakrishnan, Smitha. 2005. "'Time to Show Our True Colors': The Gendered Politics of 'Indianness' in Post-Apartheid South Africa." *Gender & Society* 19 (2): 262–81.

Warner, Michael. 2005. *Publics and Counterpublics*. New York: Zone Books.

Whitesel, Jason. 2014. *Fat Gay Men: Girth, Mirth, and the Politics of Stigma*. New York: New York University Press.

Mapping Beauty, Fashion, and Femininity:
Recent Contributions by Blain Roberts, Marcia Ochoa, and Vanita Reddy

Marcia Ochoa's *Queen for a Day: Transformistas, Beauty Queens, and the Performance of Femininity in Venezuela*, Durham, NC: Duke University Press, 2014

Blain Roberts's *Pageants, Parlors, and Pretty Women: Race and Beauty in the Twentieth-Century South*, Chapel Hill: University of North Carolina Press, 2016

Vanita Reddy's *Fashioning Diaspora: Beauty, Femininity, and South Asian American Culture.* Philadelphia, PA: Temple University Press, 2016

Manuel G. Avilés-Santiago

Until recently, beauty, fashion, and femininity have, for the most part, been overlooked by academia in spite of their sociocultural and political meaning, implications concerning power, role as instruments of modernity, and status as technologies of neoliberalism. Instead of recognizing the critical potential of these subjects, scholars have long disregarded them as irrelevant and frivolous. Aside from well-known foundational projects on philosophical discourses of beauty, surprisingly little scholarship has explored these themes. Exceptions are rare but worth noting: in the early aughts, two case studies of the Miss America Pageant were published (Watson and Martin 2004; Banet-Weiser 1999) and preceding those was a single edited collection (Cohen, Wilk, and Stoeltje 1996) that explored the ways in which gender ideologies are represented and reinforced in beauty pageants globally. Only now—over a decade after the last contributions to the field—have three works by Blain Roberts, Marcia Ochoa, and Vanita Reddy attempted a much-needed continuation of the debate and deepening of the analysis. These scholars' projects consider beauty, fashion, pageantry, and femininity as complex constellations of material and symbolic cultural signifiers. All three books delve into questions of how these terms and their conceptions complicate the narratives of a nation—and its diasporas—through embodiments that remap geographies of race, gender, culture, and national identity.

WSQ: Women's Studies Quarterly 46: 1 & 2 (Spring/Summer 2018) © 2018 by Manuel G. Avilés-Santiago.
All rights reserved.

In *Pageants, Parlors, and Pretty Women: Race and Beauty in the Twentieth-Century South*, Blain Roberts undertakes an extensive and meticulous historical analysis of the construction of female beauty in the South, tying her analysis to the way consumer culture informed Southern beauty via products, rituals, and pageants—all of which together reiterated and reinforced women's embodiment of the impact of the cultural and economic modernization of the most highly racialized and segregated regions of the United States. One of the most illuminating elements of her study is that, by conducting a racially inclusive cultural history of beauty, she unveils the dialogue that white and black Southern women had with each other when articulating their specific approaches to beauty.

In her introduction, Roberts defines beauty "as an expansive category that encompasses ideals, practices, rituals, labor, and even spaces" (9), demonstrating the power of this definition through the examination, historicization, and contextualization of the complex significance of beauty in women's lives during the Jim Crow era. While her first chapter explores white Southern women's attempts to reconcile modern beauty practices with the ideals of Southern ladyhood, her second chapter examines black Southern women's struggles to gain access to a black beauty culture in the face of financial instability. This analysis goes beyond products and practices to position the reader inside of the beauty salon to investigate the role of black beauticians. "Free from economic entanglements with whites, beauticians fought the intransigence of white southerners by taking advantage of the opportunities their workplace provided" (230). These opportunities, Roberts shows, often brought these women to the front lines of local activist and civil rights movements.

Many of the "pretty women" (white and black) who were created in "parlors" by beauty products, practices, and rituals, found a showcase for themselves on the pageant stage. Pageants—the most popular public ritual of Southern beauty during the twentieth century—became a medium for the region to demonstrate that "glamour, it turns out, could be cultivated in the most unglamorous places" (104)—places like the rural South. Chapters 3 and 4 trace the history of Southern pageants, particularly their role in promoting agricultural products, such as tobacco and cotton, during the Depression. For white women, competing in pageants was part of an agenda of Southern modernization; black women used pageants to help embody respectability politics through beauty while strengthening the financial stability of local organizations within the black community.

In her conclusion, Roberts chronicles a paradigm-shifting moment in the notion of Southern beauty when in 1968, in the contexts of the civil rights, anti-war, student, and women's movements, a feminist protest against the Miss America pageant served as a frame for the celebration of Miss Black America as an extension of the Black Is Beautiful movement. For decades, however, in pageants like Miss America and Miss USA, Southern white women "outperformed women from other regions, mainly because of expectations that they would and because of strong southern state pageant systems" (272).

Roberts's story of Southern women is not unique. Rather, it is shared, on a global stage, with beauty pageant participants around the world, including in Venezuela. With seven Miss Universe, six Miss World, and seven Miss International wins over six decades, Miss Venezuela is a national event with transnational circulation that has become an instrument for the development of Venezuela as a modern nation as well as a critical site for constructing femininity. Marcia Ochoa's *Queen for a Day: Transformistas, Beauty Queens, and the Performance of Femininity in Venezuela* studies Miss Venezuela's "misses" (cisgender beauty queens) and "*transformistas*" (a category best approximated by transgender) in the context of the production of a national femininity "with similar symbolic resources, in dialogue with shared discourses, and employing similar kinds of techniques and technologies" (5). To disclose and interpret this complex dialogue, Ochoa engages in rich anthropological work in Venezuela that intertwines the methodologies of observation, interview, textual analysis, and archival research with sophisticated theoretical interventions. For example, one of the greatest assets of the book is Ochoa's furthering of Jesús Martín-Barbero's notion of mediation. For Ochoa, the bodies of misses and transformistas mediate national gender ideology; they display how media spectacles like Miss Venezuela inform the everyday production of femininity.

Queen for a Day is strategically divided into three parts. The first section, "On the Transnational," looks at how Miss Venezuela—as a national and transnational product—has become a way for the nation of Venezuela to imagine itself, creating a national brand that erases class and race even as it reveals "tensions in center and periphery, national and social relations in Venezuela" (46). The second section, "On the Runway, on the Streets," takes the reader to the pageant runway of the Miss Oriente preliminary competition and to the spontaneous city runway of Avenida Libertador in Caracas. Ochoa reveals both runways to be platforms upon which misses and transformistas can project ideas of glamour, beauty, and femininity to both imagined and real audiences. The final section of the book, "On the Body," analyzes the corporeal mediations of national, transnational, racial, and gender ideologies through both plastic surgery and spectacular femininity.

In the mode of spectacular femininity, the Miss Venezuela 2017 national costume for Miss Universe, Venezuelan Warrior, "represents the brave Venezuelan women, authentic and warrior-like, who rise to [meet] the adversity of the present and the future" (*El nacional* 2017; translation my own). As Ochoa indicates, the beauty queen as the embodiment of the nation uses beauty and glamour to negotiate power (as well as marginality) and displays the national brand on the transnational stage—at least for a day.

Just as the image of Miss Venezuela in her "traditional" costume allows for the materialization of a spectacular projection of national femininity, Vanita Reddy argues that beauty and fashion, as diasporic embodiments, have produced an idea of India that maps out a territory of belonging while working as a series of technologies of neoliberalism, individualism, and consumption. Reddy's *Fashioning Diaspora: Beauty, Femininity, and South Asian American Culture* explores how South Asian standards of beauty and fashion move to and transform in a U.S. context, serving as instruments by which the South Asian diaspora can challenge, resist, and adapt their cultural identities and senses of belonging. The volume opens with the online backlash against the historic crowning of Nina Davuluri as Miss America 2014, the first South Asian American to win the pageant. Referred to as a terrorist and called both Muslim and Arab, Davuluri experienced a win that ignited cyberracism on a grand scale and exposed the anxieties produced by the "browning of America." Intrigued by how an "Indian feminine beauty animates the social" (2), Reddy expands the scope of her analysis beyond the pageant industry to consider less obvious representations of Indian beauty and focus on diasporic embodiments that prompt diasporic subjects to engage in "practices associated with beauty [that] are socializing in the way that they make possible new racialized subject formations, affiliations, and forms of diasporic belonging" (17).

Even though the volume is organized around two main themes—beauty and fashion—its objects of study are varied, and include a contemporary diasporic young adult novel, visual and performance art, and, of course, the beauty pageant motif. One of the highlights of *Fashioning Diaspora* is its approach to beauty not as a one-dimensional abstract ideal but as a system. Departing from the idea of assemblages—and in conversation with theorists including Gilles Deleuze and Félix Guattari—Reddy defines "Indian beauty" as a dynamic concept that encompasses "a network of bodies, desires, events, performances, clothing and adornment practices, and commodities that are negotiated within a specific set of conjunctures in diaspora" (7).

These three books approach different regions and form a diversity of liminal spaces; nevertheless, they all see beauty as a mobile and multidimensional system that can be employed as a means of mapping race, gender, and national identity. The interdisciplinary methodological approaches taken by Roberts, Ochoa, and Reddy present new opportunities for the scholarly exploration of beauty; all three projects make essential interventions into scholarship not only specifically on beauty, fashion, and femininity, but also within the broader fields of transnational feminisms, gender studies, and cultural studies.

Manuel G. Avilés-Santiago is assistant professor of communication and culture at Arizona State University. He is the author of *Puerto Rican Soldiers and Second-Class Citizenship: Representations in Media*. He can be reached at maviless@asu.edu.

Works Cited

Banet-Weiser, Sarah. 1999. *The Most Beautiful Girl in the World: Beauty Pageants and National Identity*. Berkeley: University of California Press.

Cohen, Colleen Ballerino, Richard Wilk, and Beverly Stoeltje, eds. 1996. *Beauty Queens on the Stage: Gender, Contests, and Power*. New York: Routledge.

El nacional. 2017. "Traje típico de Keysi Sayago representa la lucha de la mujer venezolana." November 12. http://www.el-nacional.com/noticias/ entretenimiento/traje-tipico-keysi-sayago-representa-lucha-mujer-venezolana_211358.

Watson, Elwood, and Darcy Martin, eds. 2004. *"There She Is, Miss America": The Politics of Sex, Beauty, and Race in America's Most Famous Pageant*. New York: Palgrave Macmillan.

PART II. **THE POLITICS OF STYLE**

Style Politics and Self-Fashioning in Mamie Garvin Fields's *Lemon Swamp and Other Places*

Erica L. Ball

Abstract: This article explores Southern black women's engagement with beauty culture, fashion, and style politics at the turn of the twentieth century. Focusing on Mamie Garvin Fields's personal history, *Lemon Swamp and Other Places: A Carolina Memoir*, the article interrogates the ways that middle-class and aspiring black women designed, deployed, and enjoyed fashionable clothes and stylish creations. It argues that in addition to serving as part of a larger project of black middle-class self-fashioning, these efforts were powerful assertions of black women's humanity, individuality, and determination to thrive as black women in the context of Jim Crow. **Keywords:** Respectability, black middle class, African American women, dressmaking, domestic arts, Jim Crow

Lemon Swamp and Other Places: A Carolina Memoir has long been a cherished, if understudied, text for specialists in African American women's history. Composed of a series of interviews Karen Fields conducted with her grandmother Mamie Garvin Fields (1888–1987) in the late 1970s, *Lemon Swamp and Other Places* offers readers a rare glimpse into the day-to-day activities of a young black Southerner living in the Jim Crow South. Over a series of recollections told in loosely chronological order, Mamie Garvin Fields offered information about the lives of her enslaved grandparents and parents, mused about her relationships with her childhood friends and neighbors, and described the ways the implementation of Jim Crow laws reshaped the Charleston, South Carolina, community in the 1890s and early 1900s. She also reflected on her years as a college student and her subsequent experiences as a teacher on the South Carolina Sea Islands, her marriage to a bricklayer named Robert Lucas Fields, and her life as a wife, mother, and clubwoman in the 1920s, 1930s, and 1940s. As such,

WSQ: Women's Studies Quarterly 46: 1 & 2 (Spring/Summer 2018) © 2018 by Erica L. Ball. All rights reserved.

Lemon Swamp and Other Places provides a remarkable firsthand account of daily life in the Jim Crow South in the decades before the advent of the modern civil rights movement.

Although *Lemon Swamp and Other Places* serves as a useful point of entry for analyzing a variety of aspects of black Southern life, it is Fields's description of her work as a black beauty culturist in the early decades of the twentieth century that has received the most sustained attention from scholars in recent years. In scenes peppered throughout the second half of her memoir, Fields describes her enthusiasm for Annie Turnbo Malone's Poro method of hair care and expresses her thrill at seeing the laundress-turned-hair-care-millionaire Madam C. J. Walker give a lecture in Charleston. Fields's accounts of black women's neighborhood hair tutorials offer an invaluable insider's perspective on black women's changing hair care practices in the 1920s and 1930s. Her descriptions of the varied ways women of African descent styled their hair between the 1890s and 1940s reveals the remarkable range of styles adopted by young and elderly black women—both rural and urban—during these decades of profound change. For these reasons, *Lemon Swamp and Other Places* has become an essential primary source for those studying the history of black women's hair care practices in the early twentieth century (Gill 2010, 36–39).

If we turn our attention to the first half of *Lemon Swamp and Other Places* and widen the scope of our analysis from the focus on black women's hair care to fashion and beauty more broadly, we see that Fields's entire memoir is filled with descriptions of black beauty and personal aesthetics. An accomplished dressmaker as well as a teacher and hair care provider, Fields had an eye for beauty and a love for fashionable clothing, accessories, and handmade household goods. Over the course of her memoir, she comments extensively on the attractiveness of crocheted curtains, blankets, and dresses; delights in the memory of her own and her family members' wedding trousseaus; regrets the purchase and subsequent loss of an expensive, stylish hat; and reflects on the sensation of skirts, ribbons, and petticoats as they swished and fluttered during chaperoned waltzes and games of musical chairs. These reflections on everyday beauty are more than just passing observations. Rather, Fields's meditations on the beauty surrounding her often include her perspective on some of the inter- and intraracial political implications of elite and aspiring urban black women's style. For these reasons, *Lemon Swamp and Other Places* must be understood as a text that provides important insight into the ways rank and file black women—as opposed to more celebrated public figures and international icons like Madam C. J. Walker, Josephine Baker, or Mary Church Terrell—conceptualized the relationship between self-fashioning, beauty culture, and the dynamics of Jim Crow at the turn of the twentieth century.

As I see it, Fields's personal experiences demonstrate how deeply black women's beauty practices remained imbricated in the larger, collective campaign to push back against expressions of antiblackness during the rise of Jim Crow. First, Fields's recollections of interactions with Southern white people at the turn of the twentieth century reveal the extent to which, when faced with living embodiments of black beauty, white Southerners could perceive black access to fashion and expressions of refinement—rife as they were with connotations of middle-class or elite status—as challenges to the South's modern racial caste system at the moment of its inception. Meanwhile, from an intraracial perspective, Fields's account of her experiences between the 1890s and the advent of World War I suggests that the skill and taste required to create unique and fashionable items for the body and home remained bound up in the period's expanding racial "uplift" campaign. Finally, on a more personal level, Fields's recollections suggest that participation in fashion and beauty culture allowed middle-class and aspiring black women to pursue self-care and take pleasure in their own bodies, acts that, as late-twentieth- and early-twenty-first-century black feminist scholars have pointed out, must be understood as radical endeavors for black women living in a hostile world (Lorde 1988). *Lemon Swamp and Other Places* suggests that Mamie Garvin Fields, along with her friends and members of her family, understood this concept deeply at the turn of the twentieth century, and thus made a concerted effort to center black beauty in their day-to-day lives.

Lemon Swamp and Other Places was first published in 1983 at a moment of heightened interest in African American women's history. Originating in the early 1970s when Fields first presented a folder of letters describing her youth to her three granddaughters, and blossoming in the mid- and late 1970s as Karen Fields recorded their conversations, the project that became *Lemon Swamp* was part of wave of personal, and largely unpublished, oral histories and interviews of countless African Americans conducted with family members in the years surrounding the 1976 publication of Alex Haley's novel *Roots*, and its subsequent television adaptations in 1977 and 1979. During this period, African

American interest in genealogy exploded, and black Americans rushed to record the memories and stories of their parents, grandparents, and other elderly relatives (Morgan 2017). *Lemon Swamp* also arrived during the heyday of the new social history, a movement to capture the stories of everyday Americans, and to reframe the conventional narrative of U.S. history by telling the story "from the bottom up." For students of African American women's history, *Lemon Swamp* appeared alongside pioneering oral history collections like *Black Women in White America: A Documentary History* (Lerner 1972) and *We Are Your Sisters: Black Women in the Nineteenth Century* (Sterling 1984). It also complemented groundbreaking texts on African American women's history like Deborah Gray White's *Ar'n't I a Woman: Female Slaves in the Plantation South* (1985) and Paula J. Giddings's *When and Where I Enter: The Impact of Black Women on Race and Sex in America* (1984). Although *Lemon Swamp* seems to have made less of an impact in the field of literary studies, the text might profitably be considered alongside texts such as Alice Walker's *In Search of Our Mothers' Gardens: Womanist Prose* (1983), and understood as part of the same period's deepening interest in the study of African American women's memoir and literary history.

An account of "how we led our lives, how we led *good* lives," *Lemon Swamp and Other Places* sketches memories of a vibrant family and community, rather than an analysis of "discrimination, violence, economic pressure, and deprivation of civil rights" (Fields 1983, xix–xx). At the same time, however, Fields demonstrates a keen awareness of the political connotations of black middle-class processes of self-fashioning. In the first half of the text, covering roughly the period between the 1880s and the early 1910s, *Lemon Swamp* contains numerous examples of Fields's perspective on the political significance of African American women's embrace of fashion, domestic arts, and modern beauty culture. From an early age, Fields understood that fashionably adorned black bodies often elicited negative responses from those Southern whites who believed feminine beauty and style were privileges for white women and girls alone. In the early 1890s Fields noticed the suspicion generated by her particularly fetching outfits:

> Once [Mother] crocheted a dress for me, a white dress, and . . . put yellow under it and passed yellow ribbons through it. My hair was long and curly, and when I wore that little dress, my mother would put a big yellow bow in my top plait and take me out. Well! The white people

stopped her in the street to ask where she got it; they thought maybe she was a laundress and stole it from some white woman. (9)

As Fields understood it, some white Charlestonians had difficulty entertaining the notion that her mother might be accomplished in dressmaking and other domestic arts, and moreover, inclined to dress her own children in her handiwork, rather than designing such wares for white women. Fields's description also suggests that these white observers experienced a sort of cognitive dissonance at encountering a black girl arrayed in the type of dress and ribbons that, in their mind, "belonged" to white women and girls. To build upon Shirley Tate's analysis of reactions to Michelle Obama's tenure as first lady, the pretty, crocheted dress and plaited hair of young Fields marked her as a black female body "out of place" in turn-of-the-century, Jim Crow Charleston (Tate 2012, 232). That this should happen during the rise of de jure segregation is not inconsequential. Indeed, as Barbara Young Welke (2001) has demonstrated in her study of American railways and the law during this period, it was the presence of neatly dressed, first-class-ticket-holding, "respectable" black women in the "ladies' car" of trains in the 1880s that undercut what conductors expected to be a straightforward system separating black and white passengers. Moreover, it was precisely because these same respectable black ladies repeatedly sued for the right to be accommodated in the ladies' car that Southern states responded by passing legislation mandating the segregation of the races on railway lines in the 1890s and 1900s (280–322). By showing themselves to be beautiful in interracial public spaces, young Mamie Garvin Fields and her mother became disruptive black bodies out of (their) place. And in doing so, they troubled and threatened the emergent Southern racial caste system.

As Fields's comments further suggest, these incidents were not solely about beautifully adorned black bodies. A black woman's display of such domestic skill and artistry *for herself and her family* turned the notion of white supremacy on its head. Domestic artistry and aesthetic sensibility served as important gender-specific indicators of respectability and elegance at a moment when cheap, ready-made articles of clothing were worn by poorer, urban African American and European immigrant women alike. By contrast, skills like dressmaking and crocheting, along with the other domestic arts, were key courses of study in black women's colleges and black women's urban settlement work at the time. Thus, they held special value and possibility for someone like Fields, who was the brown-skinned daughter of a carpenter and a member of a community that might best be described as respectable, middling, strivers, or "aspiring" (Mitchell 2004, xx) African Americans: men and women who were not members of the city's light-skinned elite, yet were active in churches and mutual aid societies and attentive to education, self-improvement, and racial "uplift" (Higginbotham 1993; Shaw 1996; White 1999).

After arriving at Claflin University with her sister, Fields found that "girls were still learning the crafts my mother had learned—crocheting, tatting, embroidery—but there were new things too." She recalled that

> Hattie learned "battenberg," which was very intricate work looping braid into various designs and sewing it down with a tiny stitch in linen thread. This work was very fashionable at the time. Hattie made a beautiful white battenberg tablecloth, which she put away for her trousseau. I was fond of needlework, and I liked drawing, but my favorite art classes were millinery and dressmaking. (Fields 1983, 87–88)

Fields also indicated that she chose to study dressmaking even as she worked toward her teaching certificate in an effort to expand her economic opportunities. "Many other times in my life, that training made it possible for me to earn money while staying at home . . . . Claflin gave me a trade, as well as my profession" (90). As Fields's experiences suggest, black women's facility with the domestic arts served multiple functions, simultaneously serving as potential pathways to economic independence, tools for personal and collective self-improvement, and evidence of respectability and middle-class status for aspiring African Americans.

For the rural poor, who often had little time to acquire such skills and no access to formal or informal networks of women to learn from, the creation and use of fine, handmade goods for the home and body signified urban culture and modernity as well as a black middle-class identity. Fields understood this dynamic, and elaborated on this phenomenon while reminiscing about summer visits to her extended family in the countryside as a child. After learning that her younger country cousins weren't taught to crochet the delicate items associated with the domestic arts, Fields was determined to give them lessons and insisted—over her cousins' initial objections—that they take the buggy into town to purchase crochet needles from the general store. Upon arriving in the town of Ehrhardt, Fields quickly learned that not only had she violated the town's Jim Crow custom limiting black shoppers to Saturdays but also transgressed white residents' racialized gender norms. She recalled, "We went on into the store, to a woman named Ruth. Ruth looked awhile and said to me, 'Whar ye cum frum?' (You know how some of those folks talk.) 'I come from Charleston.'" Ruth responded, "Um hum." Fields continued:

> So Marie and I stood there quiet, waiting for Ruth. "Well, why you ain't out thar in the fieeyuld pickin' cawtun," she wanted to know, "so much cawtun to pick?" "I don't know how to pick cotton. We don't have cotton where I come from. I like to pick cotton and have fun visiting here. But I came down to the store for a crochet needle." Silence awhile and still squinting.
> "A crochet needle. Who crochets?" she said, surprised to find somebody know how to crochet, I guess. Oh, they were begrudgeful, some of those crackers. They didn't like to see a colored child know about crocheting. Too refined. (Fields 1983, 71–72)

In recalling the incident, Fields made the connection between the racialization of the training (and spare time) necessary for the production of elegant accessories and articles of clothing and the maintenance of white supremacy. She explained:

> Really, certain whites didn't like to think you had leisure to do anything but pick cotton and work in the field. Even the children weren't supposed to. That's one reason why the Negro children had only a two-month school (the white had seven months), and it started after picking. Many black grown-ups were supposed to work every year for this or that white person. Just generally, if you were black, you were not supposed to have either time or money, and if you did, you ought not to show it. There were what we called "bad crackers" in Ehrhardt, who had the reputation of enforcing that sometimes. They'd whip a person or do something else humiliating, maybe even lynch you. But then, I didn't know enough that particular day to be afraid; I thought we could just go down and get the things for crocheting. (1983, 72)

For Fields, the ability to share the skills taught to her by her mother, and to crochet stylish accessories were markers of her status as a middle-class black girl, and her ability to style herself as such allowed her to create a modern, educated, urban sense of self that distinguished her from the rural, uneducated whites who sought to exercise power over her. These were skills associated with ideal black femininity and the behaviors aspiring black women and girls were instructed to emulate. This may well have informed her desire to share her knowledge and expertise with her cousins. Whatever the case, she was clearly aware that in the context of a small, rural Deep Southern town at the turn of the twentieth century, beauty, along with the skill to create it—much like education and respectable behavior—challenged white perceptions of what black girls like herself "ought to be and to do" (Shaw 1996, 24).

In addition to demonstrating just how charged black women's beauty could be for white observers, Fields's insistence on enjoying fashion and sharing knowledge of the domestic arts with friends and relatives invites us to further interrogate some of our assumptions about how African Americans practiced "style politics" in private, intraracial spaces. Whether it was former slaves claiming new articles of clothing for themselves in the wake of the Civil War (Glymph 2008, 204–9), black washerwomen and domestic servants dressing their best to enjoy their leisure time in the dance halls of turn-of-the-century Atlanta (Hunter 1997, 182–83), or later, when working-class men and women embraced the zoot suit in the 1930s and 1940s (Kelley 1994; Peiss 2014; Ramírez 2009), historians have found that members of the black and Latinx working classes engaged in style politics by creating their own idiosyncratic forms of fashion within their communities (White and White 1998, 190). They argue that in addition to providing a tremendous source of pleasure to the wearer, certain distinctive styles helped to bind together members of communities and subcultures, and marked the wearer as liberated, modern, and unencumbered by the marginalized status conferred upon them by white Americans (Kelley 1994; Chapman 2012).

Fields's embrace of fashion, as well as her clear sense of pride in her expertise as a dressmaker, suggests that much like their poor and working-class counterparts, middle-class and aspiring black women engaged in their own form of style politics during the early years of Jim Crow. This interpretation of black middle-class style politics is especially apparent in Fields's description of her and her sister Hattie's determination "to look just as good as anybody else" going off to college. Although they were "dressed to a T" when their father dropped them off at the station, they soon found that "looking just so after riding on the train wasn't easy." As she explained, "the train was segregated" and "white people were given the privilege of riding behind," away from the "dust and cinders" of the locomotive. "Up in front we had to fight to keep ourselves clean," she recalled. And as the train slowed on the approach to each station, "everybody would get up and commence to shake and brush and turn around, ask their neighbor to look over the coat, try not to offend anybody by shaking dust on them, so forth." As she put it, "Back then, we dressed. We had the idea that the way you looked when arriving reflected where you came from and how your people carried themselves. Because of that, everybody cleaned up the best they could just before arriving" (1983, 85–86). Declarations such as these must be understood, as Shane White and Graham White have argued, as "not merely vivid repudiations of black physical and aesthetic inferiority, but salutary expressions of African American pride" (1998, 218). Thus, to ensure that they made a good impression on the cousins who planned to meet them at the station, "Hattie and I fixed one another's things when we got near Orangeburg" (Fields 1983, 86). References such as these suggest that Fields, her family, and her friends defined their self-presentation in terms of their own families and communities, and more significantly, made their personal fashion choices and determination to be stylish part of an ongoing refusal to be limited by or measured according to the yardstick preferred by hostile white observers.

This distinctive version of style politics is especially apparent in one story involving Fields and her friends. Given its complexity, it is worth discussing at length. In the summer of 1913, Fields decided to accompany her godmother on an extended trip to Boston, Massachusetts, and earn extra income before her upcoming wedding to Robert Lucas Fields. By that autumn, Fields and her friend Myrtle Benton were faring very well, working at a shirtwaist factory making ready-made garments alongside European immigrant women during the day, and boarding with the parents of their friend Ellestine Lee in the evenings. All talented seamstresses, Lee, Benton, and Fields were also running their own sewing room out of Ellestine's bedroom. Christening their business venture Parisian Vogue, the enterprising young ladies "made a display of pictures cut from magazines" such as *Vogue* and installed a sign in Ellestine's bedroom window. Soon women from their Roxbury neighborhood were flocking to Parisian Vogue to purchase Mamie, Myrtle, and Ellestine's stylish made-to-order creations, garments of notably higher quality than those they manufactured in the factory during the day (Fields 1983, 150).

One day, a woman they called Sister Green came upstairs to place an order. Sister Green, as Fields later recalled, was one of those fat church sisters, the kind who wear a lot of perfume, a lot of jewelry, great big hats, and of course, "the latest" style, whatever that happens to be. Well naturally she wanted a style she saw in one of our pictures, with a long, narrow body and fitted long sleeves, just the thing she needn't wear. However, she was also the type of church sister who knows exactly what she wants, says so clearly, and is used to getting things done exactly that way. She wasn't the type you could make a suggestion to, like "I think this one with the full sleeves would be more flattering." No. Sister Green walked right in, looked at the picture of an outfit with a cinched-in-waist, and saw *herself*. (151)

Over six decades later, as Mamie Garvin Fields recounted this story to her granddaughter, she detailed the way that she and her friends set about bridging the gap between the "plump" black body of Sister Green and the slender white feminine ideal on display in the pages of *Vogue*. The task was not a simple one, Fields recalled, for when Ellestine began taking measurements, "we could see right there that where the bodice was supposed to go in, it had to go out." And "the sleeves, which were supposed to taper from wide to narrow, had to go in and then out over Sister's arms. *Um*-um-um." So "for the fittings," she said, "we covered the mirror. We were the mirror." And rather than comparing her body negatively against that of the *Vogue* model on display, they described what would best flatter Sister Green's figure. When they finished, they had designed a beautiful dress. Fields explained that, "when we finally pulled back the drape from the mirror the day she came to get the dress, [Sister Green] looked at herself for a long, long time. Then all of a sudden she began to smile, turn around, pat her hair, primp *pleased as could be*. Hallelujah! She liked it. It did look nice," she recalled. Although "the dress really didn't look a thing like the picture . . . it did fit Sister Green like a glove." Having pleased Sister Green, who was apparently "a woman of influence" whom the other women in the church "copied," Mamie, Myrtle, and Ellestine were soon inundated with orders for similar dresses; once Sister Green wore her dress to the church tea, apparently "everyone in church wanted one" (151).

Fields's description of Sister Green's experience with Parisian Vogue raises a number of additional and intriguing questions about elite and aspiring black women's engagement with fashion and style politics. How is it that Sister Green is able to look at an image from *Vogue* and see herself when she is neither the target audience for such fashions, nor is her body, by virtue of her African ancestry and weight, the standard beauty ideal? What does Fields's and her friends' collective role as Sister Green's mirror, or the churchwomen's tendency to copy Sister Green's style tell us about how we might think about black women's ways of seeing, admiring, and embodying beauty in the early twentieth century? And how does the act of creating beauty and fashion away from the white gaze, serve as an affirmation of black women's beauty and worth during the height of the Jim Crow era?

To start, the interplay between Mamie Garvin Fields, Myrtle Benton, Ellestine Lee, and Sister Green troubles the longstanding notion that fashion for respectable black young ladies and the older, influential church sisters they respected was purely imitative of white middle-class values and ideals. There is a subtle but persistent tendency to characterize the behavior and style associated with black middle-class respectability as a rejection of authentic black working-class values and a wholesale embrace of elite white ones. But what if we entertain the possibility that with style, as with other forms of expressive culture such as music, language, and dance, black women were able to create something new for themselves and their communities? Shane White and Graham White have argued that such style politics were essential for black New Yorkers transitioning from slavery to freedom in the early nineteenth century (1998, 101, 123–24). It is important to recognize that the same type of agency, skill, and creative adaptation was still at play as Fields and the other young women translated the style displayed in *Vogue* into something special, unique, and purposely designed for Sister Green at the turn of the twentieth century.

Moreover, Sister Green's behavior in Paris Vogue upends standard arguments about the ways black women negotiated white standards of beauty at the turn of the century. Scholars have long demonstrated that in the nineteenth and early twentieth centuries, "beauty culture was uniquely [political] for African American women, in large part because they confronted popular images of feminine beauty that perpetually used a white ideal" (Walker 2007, 3). This was especially true for black Southerners, who, as Blain Roberts has argued, were characterized by whites as the antithesis of beauty and refinement for white women (2014, 7). Over the course of the nineteenth and early twentieth centuries, these white ideals of beauty were elevated by advertisements marketing products for a rapidly growing beauty industry, and framed in explicit opposition to blackness, as Noliwe M. Rooks has shown (1996, 26–40). Given this context, black women found themselves constantly negotiating white ideals of beauty and intraracial colorism in the first half of the twentieth century (Craig 2002), and furthermore, as Roberts contends, engaging in a difficult and "ongoing struggle to be recognized as attractive" in the Jim Crow South (2014, 59).

But Fields demonstrates that even as black women negotiated the white beauty ideals promoted by advertisers, they did not always internalize these beliefs. In fact, Sister Green's ability to look at an image from *Vogue* and see herself suggests that black women had already devised what bell hooks calls "oppositional viewing strategies" that allowed them to appreciate and enjoy forms of visual culture and fashion not meant for them without sustaining damage to their psyche (1992, 120; 124). Indeed, market research on black consumers in the 1930s suggests that this ability was widespread by the interwar era. By this period, black women appear to have developed alternate ways of reading a visual landscape that, by in large, sought to reinscribe slavery on the bodies of black people, and to frame black servility as the key to white beauty, affluence, and luxury (Marchand 1984; Manring 1998; Peiss 1998). According to this research, black consumers evinced a deep aversion to images that endorsed slavery or black servility, or portrayed white characters as somehow superior to black figures. So instead of responding to the promise of aspirational whiteness inherent in much of the advertisements of the day, black consumers focused on the product itself (Edwards [1932] 1969). Sister Green's behavior in Parisian Vogue indicates that at least some black women had developed this way of viewing fashion advertisements and magazines at least two decades earlier, before the Great Migration and its attendant cultural and political developments. If they were like Sister Green, they could look at the image of a beautiful dress in *Vogue*, without fixating on the white model in the frame. Instead, they could see *themselves* in the product embodying their own version of black beauty.

It is also important to keep in mind the spaces in which such cultural processes took place. Indeed, one of the most striking aspects of this anecdote is that it was a closed, intimate, black woman's space: a bedroom in a private home. As scholars have shown, whether it was the antebellum slave cabin or the 1960s "soul sister's" college dorm room, it was in intimate, communal spaces such as these that black women created their own, alternative, ideals of beauty (Camp 2004, 78–86; Ford 2015, 112–116). And as Davarian Baldwin has noted in his study of Chicago during the Great Migration, "the beauty salons, kitchens, and porches" of urban black communities served as "important venues where women finalized the process of reconstructing themselves as sophisticated and modern" (2007, 62).

Moreover, as Mamie Garvin Fields, Ellestine Lee, and Myrtle Benton designed that dress for Sister Green, they allowed their respective gazes to serve as positive affirmations of their judgment, expertise, and individual sense of style. Fields tells us how they spoke to each other:

> "I think Sister Green would like it better if we shortened here." "Well, I don't know, Myrtle. What do you think?" "Let Sister Green raise her arm and tell us how it feels." And so on like that, until Sister said, "You *stylish* girls do just what you think will suit. You are the professionals." (1983, 151)

These types of interactions underscore the fact that the young women in Lee's bedroom were not simply service workers catering to the whims of an unfamiliar customer from a higher class or a different race. Rather, they were engaging in a caring ritual as members of a community of aspiring black women. Moreover, these sorts of positive affirmations accompanying communal African American women's beauty rituals serve as an important reminder that even beyond the juke joint and the dance hall, a shared sense of style and attention to self-care in private spaces helped to create and nurture black women's community.

Finally, Sister Green's love for distinctive style reminds us that fashion was not appreciated and embraced by black women solely for its utility in ongoing campaigns to uplift and reform the race. The pleasure Sister Green seemed to feel as she smiled, turned around, patted her hair, and primped before the mirror suggests that she took immense gratification in looking her best. There is a sense of almost palpable delight at the way she first allows herself to be fitted and cared for by the young women, and then revels in her joy when she finally takes a long look at herself wearing the finished product. Sister Green not only looks good, she clearly feels good too. This is hardly the type of reserved decorum required for the public displays of respectability that, scholars have long argued, dominated elite and aspiring black women's activism in this period (Gilmore 1996; Higginbotham 1993; Shaw 1996; White 1999; Wolcott 2001). And while we can't know exactly whom Sister Green might want to make such an effort to impress, it seems unlikely that her primary audience was white observers. Indeed, whiteness takes a backseat in this little tale. Remember, Sister Green was the final and ultimate judge of her own appearance. She saw herself, and she liked what she saw. As Fields explained to her granddaughter in the 1970s, "There is a lesson from the way Miss Green looked at that *Vogue* model and saw herself, and it isn't the one people always say, 'See yourself as others see you': it's 'People will see you the way you see yourself'! Plump Sister Green never thought she wasn't chic, and so nobody else did either" (1983, 152). Sister Green's ability to see her own body in a positive light further empowered her to define herself on her own terms. And as the historian Stephanie Camp has argued, these moments of self-actualization, moments where black women could take pleasure in their own bodies and beauty on their own terms, must be understood in political as well as aesthetic terms (2004, 61–92).

In framing her recollection of Sister Green in this way, Mamie Garvin Fields demonstrates just how important style politics, self-fashioning, and beauty culture were to middle-class and aspiring black women in the period. As I have argued elsewhere, black middle-class self-fashioning was a project that early-nineteenth-century elite and aspiring free black men and women engaged in an effort to define themselves on their own terms and in their own private spaces *despite the fact* that they lived in a slaveholding republic. For them, certain forms of self-improvement activities, such as literacy, institution-building, and temperance, held enormous value, helping them to define themselves—for themselves, if no one else—as the living antithesis of proslavery discourse. Beauty practices, I would argue, must be understood as the corporeal version of this project for turn-of-the-twentieth-century black women.

Lemon Swamp and Other Places demonstrates that for Mamie Garvin Fields, her friends, and her family, beauty and fashion were crucial to their sense of themselves as members of a community of modern, urban, middle-class black women. Moreover, moving beyond discussions of the negative impact of white beauty standards, *Lemon Swamp* offers a window onto those private spaces where black women crafted their own counter-narratives about black women's beauty. The memoir suggests that Mamie Garvin Fields and her community clearly understood their ability to determine, design, and enjoy their own stylish creations in both public and private inter- and intraracial spaces as a powerful assertion of their humanity, individuality, and determination to thrive as black women in a hostile world. In the process, *Lemon Swamp and Other Places* offers insight into the complex and multifaceted ways that middle-class and aspiring African American women conceptualized and deployed style politics at the turn of the twentieth century.

Erica L. Ball is professor of American studies at Occidental College. She is the author of *To Live an Antislavery Life: Personal Politics and the Antebellum Black Middle Class* and coeditor of *Reconsidering Roots: Race, Politics, and Memory*. She can be reached at balle@oxy.edu.

Works Cited

Baldwin, Davarian L. 2007. *Chicago's New Negroes: Modernity, the Great Migration, and Black Urban Life*. Chapel Hill: University of North Carolina Press.

Camp, Stephanie M. H. 2004. *Closer to Freedom: Enslaved Women and Everyday Resistance in the Plantation South*. Chapel Hill: University of North Carolina Press.

Chapman, Erin D. 2012. *Prove It On Me: New Negroes, Sex, and Popular Culture in the 1920s*. New York: Oxford University Press.

Craig, Maxine Leeds. 2002. *Ain't I a Beauty Queen? Black Women, Beauty, and the Politics of Race*. New York: Oxford University Press.

Edwards, Paul K. (1932) 1969. *The Southern Urban Negro as a Consumer*. Reprint, New York: Negro Universities Press.

Fields, Mamie Garvin, and Karen Fields. 1983. *Lemon Swamp and Other Places: A Carolina Memoir*. New York: Free Press.

Ford, Tanisha C. 2015. *Liberated Threads: Black Women, Style, and the Global Politics of Soul*. Chapel Hill: The University of North Carolina Press.

Giddings, Paula J. 1984. *When and Where I Enter: The Impact of Black Women on Race and Sex in America*. New York: William Morrow.

Gill, Tiffany M. 2010. *Beauty Shop Politics: African American Women's Activism in the Beauty Industry*. Urbana: University of Illinois Press.

Gilmore, Glenda Elizabeth. 1996. *Gender and Jim Crow: Women and the Politics of White Supremacy in North Carolina, 1896–1920*. Chapel Hill: University of North Carolina Press.

Glymph, Thavolia. 2008. *Out of the House of Bondage: The Transformation of the Plantation Household*. New York: Cambridge University Press.

Higginbotham, Evelyn Brooks. 1993. *Righteous Discontent: The Women's Movement in the Black Baptist Church, 1880–1920*. Cambridge, MA: Harvard University Press.

hooks, bell. 1992. *Black Looks: Race and Representation*. Boston: South End Press.

Hunter, Tera W. 1997. *To 'Joy My Freedom: Black Women's Lives and Labors after the Civil War*. Cambridge, MA: Harvard University Press.

Kelley, Robin D. G. 1994. "The Riddle of the Zoot: Malcolm Little and Black Cultural Politics during World War II." In *Race Rebels: Culture, Politics, and the Black Working Class*, 161–82. New York: Free Press.

Lerner, Gerda. 1972. *Black Women in White America: A Documentary History*. New York: Pantheon Books.

Lorde, Audre. 1988. *A Burst of Light*. Ithaca, NY: Firebrand Press.

Manring, M. M. 1998. *Slave in a Box: The Strange Career of Aunt Jemima*. Charlottesville: University of Virginia Press.

Marchand, Roland. 1984. *Advertising the American Dream: Making Way for Modernity, 1920–1940*. Berkeley: University of California Press.

Mitchell, Michele. 2004. *Righteous Propagation: African Americans and the Politics of Racial Destiny after Reconstruction*. Chapel Hill: University of North Carolina Press.

Morgan, Francesca. 2017. "'My Furthest-Back Person': Black Genealogy Before and After *Roots*." In *Reconsidering Roots: Race, Politics, and Memory*, edited by Erica L. Ball and Kellie Carter Jackson, 63–78. Athens: University of Georgia Press.

Peiss, Kathy. 1998. *Hope in a Jar: The Making of America's Beauty Culture*. New York: Metropolitan Books.

———. 2014. *Zoot Suit: The Enigmatic Career of an Extreme Style*. Philadelphia: University of Pennsylvania Press.

Ramírez, Catherine S. 2009. *The Woman in the Zoot Suit: Gender, Nationalism, and the Cultural Politics of Memory*. Durham, NC: Duke University Press.

Roberts, Blain. 2014. *Pageants, Parlors & Pretty Women: Race and Beauty in the Twentieth-Century South*. Chapel Hill: University of North Carolina Press.

Rooks, Noliwe M. 1996. *Hair Raising: Beauty, Culture, and African American Women*. New Brunswick, NJ: Rutgers University Press.

Shaw, Stephanie J. 1996. *What a Woman Ought to Be and to Do: Black Professional Women Workers During the Jim Crow Era*. Chicago: University of Chicago Press.

Sterling, Dorothy. 1984. *We Are Your Sisters: Black Women in the Nineteenth Century*. New York: W. W. Norton & Company.

Tate, Shirley. 2012. "Michelle Obama's Arms: Race, Respectability and Class Privilege." *Comparative American Studies: An International Journal* 10 (2/3): 226–38.

Walker, Alice. 1983. *In Search of Our Mothers' Gardens: Womanist Prose*. San Diego, CA: Harcourt Brace Jovanovich.

Walker, Susannah. 2007. *Style and Status: Selling Beauty to African American Women, 1920–1975*. Lexington: University of Kentucky Press.

Welke, Barbara Young. 2001. *Recasting American Liberty: Gender, Race, Law and the Railroad Revolution, 1865–1920*. New York: Cambridge University Press.

White, Deborah Gray. 1985. *Ar'n't I a Woman: Female Slaves in the Plantation South*. New York: W. W. Norton & Company.

———. 1999. *Too Heavy a Load: Black Women in Defense of Themselves, 1894–1994*. New York: W. W. Norton & Company.

White, Shane, and Graham White. 1998. *Stylin': African American Expressive Culture from Its Beginnings to the Zoot Suit*. Ithaca, NY: Cornell University Press.

Wolcott, Victoria W. 2001. *Remaking Respectability: African American Women in Interwar Detroit*. Chapel Hill: University of North Carolina Press.

Dying to Be Beautiful:
(Re)Membering the Women of Juárez, the Commodification of Death, and the Nonuniversal Standards of Beauty

Bernadine Hernández

Abstract: In 2010 MAC Cosmetics, owned by Estée Lauder, teamed up with a small fashion house in Los Angeles, California, called Rodarte to put out a makeup and clothing collection based on Juárez, México. The Rodarte sisters visited Juárez and fell in love with the "hazy" landscape and based this beauty collaboration on the industrial border town and the women who were coming out of work from the maquiladoras. This article is concerned with how the discourses and popular culture that surround the women of Juárez are used to not only commodify their deaths but also to construct standards of beauty at the expense of poor Mexican women. (Re)membering is not only memorializing the dead women of Juárez through veins of capital, but it is the actual re-membering of their subjectivities and bodies that clump them together as nothing more than "victims." Keywords: border, violence, transnational feminism, beauty industry, feminicides, Juárez

In 2010 MAC Cosmetics, owned by Estée Lauder, teamed up with Rodarte, a small fashion house in Los Angeles, California. Rodarte was founded in 2005 by Kate and Laura Mulleavy and is known by most in the fashion and beauty industry as a "mixture of high couture, modern femininity, and Californian influences" (Shapovalova 2015). However, as Nicole Phelps describes in an online article for *Vogue*, in 2010 they could not find much Californian inspiration and instead took a trip to the border of El Paso, Texas, and Juárez, México, to gain "inspiration" from the "ethereal" desert landscape. After the Mulleavy sisters returned from their road trip they collaborated with MAC Cosmetics on a makeup line that would coincide with their Fall 2010 clothing collection based on that

WSQ: Women's Studies Quarterly 46: 1 & 2 (Spring/Summer 2018) © 2018 by Bernadine Hernández.
All rights reserved.

trip. The sisters stated that their mother is Mexican and Italian and they wanted to get in touch with their Mexican ancestry when they stopped in the Juárez desert to tour the city. Once there, they latched on to the "hazy, dreamlike" quality of the landscape and the maquiladora workers going into the factories at night. The two decided to build an entire collection off the idea of sleepwalking and ghosts (Phelps 2010). The hazy landscape that they fell in love with was caused by the pollution from factory industrialization on the border and their obsession with the women as sleepwalkers and ghosts is layered with critiques of global capitalism, labor exploitation, and gender violence. Their partnership with MAC resulted in the same thematic idea titled the Juárez Collection. The makeup range included Ghost Town, a sheer white lipstick with white, gold, and green pearlized frost; a mineralized eye shadow called Sleepwalker that was a beige with copper, pale blue, and pale pink veining; a shimmery mid-tone blue-pink blush called Quinceañera; and a nice light-opal mint-frost nail lacquer called Factory. The photo campaign MAC released for the Juárez collection situated a ghastly looking white model with sunken eyes and a white draped dress next to a ghost shadow figure with a white pearled dress, dripping in what seems to be iridescent blood. When the press kits and preview photos of the makeup were sent to key beauty bloggers and industry experts internationally, many were struck by the "romantic" theme of the collaboration, but three beauty bloggers were outraged that the Rodarte sisters used the women of Juárez as inspiration for their collection and wrote about it aggressively until Rodarte and MAC released an apology. The three women who blew the cover off the scandal were Jessica Wakeman, a New York City–based blogger at the *Frisky*, Liloo Grunewald at *Le Petit Jardin de Liloo*, and Yinka Odusote who writes for *Vex in the City*, the latter two women working in the United Kingdom.

After the uproar in the beauty blogosphere and throughout the beauty industry, Rodarte and MAC each released their own apologies, but they came too late for some. Phelps further clarifies that for others, the "edgy and artistic" portrayal of the women of Juárez in the beauty and fashion industry was "cozy," "romantic," "beautiful," and "emotional" (2010). When beauty symbolizes death in the context of the "first world" at the expense of poor Mexican women, there is much to untangle. This production, consumption, and exploitation of subaltern Mexican female bodies and the process of (re)membering them after their death is not only the commodification of their bodies but also relies on the marketable illusion of their subjectivity to promote a conventional standard of beauty not available to women of color in the same regard.[1]

How can one woman become beautiful through the death of another? This article is concerned with how discourses and popular culture surrounding the women of Juárez are used not only to commodify their deaths but also how this discourse and memorialization is utilized to construct standards of beauty at the expense of poor Mexican women. (Re)membering is not only memorializing the dead women of Juárez through veins of capital but it is also the actual re-membering of their subjectivities and bodies that clump them together as nothing more than "victims." The irony of this whole incident is that many of the victims in Juárez work in exploitative transnational maquiladoras, which supply fabrics, clothing, and goods to the United States, and in doing so, participate in the production of the conventional standards of beauty unavailable to them. In the same vein, the Rodarte sisters, as Mexican Americans and first world subjects, can profit off of the production of "beauty" from the deaths of poor Mexican women and package it as artistic. Rodarte apologized saying, "We recognize that the violence against women taking place in Juarez [sic] needs to be met with proactive action. We never intended to make light of this serious issue and we are truly sorry. Helping to improve the conditions for women in Juarez [sic] is a priority for us" (Temptalia 2010). While Rodarte issued this apology, they still went on to stage their "sleepwalker" ready-to-wear runway show and fashion line. MAC, on the other hand, issued an apology and pulled their line from distribution, "We understand that product names in the M·A·C Rodarte collection have offended our consumers and fans. This was never our intent and we are very sorry" (Temptalia 2010). MAC also stated they would donate their projected global profits of one hundred thousand dollars to a nonprofit organization helping to end the violence against women in Juárez, but as of January 2017, there is no record of that donation.

As for Rodarte, Phelps writes for *Vogue* that she was impressed by the "arts and craft, naïve, almost random quality" of the collection, and many major celebrities had similar reactions (2010). Many of the dresses were patchworked together from vintage lace, floral chiffons, burnout velvets, and other salvaged bits from the "imagined maquiladoras' floors" and draped with strands of pearls. The deadly romantic vibe the show gave off closed with a quartet of "ethereal, unraveling, rather beautiful white dresses that alternately called to mind *quinceañera* parties, corpse brides, and if you wanted to look at it through a really dark prism, the ghosts of the victims of Juárez's drug wars." Laura Mulleavy stated that Juárez was the inspiration for the sleepwalking and ghost theme. She stated that the women on the border and the women in the show "exist in between two worlds" (Phelps 2010). The sisters wanted to translate something that was light and ephemeral, but darker at its core. Rodarte is well known for their relentlessly gothic creations and the Mulleavy's stand behind their idea that you can be scarred and still beautiful. But beautiful for whom and to what end?

For MAC and Rodarte to (re)member the victims of Juárez in this way is to bottle and sell a romanticized notion of the violence to make other women look edgy, pretty, and "natural." There is nothing natural about poverty and labor exploitation. Women in Juárez are dying and other women are wearing a product that profits off of their death. It makes sense that the Rodarte sisters talk about the landscape in terms of beauty and femininity, because that "ethereal" nature is what lured colonists thousands of years ago to plunder, pillage, and rape the land. Through historical trauma and the ideology of colonialism, subaltern, poor, and Indigenous Mexican beauty is excessive in relation to white femininity as are the subaltern, poor, and Indigenous Mexican bodies once left in the desert as things.[2] The clothing and beauty lines by MAC and Rodarte were not made for these women, but made off of the backs of their deaths and the violence that occurred to their bodies. The commodification of death is apparent and the logic of the beauty campaign is to make women look beautiful, when the standards of beauty for women of color are differentiated and come at higher costs because they are not only gendered racially, but also racially gendered as improperly feminine. It begs us to ask: What is beauty? Who can be beautiful within our society? And if we break the beauty mold, is that inclusive or tokenizing?

Global capital, the denationalization of women's rights, state-sanctioned violence, and patriarchy all serve their purpose in the exploitation and assassination of women of color in México and Latin America. The feminicides in Juárez took a steady upturn in May of 1993.[3] Since then, upwards of one thousand female bodies have been found in various forms and places, such as the desert, alleyways, water sources, and garbage dumps. Other women in Juárez and surrounding areas have gone missing and their bodies never recovered. According to the National Citizen Femicide Observatory, as of 2015, six women are killed each day in the border town of Juárez and only approximately 1.6 percent of the murders investigated lead to sentencing (Matloff 2015). The feminicides have been thrust into popular imagination by songwriters like "Tori Amos, At the Drive In, Lila Downs, Los Tigres del Norte, and Los Jaguares" (Gaspar de Alba and Guzmán 2010, 3). There are many short films, documentaries, and Hollywood blockbusters that portray the murders; and hundreds of short stories, poems, novels, visual art, performance art, scholarly articles, and countless investigative journalism pieces about the women of Juárez. The victims are generalized to be "predominately between the ages of twelve and twenty-three, young, slim, petite, dark-haired, and dark-skinned" (3). Scholars have likened the women of Juárez to the concepts of "bare life" or the "production of human waste" that Giorgio Agamben (1998) and Zygmunt Bauman (2004) theorize for other historical periods. However, I contend that these Western/European theorists cannot offer serious engagement with the power structures producing the death for the women of Juárez. Alicia Schmidt Camacho reminds us that border industrialization was a cross-border plan meant to fuse the relationship between capital, cheap labor, and service. However, she also reminds us that the constant labeling and representation of poor Mexican women as female bodies available for appropriation reinforces cultural narratives that turn these women in cadavers to be consumed then discarded (2010, 278). That this cultural narrative is persistent in the United States and México, as well as within first world social theory, is problematic as it runs the risk of erasing the organizing efforts of Mexican women, their families, and transnational feminists.

Still, there is a gendered system of cross-border legalities, deportations, and power that cement the position of poor Mexican women in society. Due to historical immigration and labor laws, like the famous Bracero Program that prohibited women and children from becoming legal braceros, migration on the border between the United States and México has historically been male centered (Hernández 2010, 202). However, what cements the Mexican woman's position in her society with regard to immigration and labor laws is informed not only by this male-centered migration history but also the fact that women continued to migrate unprotected across the border for domestic work, despite legal restrictions, because of the institutional inability to handle female migrant workers or deportees. In fact, many of the women were sexually assaulted en route to the United States or, if detained, in the Immigration and Naturalization Service facilities (202). This position is informed by the deep-seated patriarchy women have to deal with daily in México and the United States that is intertwined with global capital and state-sanctioned violence. It is also rooted in racist border policies that do not enforce bodily protection for Mexican women, but instead facilitate corporate extraction of their labor power for transnational use. Law and order was not lacking for Mexican and Central American women, but it was not upheld or negotiated since they are not perceived as important enough to attempt to combat their brutalization and murder by the United States or México. Kelly Lytle Hernández reminds us that public discourse in the 1950s and 1960s reserved brutalization for men and male juveniles (2010, 203). Even though women were "not allowed" to cross the border, these unsanctioned crossings caused the violence to shift to women and a surge in deadly situations. As more women made the conscious decision to not cross the border because of violent brutalization, border industrialization offered a different kind of gender and sexual violence for poor, subaltern Mexican women. Even before the signing of the North American Free Trade Agreement, Hernández reminds us that "many transnational corporations, which located their factories in México to take advantage of cheap labor and minimal trade barriers, did not pay a living wage, and working conditions for the overwhelmingly young and female workforce were often dangerous, if not outright lethal" (230).

The transnational context that creates the commodification of particular Mexican women is evident in border and immigration policy and was further solidified when the border-industrialization program was implemented in 1967. With border industrialization, 160 enterprises that were subsidiaries of U.S. firms sprung up along the U.S.-México border. These enterprises, or maquiladoras, employed over seventeen thousand people in México at the time of their implementation, over 75 percent being Mexican women looking for jobs because of displacement in their hometowns (Ericson 1970, 34). The Mexican government agreed to waive its duties and regulations on the importation of machinery, equipment, and raw materials for these maquiladoras, as well as its restriction of foreign capital, so long as end products, mainly assemblies of U.S. components, are exported. The only duty paid is for products not made in the United States. In this case, it is primarily the labor to assemble the products, that is unprotected under Section 708 of the

Tariff Schedule. Due largely to this lack of protection, the conventional wage in maquiladoras was typically $1.60 per hour in 1968 and 1969. U.S. companies preferred to locate their factories in cities such as Juárez because of the low-wage labor and the usage of the Programa Nacional Fronterizo facilities already built by the Mexican government.[4] The transnational economic exchange between U.S. and Mexican industrial and corporate companies and México's support for easier capital flow across borders solidifies the link between the global and the local in Juárez. This means that global capital fuels the already intense Mexican patriarchal nation-state that only legally recognizes violence against women "as crimes against the honor of the family, rather than as crimes against the personal, physical integrity and human rights of the woman victim" (Fregoso 2003, 18). The Mexican nation-state logic states that if the women were not outside of the domestic space, then they would not be susceptible to murder or disappearance. This age-old victim blaming functions as a tool of political repression sanctioned by an undemocratic patriarchal state for women living on the border. By blaming the victims for their own murders, the Mexican nation-state is able to politically claim no responsibility for the murders and keep the patriarchal state intact. And for the murder victims in Juárez, their position as denationalized and commodified subjects functions intricately with the patriarchal standards structuring the state and transnational/global capital.[5]

This transnational economic context and the gender violence central to the U.S. and Mexican states inform the further commodification of Juárez women in U.S. beauty discourses, as exemplified by the Rodarte fashion campaign. In order to think about the standards of beauty being sold at the expense of Juárez victims' personhood and bodies after death, we must examine how the social constructs of the Mexican national imaginary positions the women as a living commodity or "thing" to be consumed and discarded. To think of the women of Juárez as a commodity in the Marxist sense is to think about how they are owned. For Karl Marx, the body is the mere appendage to capital and its labor becomes a commodity external to being. The commodity has two essential factors: exchange value and use value, meaning the substance of value and the magnitude of value. However, in the case of the feminicides and the women of Juárez, how can a body be a commodity if it is not really owned by anyone or anything? In Julia Estela Monárrez Fragoso's astute essay "The Victims of Ciudad Juárez Feminicide: Sexually Fetishized Commodities," she states that "the different bodily qualities that are codified in gender, ethnicity, social class, and other means of valuing human men and women, including the degree of respect of bodily integrity and the dignity the worker's body achieves in different places, exist in an environment that is made spatially competitive through the circulation of capital" (2010, 63). The women of Juárez are represented and produced as signifiers of the racial, gender, and economic systems through a social process of value or who is worth what. These women, both before and after death, are "exterior object[s], a thing with its own properties satisfying needs of all kinds" (Marx 2011, 46). In this case, the patriarchal conditions a woman in Juárez lives under in México as well as the global capital investment in her body constitute these "needs." While she is not transactionally owned and has agency, she embodies social use and exchange value for México, the United States, and the maquiladoras. Monárrez Fragoso rereads Marx's notion of the commodity, inserts her own comments in brackets and states,

> The nature of these needs, which originate either from hunger or fantasy, [in the cultural construction of women] does not modify the problem whatsoever. . . . The same body of the commodity [the body of women] is thus of use value or a good. . . . By the same token it is necessary to reduce the exchange value of the [women/commodities] to something that is common, with respect to that which they more or less represent [in terms of social class and gender, as well as of race and ethnicity].
> (2010, 64)

Mexican cultural norms have structured the lives of women in Juárez as commodities that can be consumed and have use and exchange value. It is not that these women do not mean anything to their families and others that interact with them daily, but border industrialization in conjunction with the Mexican nation-state and the Mexican national media discuss the women in terms of patriarchy and capital. The Mexican patriarchal nation-state and U.S. industrial border factories value these women's bodies differently than first world bodies because the taking of life is not an open act to anyone. This means that homicide is illegal by law, however, the law is not upheld in relation to the victims of Juárez because of their fluctuating legal value. Thus, maquiladoras invested in transnational trade utilize the women for their productive and reproductive capacity. The transnational trade on the border utilizes racialized gender as what Ruth Wilson Gilmore tracks as racism, "specifically, the state-sanctioned or extralegal production and exploitation of group-differentiated vulnerability to premature death" (2007, 28).

The currency of death is not an anomaly for contemporary society. Marx constructs living through death when he states that "life belongs to the object . . . meaning whatever the product of his labor is, he is not" (1932, 29). There is no life in capitalism. However, there is a self that can be recuperated through the demystification of the material realities that shape society. Even through all this, the thing or "object" that Marx comes to see as a commodity is what has authority. In the case of Mexican media coverage and, more importantly, the Rodarte fashion campaigns, rendering the women of Juárez as things makes them responsible for their own position and their own death because it does not question the violent structures of power. They become the carriers of the values society places on them, which is congealed in the commodity, just as it is congealed in the Marxist sense of the commodity. Rosa Linda Fregoso reminds us that the Mexican government and media perpetuate this discourse of the commodity along with la doble vida narrative that these women were also engaged in sex work after their shifts at the maquiladoras (2003, 10). After they are used, murdered, and disposed of, their death becomes something to sell, not because people are concerned with stopping the murders, but because the romantic notion of their suffering translates to iridescent lipsticks, rosy red blush, and flowing, patchwork dresses.

Globalism, particularly in the beauty industry, fuels the commodification of subaltern Mexican females that in turn fuels an already toxic atmosphere for women in the Mexican patriarchal nation-state. This, in turn, is linked to how standards of beauty in the United States are constructed at the expense of brown women's bodies. The cheapest MAC makeup product sells for fifteen dollars and Rodarte's cheapest item of clothing is a T-shirt that sells for over two hundred dollars. In a time of racial capitalism evident by the exploitative wages of the Mexican women in the maquiladoras, the target audiences for these beauty products are white women of first-world nations. I deploy the term "racial capitalism" coined by Cedric J. Robinson in Black Marxism to understand that "racialism and its permutations persisted, rooted not in a particular era but in the civilization itself" (1983, 28). Race became the rationalization for domination, exploitation, and extermination of non-Europeans, and the interlocking structures of race and class were the basis for capitalist domination. It is no coincidence that the maquiladoras are placed on the U.S.-México border because the labor was always already devalued through racial tensions and capital.

The impact of beauty campaigns featuring lower-class women being sold to upper-class women is vast. To start, the standards of beauty that cross into México from the United States are unattainable for poor, Mexican women. In México, while the main symbol of femininity is Our Lady of Guadalupe, "darkness" is either completely rejected or delicately embraced. The mestiza "innocent" and "demure" nature of Our Lady is "symptomatic of the way in which two national concerns, the racial and the sexual, [are] inscribed on her body" (Ruiz 2002, 290). Both the United States and México have standards of beauty that favor light skin, but the "native" and colonial past of each country require a more nuanced understanding of how beauty is shaped in each place. It is evident that the Rodarte sisters and MAC Cosmetics were functioning from U.S. beauty standards with their Juárez line because there was scarce portrayal of women of color in both the beauty campaign or fashion show. This centering of whiteness exemplifies how the beauty industry is profiting off an already commodified female population who can never achieve the standard of beauty they are being used to sell. The Rodarte/MAC beauty campaign was targeting an upper-class and "light"-skinned femininity.

In México the imposition of whiteness promotes the "Hellenic beauty type" (Ruiz 2002, 291). Manuel Gamio—archaeologist, anthropologist, and judge for Mexican beauty pageants—argues that the Hellenic beauty standards are not accepted beauty ideals by a majority of Mexicans. The Hellenic type does not match the racial phenotype of the majority of the population and he states, "*Sería imposible esperar que nuestros indios y mestizos aceptarán tales cánones, porque no corresponden a su ideal de belleza*" (It would be impossible to wait for our Indians and mestizos to accept such canons, because they do not correspond to their ideal of beauty) (1921, 19; translation my own). While the Hellenic or white beauty type does not look like the majority of México's population, there is a strong anti-Indigenous sentiment that pervades the Mexican national imaginary. Indigenous features with dark skin and large noses are not considered conventionally beautiful in relation to whiteness.

Coupled with the global and transnational context of the maquiladora, female beauty standards bleed into the workforce. This is why the Rodarte/MAC controversy cannot be separated from capital. In the maquiladora, not only is production monitored but also their maintenance of proper femininity and beauty in their personal appearance. Whereas the attainment for proper femininity and beauty for white women is always accessible, the Mexican women in the maquiladoras constantly have to prove themselves in order to keep their jobs while also being open for sexualization. As Leslie Salzinger reminds us, "Apparent embodiments of availability—cheap labor, willing flirtation—these young women have become the paradigmatic workers for a transnational political economy in which a highly sexualized form of femininity has become a standard 'factor of production'" (2007, 161). Sexual assault is a structural violence and not only individualized, and the role of production and capital function interdependently with standards of beauty, sexuality, and abuse in the workplace. Production is intertwined with the "right look" for people and products alike (163). The factories that employ mostly female workers are set up in ways similar to a panopticon, where the "architecture is designed to control through visibility, a visibility that is ultimately as much about fostering self-consciousness as it is about the more mundane operations of supervision" (163). This constant monitoring of the women creates a systemic male gaze, making them always open to the particular labor and appearance standards and assault closely intertwined with production. So ultimately, the "right look" not only points to the visual rhetoric of the shop floor and product but also to how finely finished the factory women look through labor control. In this setup, the women are the main subjects of the systemic incitement of the desire in production (164). This means that production and desire are always linked and interwoven together. Thus, the maquiladoras not only reinforce a relationship with global capital but also work hand in hand with the patriarchy in México that establishes beauty, domestic, and gender norms as "common sense" in the very setup of these workforces. In a space where capital, race, and patriarchy interweave, beauty standards in the United States have a major influence on the standards of hiring for the *maquilas*. Besides being young and female, factory owners want women that are "slim, [have] thin hands, and short nails" (168). They are racially marked because of their "diminutive" hands that can work fast on the factory line. Just as workers in the Bracero Program were racialized for their arm labor power, Mexican women were hired for their small hands. Never could they occupy a white position of beauty through the conventional beauty standards Rodarte and MAC thrust them into. Brown skin, black eyes, petite frame, diminutive feet and hands, and black hair do not coincide with the ideal of beauty that Rodarte and MAC were selling, but those very physical attributes are what most maquiladoras look for when hiring women as alterable standards of U.S. beauty that are still acceptable. The maquiladoras owned by U.S.-based companies require their Mexican managers to use U.S. beauty standards and racial norms to "read" the women's bodies during hiring. However, Mexican managers specifically target women they perceive as Indigenous due to anti-Indigenous racism, which allows for maquiladora factories to not think about a high turn over rate due to disappearance, murder, or poor working conditions for Indigenous and subaltern Mexican women.

As gender, sexuality, and beauty became markers of identity on the border region during the 1990s and 2000s, it becomes harder to map the connections the process of class and racialization had on the very func-tion of gender, sexuality, and beauty within Juárez and the United States more broadly. Women of color, particularly brown and black women in the United States, thereby become differently gendered in terms of beauty standards. For MAC and Rodarte to think that beauty could be sold to all women on the platform of "bringing light" to the tragedy in Juárez is a complete fallacy. The brown woman is always in contention with and con-stitutive of various gendered formations of and through colonial, sexual violence. *Mestizaje*, darkness, or brownness is a historical positionality. As the impasse between human and nonhuman, the poor, Mexican "female" body is not acknowledged as is exemplified by the in-between state she rep-resents in the Rodarte show. The unprotected brutalization on the border that was once reserved for men and boys is now a mundane occurrence to the women of Juárez. Mexican women and their beauty only become legi-ble under capital, particularly within the historical context of the U.S. fash-ion industry's commodification of Juárez. Black feminist Hortense Spillers calls the brutalization of gender violence a form of "ungendering," a read-ing that places women out of the "traditional symbolics of female gender" while making her whole within her historical position (2003, 85). Beau-ty and gender can no longer be understood as a universal category that does not take into consideration the nuances of racial and sexual violence and the "unmarking" of certain bodies for certain ends. For the women of Juárez, their specific economic condition and the Mexican cultural and media narrative that deem them "things" ungender them and the confines of proper femininity, and beauty standards in both México and the United States render them invisible. However, this ungendering also allows for a radical understanding of the structures of power and violence that cause it. Following this same train of thought, Juana María Rodriguez states, "Like other feminine subjects, the Latina who in consenting to her own subjugation might find satisfaction in particular forms of abjection, represents the unimaginable category of racialized female masochist, daring to perform that which has already come to define her" (2014, 141). Rodriguez argues that there is a historical positionality to the subjugation of the women of Juárez. She can never embody proper beauty or femininity because of her position in Mexican society, thus tying beauty and gender to the historical process of the body and the violent systemic relations that allowed MAC and Rodarte to commodify further the brown female body. The women of Juárez live, labor, and love in the space of violence and had lives and agency before they became the inspiration for a popular makeup company and fashion line, but they were never absolved of their position within patriarchy and global capital.

MAC and Rodarte stated that they thought the Juárez campaign was acceptable because it "memorialized" the dead women of Juárez. However, this (re)membering memorializes their death as an inspiration for beauty; beauty that is unattainable for poor, Mexican women. Melissa Wright reminds us, "A focus on the narrative image of [the imagined woman performed by the Rodarte models], rather than on the lives of the murder victims, reveals the intimate connection binding these stilled lives to the reproduction value in the maquiladoras located in Ciudad Juárez" (2007, 184). The continuous slippage of value pitted against waste for the sake of propelling the beauty industry forward not only freezes the victims in time but also treads a dangerous line of further entangling the exploitative results of global capital on Mexican women's subjectivity with concepts of beauty and fashion. For the Mexican patriarchal system, the erroneous linking of modernization with women's newfound independence binds the Mexican woman's position to capital through media narratives. Mexican television news outlets, print newspapers, and online media sources distinctly blame the women for being out late at night, partying after work, or being with men as reasons for their murders. While capital, patriarchy, and state-sanctioned violence are intricately woven together, it is through the systemic nature of the beauty industry that prescribes what is beautiful, consumable, and worthwhile to individuals.

The beauty industry functions through visual media, print culture, the internet, and advertising. Rodarte and MAC maintained that the reasons for choosing to portray Juárez artistically in their fashion and

makeup line were because of its ethereal landscape; however, as Fregoso states, the concepts represent stigmatized bodies that are "gendered
[and] racialized" (2003, 2). Memory production thus becomes a performative gendered and racialized process. The women of Juárez and their
deaths were performed during Rodarte's runway show. There were only
two women of color in the show, one black and one Asian. The set was dim
with numerous wax candles lighting the runway. Each model was washed
out in white makeup and walked to the soundtrack of "Blue Moon" for the
finale. The last final models were dressed as ghost brides and styled in white
chiffon and flowing lace. While the Rodarte sisters did not state that these
models were representations of the dead women of Juárez, they did say
that seeing the women as sleepwalkers inspired this collection. Obviously,
this performance takes agency away from the actual women who experience traumatic violence, but it also fails to include the community actually
affected. Diana Taylor reminds us that performance has "staying power"
where the written word fails, but the structural power relations between
the United States and México does not allow "the transfer and continuity
of knowledge" (2003, 5). She continues, "Performance genealogies draw
on the idea of expressive movements as mnemonic reserves, including pat-
terned movements made and remembered by bodies, residual movements
retained implicitly in images or words" (5). Rodarte styled their Fall 2010
show through constructs of beauty widely determined by an industry that
perpetuates hierarchy. At the same time, the artistic portrayal and performance of the Juárez murders through cosmetics and fashion reproduces
those same hierarchal power structures. This top-down model is informed
by a patriarchal system. The commodifying of death and violence through
the United States and international beauty industry reinforces the patriarchal norms of México by reproducing the violence inflicted upon women
as problematic performances evacuated of life, reasoning for death,
and subjectivity.

And what we get in the end are sleepwalking and ghostly romantic images of violence, patriarchy, and capital. As Avery F. Gordon contends, to
confront lost bodies "is to contemplate ghosts and haunting at the level
of making and unmaking of world historical events" (1997, 63). For Gordon, the ghost and haunting provide a generative methodology to uncover
nation-state violence. However, in the case of the Rodarte Juárez collection, the making and unmaking of historical events is subsumed under the
guise of memorializing and (re)membering. The subject is quite literally

taken out of the equation of production. The "subject" or "ghost of the dead" ceases to exist and the production of material goods begins to take a more important role than the power struggles that created the conditions of violence and the actual victim. The historical ghosts that constantly haunt the aesthetics of beauty and the in-between status the Rodarte sisters attribute to the women coming out of the maquilas already mark the women as dead. Gordon goes on to write, "A disappearance is real only when it is apparitional because the ghost or the apparition is the principal form by which something lost or invisible or seemingly not there makes itself known or apparent to us" (1997, 63). In counter distinction to Gordon's theories on ghosts and haunting, the Rodarte sisters pathologize and reinforce the excess of violence on the border that needs artistic portrayal. Mary Pat Brady cautions against this type of fungible analysis and representation of the border arguing that it "invoke[s] as a marker of hybrid or liminal subjectivities, such as those that would be experienced by persons who negotiate among multiple cultural, linguistic, racial, or sexual systems throughout their lives. When the border is spatialized in these theories, the space is almost always universal" (2000, 172). The fungibility of the border and the women's ghosts are replaced with different modes of economy. The runway show and stylized photograph that Rodarte and MAC Cosmetics produced for their Juárez collection is not site-specific. The victims of the murders in Juárez then disappear from the social consciousness for a second time. For the woman located in the United States, the Juárez feminicides are abstracted as a consumable concept, but for the women of México, the violence is real, tangible, and deadly.

When asked about what was the inspiration for the Fall 2010 runway show, Kate Mulleavy stated in an interview that the idea of "this transient landscape, immediately we made an analogy to the idea of sleepwalking, almost a dream state, between states" (Phelps 2010). How inspiring to be able to cross between subjectivities willingly. Mulleavy's statement gets to the very core of how the commodified brown, poor Mexican female body functions within the realms of beauty without the same mobility as white feminists, and it isn't beautiful to say the least.

Bernadine Hernández is assistant professor in the Department of English Language and Literature at the University of New Mexico and is currently research professor at the Institute of American Cultures and the Chicano Studies Research Center at the University of California, Los Angeles, where she is finishing her manuscript "Invisible Bodies of a

New Nation: Civility and Sexual Economies on the Nineteenth Century Borderlands." She specializes in transnational feminism and sexual economies of the U.S. borderlands, along with American literary studies/empire from the mid-nineteenth century to the early twentieth, borderlands theory, and Chicana/Latina literature and sexualities. She can be reached at berna18@unm.edu.

Notes

1. In "Can the Subaltern Speak?" Gayatri Spivak (1984) is interrogating notions of the "Subject" within Western and postcolonial discourse and their ability to interact with disparate cultures. For Spivak, the "subaltern" does not constitute an identity, but rather positionality, just as the women of Juárez are not only constituted by "disposability." I utilize the term because Rodarte and MAC's act of epistemic knowing/violence is the essentialization of the other and is always the reinforcement of empire.

2. For a history of colonialism in México, Latin America, and the U.S. Southwest that engages with the perception of women and femininity, please see Juana María Rodríguez's *Sexual Futures, Queer Gestures, and Other Latina Longings,* Antonia Castañeda, "Engendering the History of Alta California, 1769–1848: Gender, Sexuality, and the Family" (1997) and "Women of Color and the Rewriting of Western History" (2014).

3. The term "feminicide" comes from "femicide" and was translated by Marcela Lagrade as *feminicidio*. Feminicide is a theoretical term referring to the assassination of women committed by men because they are women. This specific type of violent assassination relates to the inequality of the sexes and gender subordination.

4. The Programa Nacional Fronterizo (National Border Program) was established in 1961 to reinvigorate México's northern border region. This program authorized the building of new housing, streets, museums, other public works, and *maquilas* (factories). The maquilas were built to attract transnational companies with the lure of cheap labor, cheap infrastructure on the border, and tax advantages.

5. Denationalization, as Alicia Schmidt Camacho states in "Ciudadana X: Gender Violence and the Denationalization of Women's Rights in Ciudad Juárez, Mexico," is the "destabilization of the nation-state by globalization and means the logic of personhood supersedes the logic of national citizenship" (2010, 260). The state has expanded its function for social control while simultaneously weakening those institutions that provide the substance of citizenship: access to goods and services, justice, security, and political representation.

Works Cited

Agamben, Giorgio. 1998. *Homo Sacer: Sovereign Power and Bare Life*. Redwood City, CA: Stanford University Press.

Bauman, Zygmunt. 2004. *Wasted Lives: Modernity and Its Outcasts*. Cambridge, MA: Polity Press.

Brady, Mary Pat. 2000. "The Fungibility of Borders." *Nepantla: Views from South* 1(1): 171–90.

Castañeda, Antonia I. 1997. "Engendering the History of Alta California, 1769–1848: Gender, Sexuality, and the Family." *California History* 76 (2/3): 230–59.

———. 2014. "Women of Color and the Rewriting of Western History." In *Three Decades of Engendering History: Selected Works of Antonia I Castañeda*, 103–42. Denton: University of North Texas Press.

Ericson, Anna-Stina. 1970. "An Analysis of Mexico's Border Industrialization Program." *Monthly Labor Review* 93 (5): 33–40.

Fregoso, Rosa Linda. 2003. "Towards a Planetary Civil Society." In *meXicana Encounters: The Making of Social Identities on the Borderlands*, 1–29. Berkeley: University of California Press.

Gamio, Manuel. 1921. "La Venus India." *El Universal Ilustrado* 224 (5): 18–27.

Gaspar de Alba, Alicia, and Georgina Guzmán. 2010. "Femincidio: The 'Black Legend' of the Border." In *Making a Killing: Femicide, Free Trade, and La Frontera*, 1–21. Austin: University of Texas Press.

Gilmore, Ruth Wilson. 2007. *Golden Gulag: Prisons, Surplus, Crisis, and Opposition in Globalizing California*. Berkeley: University of California Press.

Gordon, Avery F. 1997. "the other door, it's floods of tears with consolation enclosed." In *Ghostly Matters: Haunting and the Sociological Imagination*, 63–136. Minneapolis: University of Minnesota Press.

Hernández, Kelly Lytle. 2010. *Migra! A History of the U.S. Border Patrol*. Berkeley: University of California Press.

Marx, Karl. 2011. *Capital: A Critique of Political Economy*. New York: Dover Publication.

———. 1932. *Economic and Philosophical Manuscripts of 1844*. Marxist Internet Archive, last updated 2009. https://www.marxists.org/archive/marx/works/download/pdf/Economic-Philosophic-Manuscripts-1844.pdf

Matloff, Judith. 2015. "Six women murdered each day as femicide in Mexico nears a pandemic." Al Jazeera America, January 4. http://america.aljazeera.com/multimedia/2015/1/mexico-s-pandemicfemicides.html.

Menkedick, Sarah. 2010. "Rodarte and MAC Create Collection 'Inspired By' Women in Ciudad Juárez." Change.org, July 29. Accessed August 30, 2010. http://news.change.org/stories/rodarte-and-mac-create-collection-inspired-by-women-in-ciudad-jurez. (site discontinued).

Monárrez Fragoso, Julia Estela. 2010. "The Victims of Ciudad Juárez Feminicide: Sexually Fetishized Commodities." In *Terrorizing Women: Feminicide in the Américas*, edited by Rosa-Linda Fregoso and Cynthia Bejarano, 59–69. Durham, NC: Duke University Press.

Phelps, Nicole. 2010. "Rodarte Fall 2010 Ready-to-Wear." *Vogue*, February 15. http://www.vogue.com/fashion-shows/fall-2010-ready-to-wear/rodarte.

Robinson, Cedric J. 1983. *Black Marxism: The Making of the Black Radical Tradition*. London: Zed Press.

Rodríguez, Juana María. 2014. *Sexual Futures, Queer Gestures, and Other Latina Longings*. New York: NYU Press.

Ruiz, Apen. 2002. "'La India Bonita': National Beauty in Revolutionary Mexico." *Cultural Dynamics* 14 (3): 283–301.

Salzinger, Leslie. 2007. "Manufacturing Sexual Subjects: 'Harassment,' Desire, and Discipline on a Maquiladora Shopfloor." In *Women and Migration in the U.S.-Mexico Borderlands: A Reader*, edited by Denise A. Segura and Patricia Zavella, 161–83. Durham, NC: Duke University Press.

Schmidt Camacho, Alicia. 2010. "Ciudadana X: Gender Violence and the Denationalization of Women's Rights in Ciudad Juárez, Mexico." In *Terrorizing Women: Feminicide in the Américas*, edited by Rosa-Linda Fregoso and Cynthia Bejarano, 275–89. Durham, NC: Duke University Press.

Shapovalova, Daria. 2015. "VIDEO | RODARTE W/F 2015." *Daria's Diaries* (blog), February 18. http://dariasdiaries.com/2015/02/18/video-rodarte-wf-2015/.

Spillers, Hortense J. 2003. *Black, White, and in Color: Essays on American Literature and Culture*. Chicago: University of Chicago Press.

Spivak, Gayatri. 1994. "Can the Subaltern Speak? Speculations on Widow-Sacrifice." In *Colonial Discourse and Post-Colonial Theory: A Reader*, edited by Patrick Williams and Laura Chrisman, 66–111. New York: Routledge.

Taylor, Diana. 2003. *The Archive and the Repertoire: Performing Cultural Memory in the Americas*. Durham, NC: Duke University Press.

Temptalia. 2010. "MAC Rodarte Collection for Fall 2010 + Official Statements." July 16. http://www.temptalia.com/mac-rodarte-collection-for-fall-2010/.

Wright, Melissa. 2007. "The Dialectics of Still Life: Murder, Women, and the Maquiladoras." In *Women and Migration in the U.S.-Mexico Borderlands: A Reader*, edited by Denise A. Segura and Patricia Zavella, 184–202. Durham, NC: Duke University Press.

Fashioning Identity Work:
The Perils, Politics, and Pleasures of Aesthetic Labor

Minh-Ha T. Pham's *Asians Wear Clothes on the Internet: Race, Gender, and the Work of Personal Style Blogging*, Durham, NC: Duke University Press, 2015

Reina Lewis's *Muslim Fashion: Contemporary Style Cultures*, Durham, NC: Duke University Press, 2015

David A. Sanchez-Aguilera

One of the conceits of the fashion industry is its traditionalism and hostility toward change. Bloggers, for the most part, bear the brunt of fashion editors' and journalists' ire and reluctance to adapt to the industry's digital coming of age. One illustrative example comes from a recent article on Vogue.com where several editors reviewed Milan's Spring/Summer 2017 runway collections, but not before the conversation briefly devolved into bizarre asides and invectives directed against bloggers. Sally Singer, creative digital director, went so far as to literally spell out the ill will, "Note to bloggers who change head-to-toe, paid-to-wear outfits every hour: Please Stop. Find another business. You are heralding the death of style" (*Vogue Runway* 2016).

This recent example, published months after Minh-Ha T. Pham's book, proves the need to understand how social and occupational roles in the global fashion industry are reformulated in network capitalism. *Asians Wear Clothes on the Internet* effectively contextualizes the rise of the figure of the blogger in the informational age and claims it has "democratized" the field of fashion. Pham not only dispels the rumor that social and occupational positions in the global fashion industry can ever be truly democratized but also convincingly argues that blogging and the antagonism it has incurred by critics in fashion publishing are both raced phenomena. Rather than construe Asian fashion bloggers as distinct from the Asian garment workers who perform the majority of the industry's manufacturing labor, Pham compellingly argues that both groups occupy similar social and occupational roles within fashion even as they are placed in distinct spheres of labor.

WSQ: Women's Studies Quarterly 46: 1 & 2 (Spring/Summer 2018) © 2018 by David A. Sanchez-Aguilera.

Asians Wear Clothes on the Internet begins by noting a cadre of Asian superbloggers' whose influence on the fashion industry the mainstream press paints as helping to define fashion's blogging moment. Pham focuses her attention on the personal style blogs of three superbloggers in particular, London-born Hong Konger Susanna Lau, mixed-race Japanese American Rumi Neely, and Filipino Bryan Grey Yamboa. In noting the inordinate levels of attention, clout, and acrimony they have attained in the industry, Pham seeks to understand how these bloggers rose to prominence, why their taste has become so valuable to the Western fashion industry, and how they articulate their identity through their digital labor.

In answering these questions, Pham employs a mixed-method approach that begins by historically situating how neoliberal trade practices have culturally and economically reshaped Western consumers' taste for Asianness. The rise of *kawaii* or Japanese cute culture—so perfectly encapsulated in material form by Hello Kitty—and Western taste for these products are situated in the context of the rise of Asian markets and the consolidation of China and Japan as superpowers. From the analysis of cultural political economy discussed in chapter 1, the ensuing chapters take a cultural and media studies approach to dissecting the constitutive elements of bloggers' digital posts. Chapter 2, for example, focuses on the discursive elements of blogger style stories, whereas chapters 3 and 4 focus on the visual and aesthetic components of outfit posts, including the formal aspects of outfit photos and the poses bloggers strike.

This book proves an invaluable tool for scholars of fashion, consumer, and media studies due to the sophisticated ways it thinks through the ways value accrues and is disseminated in the digital era. In particular, Pham's insights on the ways social media has influenced communication patterns—with its values of connection, relatability, and collaboration—go a long way in explaining the rise of blogging as a phenomenon and even the stagnation or ascent of certain fashion brands or business models. One has only to look at the fashion house Gucci's brand revitalization under creative director Alessandro Michele in 2015, including his innovative practice of having different artists take over Gucci's Instagram account, to see the insight Pham's work sheds on neoliberal practices of corporate branding.

Where *Asians Wear Clothes on the Internet* may have the most profound impact is on the fields of ethnic and labor studies. Pham is correct in noting that the digital labor these superbloggers perform confounds classic labor categories. Her observation that the bloggers' performances cut across material, immaterial, commercial, and affective forms of labor reveals these boundaries as porous and mutable. It also provokes questions of identity work—the management and presentation of the self in neoliberalism, where the blogger is worker par excellence—as a form of labor that interpolates the common user and is performed in all manner of social media communication. For example, the ways that businesses rely on internet users to review, share, and browse to accrue capital.

Pham's notion of racial (after)taste will prove fruitful for analyses of raced creative workers in the culture industries. Central to Pham's theoretical approach is the notion of taste, à la Pierre Bourdieu, as a disposition that both distinguishes and is distinguishing. The author illuminates the taste work bloggers perform—expressed in a variety of forms from their own self-styling to the way they curate their blogs—as a form of identity management hedges raced, classed, and gendered assumptions imputed on Asian bodies, rearticulating these categories on blogger's own terms. In doing so, Pham convincingly argues that race becomes a distinguishing mark for Asian superbloggers and the point from which they articulate an aestheticized identity that helps to accrue their brand worth.

Turning the phrase, Pham notes that the massive success of Asian bloggers has turned to racial distaste for some of the fashion industry's vanguards. This notion of a taste for that sours proves incredibly rich for thinking through the ways liberal multiculturalism creates spaces for difference while careful gatekeeping keeps raced, classed, and gendered workers from wandering too far from their subordinate social positions. Ultimately, *Asians Wear Clothes on the Internet*'s most provocative insights illuminate how the value of entrepreneurialism under neoliberalism encourages an identity work that insists upon branding one's difference and risks neutralizing it as mere bland commerciality.

Like *Asians Wear Clothes on the Internet*, Reina Lewis's *Muslim Fashion* seeks to understand the complexities of subject formation in a neoliberal consumer context where patterns of consumption have saturated most aspects of everyday life. Where Pham orients her inquiry more toward race and the matter of racial aftertaste, Lewis foregrounds a gendered analysis in her study of Muslim women's activities in fashion and fashion subcultures—in the forms of modest dress and hijabi style—in Western Europe and Northern American (WENA) territories. Pham is aware that she has chosen a group of elite Asian superbloggers as the subject of her work, and because of this stays within the ambit of high fashion (in the sense that Lau and Yamboa are unabashedly Western in their fashion choices, always sporting the latest looks from Paris and Milan fashion weeks). Due to the transnational scope of Lewis's project, and perhaps also due to the heavily ethnographic bent of her book, *Muslim Fashion* contends that there is no one fashion system, but multiple systems that Muslim women negotiate at the global, transnational, and local levels. At the heart of both *Muslim Fashion* and *Asians Wear Clothes on the Internet* however, is the belief that aesthetic work, a healthy regard for the beautiful or for one's own beauty, is not simply "false consciousness"—a charge frequently levied at fashion studies like these. Rather, what these authors make clear is that taste work is a crucial strategy in the active negotiation of race, class, gender, and, as Lewis's study importantly adds, religious subject-identities.

Lewis's groundbreaking book is an ambitious trek through the terrain of a properly Muslim fashion field that, as Lewis makes clear, sometimes includes veiling and sometimes does not. She situates her work—much of the research took place between the years 2005 to 2012—both in a moment where Muslim women are broadly perceived as existing outside of the mainstream fashion system and in the context of Muslim revivalism in WENA territories where younger generations of Muslims are taking to the reactivation of a transnational *umma*, or "a community of Muslim believers . . . contributing to new forms of 'European' or 'global' Islam" (37). Her book asks "how and why young Muslim women are using their engagement with mainstream fashion to communicate their ideas and aspirations about modern Muslim identities to coreligionists and to majority non-Muslim observers alike" (3). In answering these sweeping questions, Lewis crafts a framework that is heavily indebted to cultural studies, globalization studies, fashion studies, and sociocultural anthropology. For example, Lewis situates the experiences of the Muslim women she interviews as having to negotiate between different scales of power at the levels of nation-states, global corporate capital, supranational (e.g., religious) forces, and the local (where parental and religious elder opinion frequently intervene). Furthermore, Muslim fashion is treated in the subculture-studies parlance of style as an act of agentive articulation with women crafting forms of modest dress that draw from mainstream fashion markets, niche local and transnational ethno-religious markets, and negotiated cross-generationally. Drawing also from Stuart Halls and Paul du Gay's circuits of culture model that pays attention to the interrelation between production, distribution, and consumption (as a correction to the

Marxist tradition of privileging production), Lewis's work treats print and digital images of Muslim fashion and discourses regarding proper modest dress as equally central alongside more traditional considerations of how modest dress is produced and distributed to consumers. With regards to consumption, Lewis's chapter on Muslim women's experience working and shopping in Britain's High Street retail stores, for example, centers a spatial analysis that understands fashion as both embodied and situated in terms of time and place.

Lewis's sophisticated methodological weft is reflected by the diversity of topics addressed in each chapter. To this end, the only issue I had as a reader was the disorderly relation of the chapters to each other, with one discussing Muslim Women's retail experiences on High Street and the next moving to discuss transnational Muslim women's digital activities running modest fashion blogs. These moves can form a discontinuous reading experience. To this end, I would recommend thinking of chapters 2 and 5 together as they discuss Muslim women's retail experiences in Turkey and Britain respectively, and pairing chapters 3 and 6 as the former discusses various transnational Muslim lifestyle magazines that were founded in the early 2000s and the latter current Muslim fashion blogs run by women throughout WENA territories who are able to build transnational digital communities of support and guidance regarding modest fashion.

Ultimately, *Muslim Fashion* is a crucial intervention in the fields of both fashion studies and cultural studies. Her work demonstrates how the discourse of neoliberal choice, related to the formulation of the human and citizen as a consuming subject, are employed by Muslim women to create transnational bonds of solidarity with one another that are at once multiethnic and coreligionist, and hence contests the commonly held notion of the neoliberal subject as necessarily alienated. Further, her work calls the field of fashion studies to be critical of the ways it has constructed certain geographies, ethnicities, and religions as existing outside of mainstream fashion or unable to directly influence this field. Chapter 7 of *Muslim Fashion* confronts this head on, considering how Muslim style is making increasing inroads in the field of high fashion and reflecting on the commodification of Islam more generally. Finally, Lewis's book engages the important political project of deexceptionalizing Muslim women by countering images of them as "inevitably veiled" and demonstrating how these women's religious affiliations and practices are often matters of personal choice and preference (124).

David A. Sanchez-Aguilera is a PhD student in the Department of Ethnic Studies at the University of California, San Diego. His research looks at racial fetishism in the Paris and New York fashion industries. He can be reached at das027@ucsd.edu.

Works Cited

Vogue Runway. 2016. "Ciao, Milano! Vogue.com's Editors Discuss the Week That Was." September 16. https://www.vogue.com/article/milan-fashion-week-spring-2017-vogue-editors-chat.

Picture Perfect: Lessons in the War for Self-Love

Jodi M. Savage

"The CEO doesn't like your picture. He wants you to take another one," my female supervisor told me with a hint of apology in her voice.

It was the second time my photo was found wanting.

I had just started as the Equal Employment Opportunity Officer at a local hospital. I was responsible for investigating employment discrimination complaints and required to post my picture and contact information throughout the hospital so employees would know where to find me. Wearing a Hillary Clinton power suit from Macy's, I had gone downtown to one of those places where you stand in front of a white screen and somebody takes your photo. I was a barefaced twentysomething and my straight black hair fell to my shoulders. I flashed my brightest happy-to-be-alive smile for the camera.

But when I showed the passport-sized prints to my boss, she told me I needed to have the photo taken by a guy in the communications department. I dressed the same way for the second photo: suit, straight black hair, no lipstick or makeup. I stood in the hospital hallway against a shiny, tan tile wall and he took multiple pictures. We finally got a good one, or so I thought, until I found out about the CEO's reaction.

"What's wrong with it this time?" I asked my boss. She didn't have an answer. From her silence, I could only draw one conclusion: I was too plain. She was implying I should wear makeup or glam it up some other way. To say the CEO didn't like my picture meant that he, and perhaps even my supervisor, found something inherently unacceptable about my face—about me. But my boss couldn't say these things to me, the person in charge of investigating employees' discrimination complaints.

This wasn't just about me playing nice and taking a pretty picture. It

WSQ: Women's Studies Quarterly 46: 1 & 2 (Spring/Summer 2018)

was about something much bigger. It was about the spoken and unspoken rules concerning how women should look in the workplace. The ways we comment on and criticize a woman's appearance even when it's irrelevant. It was about the many ways women's autonomy and bodies are infringed upon every single day.

But first, it was about my own complicated struggle to meet others' expectations and accept my skin. My color. My hair. Myself.

As a kid, I sat on the side of our aqua-green bathtub scrubbing my knees and elbows with Ajax until they began to bleed. Granny stood in the threshold of our small bathroom and looked down at me with pursed lips as she monitored my progress.

"They're too dark," she said. I cried silently because my skin was still black beneath the blood-streaked paste, because my raw skin hurt, and because I had disappointed Granny.

When I was in junior high, I learned to hide my face. Granny made me wear my Aunt Jennye's makeup to cover my acne and the dark patches around my mouth. But it wasn't just any makeup. It was Dermablend, which people with skin pigmentation diseases use to even out their complexion. Aunt Jennye, Granny's older sister, had vitiligo—white spots covered her Hershey's Kisses–colored skin.

I'm surprised Granny allowed me to wear makeup, because I grew up Pentecostal. According to the church, it was a sin for women to wear makeup, lipstick, fingernail polish, or anything that enhanced our natural appearance. Perhaps she thought God would forgive a woman for wearing makeup if its purpose was to cover up her flaws.

I stopped wearing Dermablend after an incident with another aunt. One day, while wearing a full face of makeup, I reached down to give Auntie Annie Lou a hug and got makeup all over the shoulder of her baby-blue silk dress. Everything stopped. I felt the temperature rising in my face. I just wanted to melt into a puddle of brown makeup soup and slide into the gutter.

"I'm so sorry, Auntie!" I kept saying.

"That's okay, baby," she replied.

She smiled and never mentioned it again. But covering up my imperfections wasn't worth the embarrassment of leaving my face on other people's clothes. I wouldn't wear makeup again until over ten years later for a friend's wedding.

During high school, I once bought a bunch of acne products from Duane Reade for my birthday. This would be the year I got my face together. I've tried them all, Proactiv, Noxzema, Sea Breeze, Clearasil, some cucumber-smelling cream from the health-food store. None of it worked.

"Your skin cells renew themselves every seven years," Ms. Johnson, my high school librarian, used to tell me. "Don't worry. You'll have a brand-new face in seven years." I saw her almost every day because I worked in the library during my lunch period. She reminded me of Susan L. Taylor, a former editor in chief of *Essence* magazine, who always wears long, thin, black braids down her back. Ms. Johnson was a walking embodiment of self-assurance and pride: Taylor-like braids, mahogany-colored skin, red lipstick, and long painted fingernails. A literary rebel, she would always order books related to black history without asking the head librarian's permission. She'd let me read the new books before stocking them on the shelves for the rest of the students. Because of her stern demeanor, most of the kids and school employees thought Ms. Johnson was mean, but I think she had built a hard exterior because she knew we lived in a world that made little black girls and women feel ugly, unseen, and unheard. She gave me hope and free books.

Granny bought me Nadinola skin-bleaching cream to get rid of the dark spots the pimples left behind. I sometimes used Ambi fade cream too, somehow feeling better because the picture of a black woman on the box made me think it was manufactured for black people by a black-owned company. According to my teenage logic, if the cream was made by and for black people, using it didn't mean I hated myself or was trying to be white. I was simply using another beauty product, like Oil of Olay lotion or antiaging cream. Years later, I learned that several countries have outlawed bleaching creams because of their harmful effects, including skin cancer, thinning skin, and burns.

Skin-bleaching creams weren't the beauty panacea I had hoped for. Instead of getting rid of the dark spots that had freckled my face, they only lightened the skin around the blemishes. There was only one rational thing left to do: apply the cream to my entire face.

During my freshman year of college, a friend asked me about my skin color as we washed our hands in the dorm bathroom.

"You usin' skin bleach?"

"No." I feigned surprise and offense at her accusation. *What did she know about these creams,* I wondered. She had smooth, flawless, sandy-brown skin.

"Yes, you are," she replied. I heard judgment in her voice and felt ashamed. Besides, I just wanted my skin to be blemish-free, not lighter. I stopped using bleaching cream after that.

I knew why Granny was so obsessed with my appearance. She had spent her life struggling with her own. At four years old, while she played in the kitchen as her mother cooked, a pan full of hot fish oil fell on Granny. Poor and living in the backwoods of South Florida, near the Everglades, Granny's mother didn't take her to the hospital. Instead, she used home remedies. As a result of the accident, Granny lost her hearing in one ear and scars covered that ear, a portion of one side of her face, and part of her head—leaving nothing but shiny, peach-colored skin where hair should have been. While her facial scars lightened over time, the scar tissue on her head remained and she wore wigs and hair pieces to cover it as an adult.

"They called me 'burn up in sin,'" Granny would tell me about the kids who used to tease her. Although she laughed when retelling these stories, her twin brother and other family members told me about the fights she frequently got into with the kids who picked on her. Granny had spent her childhood feeling ugly and spent her life trying to hide, and perhaps compensate for, her perceived imperfections. It's no wonder she worked so hard to hide mine.

I spent a lot of time worrying about my hair. Like many other black women, I learned early on that only straight hair is acceptable. When I was a little girl, I used to sit on our red shaggy rug between Granny's knees as she straightened my hair with a hot comb. She would rub green Dax grease on my hair and scalp to insulate them from the heat. My hair would crackle like corn popping as she worked the hot comb through my thick, tightly wound coils. By nine, I had graduated to getting my hair straightened with relaxers.

In the eleventh grade, I decided to stop getting my hair relaxed. "You can't go natural. You don't have hair like mine," a friend said to me one day. Although she was also black, her hair texture was silky, wavy, the kind of hair that made people ask "What are you?" or "You got Indian in yo' family?" We took graduation pictures that year. Instead of getting a relaxer, I wore my two-textured hair with a part down the middle, each side pinned down behind my ears. Kinky waves stretched into frizzy, trying-hard-to-stay-straight ends I curled under. The big-eyed, sixteen-year-old girl wearing a black velvet top and tentative smile was beautiful. But not everyone thought so.

"You should've gotten your hair done for those pictures. It's too nappy," my mother told me when she saw the pictures that summer.

"Well, you didn't pay for these pictures; my granny did. So I don't care what you think," I replied with all the sassy confidence of a teenage girl. What I wanted to add was "You didn't even raise me, so you should just be happy you're getting a picture." What I really wanted to hear from her was "You look so pretty. I'm so proud of you." My natural hair phase was short-lived.

In law school, I again contemplated going natural but decided not to because I was afraid my hair would frighten prospective employers and clients. For the most part, my black female classmates were equally cautious. We viewed our classmates with loose natural hair as rebels or eccentric. Their short afros went perfectly with their Afrocentric views or funky wardrobe. Some students wore dreadlocks, which we thought were exotic enough to be palatable to white folks. However, they always put their locs in a ponytail or pinned them into elaborate styles before job interviews just in case prospective employers weren't so liberal or forgiving—as if our hair was something to apologize for. While taking an employment discrimination class, I read court cases about black women who were fired for violating their employers' grooming policies. These companies claimed certain hairstyles were unprofessional, unpolished, or made "clients" feel uncomfortable. Although they hid behind the "we apply these rules to everyone" defense, black women are more likely than any other group to wear afros, braids, and dreadlocks. What these employers really meant was that black women's natural, unstraightened hair scared white people.

Never mind that hair straightening isn't the most comfortable experience for black women. Just ask any black woman who has ever had her ears burned while getting her hair pressed or while getting a blow out as the smoke rose from her hair. Just ask any black woman who has ever smelled lye in her hair or felt the burning and scabs from a relaxer left on too long or experienced alopecia, which sometimes creeps along the hairline after many years of relaxing one's hair. And yet, other people's comfort was the barometer for professionalism and legal redress. I knew these court cases were hard to win. I kept relaxing my hair because straight hair made others feel safe. Being able to repay my student loans was more important than accepting myself.

As a law student, you learn to dress conservatively. My classmates and I had traded our T-shirts and jeans for grown-up lawyerly black, blue, and gray suits and uncomfortable Nine West pumps. For me, and other black women "baby lawyers," the quest to look the part meant ensuring that our makeup, clothes, and behavior weren't viewed as too loud, too much, or too "black." I preoccupied myself with such trivial details as whether or not to wear lip gloss or lipstick. *Would lip gloss make me seem too young or immature?* Whether to wear neutral-colored lips—pinks and browns, or popping plums and reds. *Would color make me seem too flashy? Does red lipstick even look good on black women?* I thought I needed to mute myself, to hide my personality and fade into the background to be deemed professional. Post earrings or dangling ones like the brown, wooden earrings I bought at an African street fair in Brooklyn? *Dangling earrings might seem "ghetto" or too casual, more appropriate for a Friday night out.*

And then I had race to add to the mix. Every black child has been told, "You must work twice as hard as everyone else to get half as far." Granny used to always tell me, "You can't do what those white kids do." These tenets applied to one's appearance, as well as one's work ethic and accomplishments. I didn't have the privilege of being adventurous or unconventional. I couldn't take any chances with afros and fuchsia lipstick and big earrings.

Singer Alicia Keys caused a stir in 2016 when she decided to stop wearing makeup. Admittedly, I gave her serious side-eye at first. I remember her battle with acne and appearing in commercials for Proactiv. *It's easy to proclaim that you won't wear makeup when you're rich and famous, and probably get fancy facials,* I thought. But sometimes the most revolutionary thing you can do is show your face to the world.

There are studies that say women who wear makeup earn more than women who don't. But it's a pipe dream wrapped in nylon stockings and high heels, because women still make less than men for the same jobs. Whether women wear makeup or not, their looks are often the subject of debate and discussion, the target of ridicule and criticism in cruel and unnecessary ways. When we disagree with women, we attack their appearance. For example, rather than addressing the substance of Congresswoman Maxine Waters's comments, former TV commentator Bill O'Reilly said he "didn't hear a word she said" because he was "looking at the James Brown wig" she wore. During his presidential campaign, Donald Trump said of Republican rival Carley Fiorina, "Look at that face. Would anyone vote for that? Can you imagine that as the face of our next president?" He also said Democratic opponent Hillary Clinton didn't "look presidential." After the election, Clinton gave a speech at the Children's Defense Fund wearing little or no makeup. "She looks more authentic and relatable," people said. "I wish she would've gone without makeup during the campaign," others added. But the sad truth is that if Clinton had regularly appeared on the campaign trail without makeup, the media, public, and her competitors would have berated her and been even more critical than when she wore makeup; because that is the unfair scrutiny to which women are subjected every day.

And when women finish fixing our faces just the way others like, people will kindly tell us that something else about our appearance is displeasing to their eyes or offends their sensibilities. And they may even tell us this with a smile, or think they have good intentions. They will use fancy words like "corporate culture" and "image" and "polished" to explain their overreaching. And courts will use such legalese as "mutable characteristic" and "immutable characteristic" to justify such overreaching.

Black women are still being told we aren't professional unless we blend in and deny some part of ourselves. Black women like Chastity Jones, who was offered a job at a company in Alabama and then told she'd have to get rid of her dreadlocks because they didn't project a "professional and businesslike image." The Eleventh Circuit Court of Appeals agreed with the company, stating that discrimination on the basis of black hair texture (an immutable characteristic) is prohibited by Title VII of the Civil Rights Act of 1964, while discrimination on the basis of black hair*styles* (a mutable characteristic) is not prohibited.

Rachel Sakabo was fired from her job as a concierge at a New York City hotel after less than two weeks because she wasn't a "good fit" for the hotel's "culture." Not long before the hotel terminated her, a manager told her she couldn't wear braids at the front desk. When Sakabo explained that they were dreadlocks, the manager asked whether she could "unlock" them. Yes, it is revolutionary to be yourself and to say to the world, "This is who I am."

The problem with chasing other people's expectations of us, whether expressed or implied, is that the bar keeps moving. You will exhaust yourself and always be that hamster running on the wheel, and you will never know when you've met their expectations. And chances are, you never will. And you won't even recognize yourself.

"I don't need to be fuckable," I said to my supervisor after she told me the CEO didn't like the second picture I had taken. "People just need to know what I look like and how to find me." Her eyes widened in disbelief. I'm pretty sure she thought I was crazy. But I was fed up. Fed up with jumping through hoops to change myself whenever other people didn't like something about me.

I had seen pictures of my white male predecessor, and his were not glamour shots. If I were a man, would I have been asked to take multiple pictures until I got the perfect shot or took the hint? Of course not. And so I said a resounding, "No." No, I am not going to take a million pictures until it meets some unspoken standard of acceptability. No, being sexually stimulating is not part of my job description. Hell no.

Refusing to take another picture that day was my way of asserting power. Of choosing my battles in the war for self-love in a world that tells women that no matter how smart or qualified they are, they are not worthy unless they look a certain way. It was preparation for the many other times in my life when I would need the strength to say no. My way of making up for all the times when I didn't or couldn't say no.

No one ever said another word to me about retaking my picture. That second photo of me—smiling, courageous, without makeup—hung in various hallways of the hospital for the next six years.

More than ten years later, I am still evolving. After a too-tight weave and a bout of inflamed hair follicles, bald spots, and a thinning hairline, I eventually cut off my relaxed hair one Saturday night after a three-hour detangling session. Thanks to my friend Tiffany, I fell in love with lip gloss and lipstick. I finally learned to apply mascara a few years ago during a trip to Sephora, but I only know how to apply it to my top lashes. I still don't know how to apply eyeliner. I found a makeup line and shade that doesn't make me look like a clown or corpse, although it's been a few years since I've worn foundation. I wear dresses and short-sleeves, and show off my dark elbows and knees whenever I please.

I have not reached the mountaintop of self-acceptance. My face's ongoing rebellion has made me a regular at my dermatologist's office. When one doctor prescribed a cream for hyperpigmentation that contained the skin-bleaching agent hydroquinone, I used it a few times. And then I remembered the Nadinola and Ajax and Dermablend. I threw the expensive cream away and found a new doctor. At various points, I began wearing foundation regularly to cover whatever skin emergency had popped up, like the chemical burn from a "natural" face wash I bought at a flea market (bad idea, I know). And then I stopped wearing makeup because I began to dislike the face beneath the mask, and because wearing and removing makeup every day is too much work. A white male colleague once accused my small afro of being an "angry hairstyle"—my 'fro was just minding her own business. Over the years, other people have expressed a similar, albeit more subtle, aversion to my natural hair.

But I love myself enough to define my own standard of beauty. I love myself enough to say no. No, I won't contort myself into someone else's brand of sexy. No, I don't feel like worrying about what others think of my face or hair or some other part of my body. No, don't tell me how to dress or when to wear makeup or how to be picture perfect. Not today, patriarchy and racism. Not today.

Jodi M. Savage is an employment discrimination attorney and writer in New York City. Her writing has appeared in *Catapult* and *The Establishment*. Jodi's writing focuses on social justice, feminism, Alzheimer's disease, and caregiving. She graduated from Barnard College and Seton Hall University and can be reached at jodimsavage@gmail.com.

PART III. **MEDIATING BEAUTY**

Remnants of Venus: Signifying Black Beauty and Sexuality

Janell Hobson

Abstract: "Remnants of Venus" examines popular representations of the "big booty," often associated with and serving as a stand-in for black women's sexualities. This essay calls into question whether such representations, embodied through racial appropriations by non-black women or satirized by black women like Kara Walker and Nicki Minaj, can exist beyond "signs" of sexual excess or whether they can be mobilized toward black sexual freedom and an aesthetic of black beauty, as other artists have attempted, from Janelle Monáe to Beyoncé to young women "twerk" dancing. **Keywords**: blackness, beauty, feminism, aesthetics, popular culture

When *Vogue* proclaimed the "Era of the Big Booty" in 2014, they seemed more than a few decades late. After all, the big booty had amassed praise and celebration since the inception of such musical genres as funk and hip-hop—think The Commodore's "Brick House" (1977) and 2 Live Crew's controversial *As Nasty as They Wanna Be* album cover (1989). Indeed, as Tricia Rose notes, "the black behind has an especially charged place . . . [in] black sexual expression," that precedes funk and hip-hop, although the increased popularity of the latter gave this body part more centrality in the culture at large (1994, 167–68). However, we would not know this from the *Vogue* article (Garcia 2014), given the focus on mostly white and Latina women and their enviable curves—including Jennifer Lopez, Iggy Azalea, and Kim Kardashian—even though these same women have been or are currently romantically linked to black male rappers who have directed the prominent cultural gaze to their curvy backsides. Incidentally, black women pop stars such as Rihanna, Beyoncé, and rapper Nicki Minaj—the latter garnering widespread attention with her ode to big-booty women in

WSQ: Women's Studies Quarterly 46: 1 & 2 (Spring/Summer 2018) © 2018 by Janell Hobson. All rights reserved.

the record-breaking music video "Anaconda"—were given curt mention in the same article, prompting outrage from various women of color on social media.

Although such beauty narratives manage to sideline women of African descent, the sexualized history of these women is often invoked in other instances. For example, in the wake of Kardashian's controversial *Paper* magazine cover depicting her derriere balancing a champagne glass in a recreation of a 1976 photograph of black, nude model Carolina Beaumont by French photographer Jean-Paul Goude, Cleuci de Oliveira wrote for the feminist blog *Jezebel* that Saartjie (or Sarah/Sara) Baartman, widely known as the "Hottentot Venus," was the "Original Booty Queen" (2014). While *Vogue* angered women of color for its marginalization of black womanhood, *Jezebel* enraged them even more for misrepresenting Baartman's history of racial dehumanization. Because of her exhibition in European cities like London and Paris from 1810 to 1815, as well as her posthumous dissection for scientific study—both actions that fetishized Baartman's so-called large behind and genitalia—some women of color accused Oliveira of minimizing Baartman's history when she suggested it mirrors the attention-seeking antics of Kardashian.[1]

These discourses on racialized beauty and sexuality highlight the ways that, firstly, black women serve as the subliminal signs for sexual excess that prominent backsides supposedly engender and, secondly, Baartman's historic role as the Hottentot Venus is still name-checked for big booty conversations. Nonetheless, while *Vogue* downplayed black women in its "Era of the Big Booty" article, it did choose to include indie artist Solange Knowles's New Orleans–based "white wedding" photographs online, thereby beautifying black women's bodies through the veneer of elegance and sophisticated chic that contests stereotypes of blackness as only signifying sexual excess, "ratchet" low culture, and vulgarity. Knowles's portraits of black womanhood were widely celebrated on the social media network called "Black Twitter," as the images highlighted her stylish bridal white-cape gown and other black women in elegant white attire, including her mother, her sister Beyoncé, and R&B artist Janelle Monáe.

While Solange is known for her daring style and for pushing against the mainstream in contrast to her more popular big sister, Black Twitter and others on social media commended her for projecting black bougie cool, which appropriates white fashion elegance to heighten black women's beauty and style. Nonetheless, the specter of elegance and thinness through which *Vogue* assimilates the black subject into sophisticated whiteness is represented by the slenderized white-wedding aesthetic of Knowles and even in the celebration of svelte, dark-skinned Kenyan actress Lupita Nyong'o, who landed her first *Vogue* cover that same year with subsequent appearances in 2015, 2016, and 2018. Such aesthetic preferences illuminate how the real beauty challenge for women of African descent is not their skin color but their curves. Indeed, *Vogue*'s first black cover girl, Beverly Johnson, developed an eating disorder to maintain a thin figure in the wake of her success, and Beyoncé, who landed her first *Vogue* cover in 2009—with the headline "Real Women Have Curves"—in her interview emphasized the extent to which she lost weight to conform to *Vogue*'s beauty standard since "I'm not a naturally stick-thin girl" (quoted in Van Meter 2009).

This essay explores how black women's beauty is intrinsically connected to booty size, which exists in a complex history of racialized and sexualized meanings. That is, their bodies continue to signify sexual excess (supposedly conveyed by a large behind) more than black sexual freedoms. I further analyze the rhetoric and imagery surrounding black women's bodies in other art and popular culture, including the work of artist Kara Walker and Nicki Minaj. Finally, this essay explores the possibility of a black sexual freedom, using the examples of Beyoncé, Janelle Monáe, and young women engaging the sexually provocative twerk dance, that can be rescued from an oppressive history of objectification and marginalization.

While much has already been written concerning the life and meaning of Baartman, her iconography as the Hottentot Venus is often recycled in present-day discourses as a reminder that such iconicity continues to inform black women's sexualities. It is in the recognition of this racialized beauty and sexual politics that I wish to examine the limitations and possibilities of representations of black women's sexualities by critiquing configurations of the ubiquitous booty, which is routinely associated with black women's bodies even though the bodies of nonblack women are racialized and, subsequently, aestheticized in similar yet different ways.

Given these aesthetic treatments, how can black women in the United States and elsewhere see themselves more holistically? What are other ways of representing black women's bodies? Moreover, can they ever exist beyond what Hortense Spillers argues is our "New World, diasporic plight [that] marked the *theft of the body*—a willful and violent ... severing of the captive body from its motive will, its active desire" (1987, 67; emphasis in original)? This historical theft, dating back to slavery, renders difficult any claims to a liberated black female sexuality since, as Spillers also argues, black women remain "unvoiced, misseen, not doing, awaiting their verb" (1984, 74), mobilized for others to define their own sexualities. The few black women artists analyzed here are attempting to reclaim their bodies.

Remnants of Blackness

The representational politics that framed the Hottentot Venus figure in the nineteenth century is specific to the era, but remnants abound in twenty-first-century imagery concerning beauty, sexuality, and racialized gender. It is precisely the racial essentialism embodied in the big booty that, when projected onto the bodies of nonblack women, can racialize these women in similar yet distinct ways, even when our culture's racial hierarchies often relieve nonblack bodies from associations with racial "deviance." When white pop stars such as Miley Cyrus, Iggy Azalea, and Taylor Swift populate their music videos with twerking black women in the background—as occurred with Cyrus's "We Can't Stop," Azalea's "Work," and Swift's "Shake It Off," all released in 2013 or 2014—they are engaging in racial tropes that mobilize black women's sexualities.

The behinds of the background dancers in these videos become racial signifiers through the fetishistic treatment of their twerking, thus suggesting a close proximity to "black cool," in the cases of Cyrus and Azalea, or a racial contrast that provides stark contrast to the perceived whiteness of the central figure, in the case of Swift, who awkwardly and comically dances with no rhythm in her video and, to some extent, Cyrus, whose own "booty" is non-curvaceous despite her eager embrace of booty-enhancing dances. The spectacle of twerking—a dance known for its rapid up-and-down movements of the derriere, which had so many parents across the United States concerned about the hypersexualization of our culture ever since Cyrus introduced it to the mainstream at MTV's 2013 Video Music Awards—amplifies this racial difference. That twerking originated in the heavily policed black communities of New Orleans and reached a global audience via YouTube, reinforces white fears of black bodies—be they sexualized or criminalized.[2] This is how dance floors become sites of contestation, reclamation, confrontation, and "battles." Twerking is the latest weapon in making legible what Carolyn Cooper (1995) calls the "vulgar body" in the public sphere of subversive body politics.

Sander L. Gilman, who arguably inaugurated academic attention to Baartman's history, notes that historically the Hottentot Venus figure visually connotes "deviant sexuality," and when paired with a white central figure, the black presence "implies their sexual similarity," so much so that, eventually, the black female figure can disappear altogether while the white woman's body, presented with an endowed behind, serves as a palimpsest of the black woman's body (1985, 209). Such is the case when Cyrus, in the quest to shed her former good-girl *Hannah Montana* image, succeeds by surrounding herself with the twerking bodies of black women, who eventually disappear from subsequent songs and videos once Cyrus's sexually mature persona was established and she no longer needed to rely on these women to signify her transgressions. This was reiterated when she denounced hip-hop as too misogynistic in a *Billboard* interview (quoted in Norris 2017), at a time when she reinvented herself once again as a softer, more mature singer-songwriter.

White rappers like Iggy Azalea still signify blackness in their music and videos, which situate her within urban "street" culture replete with booty-shaking black female dancers who authenticate her connections to hip-hop's blackness. Interestingly, Azalea's "Work" video (2013) further situates her own rural Australian working-class background—alluded to in the visuals—in a way that complicates the way her body enters and bridges these disparate settings and the positioning of her dancing white body when compared to the black background dancers. However, Azalea's video for her crossover hit, "Fancy" (2014), featuring white pop star Charli XCX, reified her whiteness in its homage to the white middle-class teenage film *Clueless* (1995), even though echoes of her appropriated "blackness" remain from her endowed behind to her affected Southern black-girl accent.

When Azalea collaborated with Jennifer Lopez—famous for her curves—for the song and music video "Booty" (2014), they are positioned as ideal beauties, due in part to their curvy but more slender booties, in the style of the ancient Roman Venus Callipyge, wrapped up in sensual desirability, in stark contrast to the derided Venus Steatopygia, couched in the sexual pathology, racial deviance, and fat shaming that framed Minaj in the reception of her music video for "Anaconda." The marginalization of black women in these representations of sexual desirability is much like what Mireille Miller-Young has described of "brown sugar," the metaphor for black women's sexuality: "Like sugar that has dissolved without a trace, but has nonetheless sweetened a cup of tea, black women's labor and the mechanisms that manage and produce it are invisible but nonetheless *there*" (2014, 4; emphasis in original). Venus Steatopygia functions as the hidden text while Venus Callipyge is visibly rendered as "white." Once again, we witness the theft of a black woman's body.

Venus Mis/Seen

Porn studies scholar Miller-Young elaborates further on the brown-sugar metaphor: "Black women, like brown sugar, represent a raw body in need of refinement and prone to manipulation. . . . While processed white sugar is held up as the ideal, there remains a powerful desire, indeed a taste, for the *real thing*" (2014, 5; emphasis in original). Such parameters inform the work of artist Kara Walker, who installed *A Subtlety, or the Marvelous Sugar Baby* at the old Domino sugar refinery in Brooklyn from May 10 to July 6, 2014, before the factory was demolished. Her "Sugar Baby," also known as the Sugar Sphinx, refers to a seventy-five-foot-long and thirty-five-foot-tall white sugar coated sculpture. Walker is known for creating paper cutout silhouettes that simulate scenes from the antebellum South in what Michele Wallace describes as "a kind of repressed theme park, a riotous, operatic hyperactive brothel of the brain that lurks barely hidden behind our more polite and publicized racial arrangements" (2003, 177). Walker's public installation craftily engages similar themes intersecting race and sexuality.

Documenting her creative process, Walker suggested through a pictorial collage that the inspiration for the Sugar Sphinx came from an amalgamation of the ancient Giza sphinx in the Egyptian desert and a lingerie-clad black model crouched on all fours and jutting out her behind for maximum exposure (Creative Time 2014). The latter image is ubiquitous in hip-hop magazines, music videos, and pornography. Combining an ancient symbol of mysterious deity—part woman, part lion—with a contemporary scene of black sexual fetishism, Walker connects contemporary black women's bodies to a history of animalizing the bodies of women and Africans, as well as to a history of empire and New World slavery (specifically its legacy of sexual politics, racial ideology, and global exploitation represented by sugar industries fueling slave labor and the "refining" process of natural resources such as sugar cane into, first, brown sugar, then powdery white sugar). Walker has stated that the mammy-like face of the sculpture, replete with bandana head covering, is a throwback to the "Aunt Dinah" image used to sell molasses, which projects a different consumptive image of digestive and servile "sweetness" (quoted in Laster 2014).

Reflecting on the legacy of slavery in the production of sugar in the New World, Walker's Sugar Sphinx, literally white-washed and coated in forty tons of sugar, illuminates the grandiose and grotesque nature of our racial history: a whitened, "sugar-coated" history based in the erasure of exploited slave labor (horrifically captured in the melting sculptures of overworked molasses-covered boys that accompany the larger sculpture) as well as in the hypervisibility of black female sexuality, which is simultaneously valued and devalued within the economies of slavery through black women's productive and reproductive labor. However, the fact that so many visitors elided this history and reduced (or aggrandized in this case) the Sugar Baby to comical spectacle suggests that black women's bodies cannot be seen in their entirety; even when, or especially when, standing in the presence of a massive booty. Because of its gigantic backside, which many visitors captured in selfies and Instagram photos, critics couldn't help but recall the objectifying history of the Hottentot Venus (Newman 2014). Slavery and the women absorbed and distorted by that legacy remain as incomprehensible as a sphinx.

Nonetheless, if art critics and audiences were willing to recognize Walker's genius in capturing the racialized and sexualized legacy of sugar and slavery in her artwork, they were less accepting of Nicki Minaj's art. Instead, numerous commentators and hip-hop fans chastised the rapper who, just one month after Walker's exhibit closed, posed in a G-string revealing her ample behind in the cover art for "Anaconda" (2014), released ahead of its equally provocative music video. There is a distinction to be made between merely crafting images of hypersexuality, as Walker has done, and embodying these images, as Minaj's performance illustrates.

This is not to suggest that Walker herself escaped similar outrage. Indeed, the artist also received criticisms and condemnation for recreating stereotypes of the big-booty black woman. However, Walker can still be recognized for her artistry and subsequently be cast in the genre of high art; whereas, Minaj's very embodiment of the stereotype cast her into the realm of the pornographic. Judging from the various outraged responses to Minaj's cover art from fans and naysayers on the internet to feminists and hip-hop website owners, the spectacle of the rapper as a big-booty woman simultaneously elicited awe and repulsion. When greeted by the sight of a black woman emphasizing her posterior, certain critics made the usual historical parallels between the Hottentot Venus and her twenty-first-century descendants, which includes Minaj. However, refusing to be an iconic throwback, Minaj responded to criticisms by pushing back through Twitter and Instagram.

In juxtaposing her "unacceptable" image with the more "acceptable" images of similarly clad slender, white *Sports Illustrated* models, Minaj challenged her critics to question just what it was that made *her* body more morally questionable than her slender white counterparts. She critically interrogated the public gaze that judged her in terms of race, gender, and size politics, whether in the various comical memes of her cover art that sought to diminish its sexual appeal, or in intellectual criticisms that reductively dismissed her body as pornographic, as Gail Dines (2014) asserted when she described the rapper's image as "little more than a big butt" reminiscent of the Hottentot Venus. Minaj's posts challenged viewers to consider her erotic appeal, sexual agency, and ironic performativity.

In the cover art for "Anaconda," Minaj's gaze is defiant as she looks directly at the camera and disrupts stereotypical notions of femininity by sporting blue Jordans in lieu of stiletto heels. Her image is aggressively raunchy instead of submissively "come hither" sexy. It is no wonder, then, that the memes on the internet have sought to neutralize its sexual power. However, Minaj's own defense against charges of vulgarity is not to distance herself from hypersexual images but instead to embrace them, to poke holes in them, to remix and then signify on them. Given the ways that black women's booties are often hidden sexual subtexts and relegated to the background, Nicki Minaj brings them to the foreground.

As the hook to the song "Anaconda," Minaj samples the "white girl" vocals from Sir Mix-A-Lot's "Baby Got Back" (1992), "Oh. My. God . . . Look at her butt!" This sampling illuminates her efforts at confronting the objectifying gaze of black men, as implied by Sir Mix-A-Lot's infamous line—"My anaconda don't want none unless you got buns hon"—and white women, indicated by the hook. Both groups have perpetuated ideas of gender and racial difference to bolster their placements within gendered and raced hierarchies. Here, Minaj provides oppositional space in her song and video for black women's sexual agency and a complicated response to those who would insist that "all the women are white, all the blacks are men."[3] To argue that Minaj signifies on the stereotype of the oversexed big-booty black woman suggests a complex engagement with the ways black women's bodies are made visible and legible while she simultaneously rewrites the script.

What begins in the video as a scene in the colonialist jungle of darkest Africa (or perhaps the tropical Global South) continues with a montage of different feminine spaces for women's reclamations of the body, from a pink workout room to a kitchen, where Minaj satirically dons a sexy French maid costume while spraying herself with whipped cream, just before symbolically castrating the phallus in her slicing up of a banana—an allusion to the same phallic symbol used in Sir-Mix-a-lot's video. That she slices the banana while staring directly at the camera in bemusement suggests, much like her cover art, her confrontation with the male gaze and a confounding of these visual parameters through breaking the fourth wall. However, it is on a soundstage where she simulates a lap dance for rapper Drake. Intriguingly, Minaj engages in parody, but her body becomes the subversive signifier of excess sexuality which she simultaneously denies to the male gaze at the end of the video. Minaj also aligns her own body with her backup dancers representing different races and ethnicities, and subsequently creates a multiracial sisterhood with other booty-shaking women, especially in their twerking—a stark contrast from the videos of Cyrus, Azalea, and Swift.

Much can be said about the subversive potential of twerking. Despite the credit given to Miley Cyrus for popularizing twerking in the wider culture, Big Freedia, a black queer rapper from New Orleans and self-proclaimed queen of bounce music, is renowned in street culture for introducing twerking. Locating a "street" expression within the queer black body, twerking conjoins the bodies of black queer men, women and nonbinary genders, and black straight women in a "queer" sexuality that, as Cathy J. Cohen suggests, redefines "the lives of . . . women of color . . . [who] may fit into the category of heterosexual, but [their] sexual choices are not perceived as normal, moral, or worthy of state support" (1997, 442). Given the different meanings of the black booty in contexts of same-sex versus heteronormative desire, the site of both queer and straight black bodies mobilizes alternative aesthetics, erotic agency, and resistance to dominant modes of sexualities.

Where Nicki Minaj proves most subversive is the way in which she exposes the artificialities of race and sexuality, from the pastiche jungle set opening the "Anaconda" video to her deliberate portrayal of her allegedly surgically altered body as a "realness" worth emulating and playfully dressing up in high fashion or sex play. Yet, when her music video was overlooked for a Video of the Year nomination for MTV's Video Music Awards, Minaj reacted on Twitter in a way that suggested her race, gender, and size prevented her from being recognized, despite the obvious influence it had on the wider culture. Such occurrences may reveal how these embodied performances are not recognized as such despite Minaj's attempts to destabilize their meaning.

While the snub briefly stirred controversy, the aftermath of her song and music video revealed more concretely the social impact of "Anaconda." One example includes the wax figure of Minaj at Las Vegas's Madame Tussauds, which depicts her in the likeness of her "Anaconda" image—crouched on all fours—that attracted several onlookers to take racy pictures with it, much like the visitors at Kara Walker's *A Subtlety* exhibit. When these pictures surfaced online they caused outrage among some who were made uncomfortable by the sexualization of black women's bodies, but Minaj was "flattered" (quoted in Wilson 2015), insinuating both her own refusal to embrace respectability politics and her appreciation that her curvaceous replica elicited desire—a desirability that was undercut by both *Vogue*'s "Era of the Big Booty" article and MTV's Video of the Year snub.

Representing Black Sexual Freedom

While Nicki Minaj has eschewed respectability politics, other entertainers such as Beyoncé and Janelle Monáe have intentionally blurred the lines between respectability and what the Crunk Feminist Collective calls "disrespectability politics," which defies the constraints of both African American calls for public respectability on the part of black bodies and the dominant culture's refutation of that same body as worthy of such respect (Crunktastic 2012). Specifically, the mobilization of twerking on the part of Beyoncé and Monáe provide complex articulations of a liberatory black female sexuality that situate their booties beyond satire in a more energizing expression that resists mere objectification. Beyoncé's celebrated self-titled visual album reminds her listeners that she is now a "grown woman" who "can do whatever I want," from defying the conventions of album releases to proudly displaying and raunchily shaking her glorified "Bootylicious" body. Her bonus video for

"Grown Woman" specifically documents through grainy video footage and psychedelic animated sequences how she has evolved from a young girl to Destiny's Child young adult to a more mature woman and mother (Beyoncé 2013). Her twerking fuses traditional dances from Africa, which expands her dance language from the more homegrown moves of a young Beyoncé in the local and nostalgic sphere of Houston, Texas, into her more global and diasporic choreography.

However, Janelle Monáe, having released her single "Q.U.E.E.N." featuring Erykah Badu (2013) earlier that year, further complicates the politics of twerking within contexts of Afrofuturism and counter-aesthetics. As Jennifer Williams observes, "It is far too easy to imagine that Monáe and Beyoncé represent two opposite poles because of the different ways they perform their sexualities," and subsequently, we are inclined to miss the important work both artists are doing when they "illuminate the possibilities of a feminist politic that is embodied and sexual" (2014). Here, Williams refers to Monáe's lyrics in "Q.U.E.E.N.": "You can take my wings but I'm still gonna fly / And even when you edit me, the booty don't lie." It is striking that Monáe reiterates this line in response to Erykah Badu's earlier verse: "But you gotta testify / because the booty don't lie."

In a culture predicated on hypersexual representations of big booties, which are burdened by stereotypes and myths, Monáe presents her own body—in stylish black-and-white skirts, tight pants, and a tuxedo during her rap—to complicate portrayals of the booty. She thus embodies her own truths when proclaiming "the booty don't lie." Monáe's song and video suggest a crafting of identity, an actualization of the self: "Is it peculiar that she twerk in the mirror? / And am I weird to dance alone late at night?" That she responds to her questions with "And I just tell 'em, 'No we ain't,' and get down," indicates her rejection of external meanings and categorizations in pursuit of her own desires and self-affirmation as well as the wider affirmation of collective black womanhood. Tellingly, a voiceover in the video for "Q.U.E.E.N." presents Monáe and her Wondaland crew in the distant future in a "living museum where legendary rebels throughout history have been frozen in suspended animation," on exhibit alongside carefully placed human skulls and "primitives" covered in white paint (perhaps to symbolize ancestry in an African context, versus the "savage" of the European imagination). At once reframing histories that resemble Baartman's, who was similarly exhibited in a museum—but in death, not in "suspended animation"—Monáe embodies history and enters this colonialist space to literally animate the body through vibrant counternarratives: including musical revival, fashions varying from feminine to masculine, and "freedom movements . . . disguised as songs" (Monáe 2013).

Equally telling is the way Monáe and her black background dancers, bedecked in tight-fitting black-and-white outfits, don't twerk for the camera, even though they pose before mirrors and bump and grind in the style of funk choreography. Monáe thus sings about "twerking in front of the mirror" without satisfying the viewer's gaze and anticipation for a sexualized spectacle. She consciously stylizes the booty while simultaneously containing it through traditional black choreography and expression. In doing so, Monáe eschews parody for prophecy in her Afrofuturistic vision, which prefers using the distant future to redefine black sexuality rather than the racialized and colonized space of the past in Nicki Minaj's jungle setting for "Anaconda."

Both Beyoncé and Monáe articulate a discourse of black sexual freedom, whether in Beyoncé's hook, "I can do whatever I want," or in Monáe's empowering rap verse, "Categorize me, I defy every label." As such, they enter into the public sphere a defiant and declarative space for becoming and for demanding their own sense of personal and collective identity. Because such narratives coexist in the wider culture of popular songs and videos that constantly reduce the dancing black body to mere object, we are reminded of the work needed to engage with and ultimately resist the dominant discourse that continues to negate black women's beauty, pleasure, desire, and desirability, or to curtail such desires through rigid moral codes. As Monáe further posits, her "Project Q.U.E.E.N.," an acronym for Queer communities, the Untouchables, the Emigrants, the Excommunicated, and the Negroid (cited in Benjamin 2013), is a "musical weapons program," designed in defense of black womanhood and in the interest of challenging the meanings of the black female body. At once redefining the respectability politics of "queen," often asserted in black nationalist discourse to describe conservative ideals of modest black womanhood, Monáe rejects these conventional labels for a more futuristic and visionary definition of a black female sexuality that exists beyond heteronormativity.

These declarations are not just "weapons of resistance"; they are survival strategies, for the dominant discourse of racism and misogyny exists to discipline, punish, and condemn black women's sexualities. An example of this is in the scholarship competition, sponsored by rapper Juicy J, which occurred the same year as these releases by Beyoncé and Monáe. Juicy J's single, "Scholarship," in which he raps about a young college student working at a strip club and twerking to pay for her college tuition, became the basis for his sponsorship, in conjunction with *WorldStarHipHop*, of a fifty-thousand-dollar scholarship awarded to a college student who entered a twerking competition by submitting an online video that highlighted her twerking skills. Yet, Juicy J eventually awarded the scholarship to biology student Zaire Holmes, who ironically did not twerk in her video; while proudly announcing the winner, he also admonished other applicants for "not reading the fine print," which stated that twerking was not required.[4] His derision expressed toward those applicants who engaged in twerk videos was the worst display of misogyny combined with respectability politics, which encouraged sexual spectacle while simultaneously dismissing women for participating in said spectacle.

One of the young women who entered the competition, Kimora Carter, specifically produced a subversive video that framed her own twerking performance by declaring: "I'm not just a twerker, and I'm not here for your hypersexual consumption . . . I'm an intellectual, I'm an artist, I'm an activist, and I'm a student" (2013). Embodying the young black woman who "twerks in the mirror," as she is shown in her video, both in the privacy of her own room and in a dance studio where she dances with other young women, Carter redefines her body for herself. Interestingly, her video also juxtaposes a cartoon of the Hottentot Venus with her own body in various states, meditating in a yoga pose, twerking while reading one of her many college textbooks, and dancing with abandon at a club, thus suggesting her own historical consciousness of how her body might be objectified in similar ways and how she attempts to reframe this visual spectacle. Such multifaceted ways of being situate her own body against Juicy J's song, playing in the background with such glib lyrics as "You a college chick, you a college chick / Keep twerking baby, might earn you a scholarship." As such, Carter's engagement with the sexist framing of her body by entering Juicy J's competition, serves as a counternarrative that subverts the dominant discourse. What is equally fruitful to consider is the way black women see themselves, as these videos, "Grown Woman," "Q.U.E.E.N.," and Carter's video entry, all depict black women dancing before a mirror, which is an intriguing motif and gesture toward self-affirmation.

The narratives surrounding black women's sexualities are ultimately bigger than twerking or Nicki Minaj or Sara Baartman. Nonetheless, the collective angst over black women's bodies is predictable and must be challenged. It is past time that we develop new ways of engaging these sexual politics. When we consider the horrific histories that enabled these systems of inequalities—from New World slavery to the treatment of Baartman—the grand theft of the black woman's body requires careful and painstaking reassemblage of missing parts and new interpretations. Indeed, both Solange and Beyoncé have attempted more daring representations, as seen in their respective 2016 albums *A Seat at the Table* and *Lemonade*, while Monáe has ventured into protest music and cinema. Their artistic engagements remind us that once we proclaim that "the booty don't lie"—despite the incredible lies told on the black booty—we can dance in the space of our own truths, reclaim our bodies, assert our beauty, and redefine our sexual selves on our own terms.

Janell Hobson is associate professor in the Department of Women's, Gender, and Sexuality Studies at the University at Albany. Her research focuses on black women's histories and representations. She is the author of *Venus in the Dark: Blackness and Beauty in Popular Culture*. She can be reached at jhobson@albany.edu.

Notes

1. See for examples Callahan 2014 and Glenn 2014.
2. Ethnomusicologist Kyra Gaunt (2016) connects the displacement of black New Orleans residents in the aftermath of Hurricane Katrina in 2005 with the creation of YouTube that same year, thus observing the significance of technology in visually constructing local longing via globalized processes while simultaneously circulating images of black hypersexuality.
3. See Hull, Bell Scott, and Smith 1982.
4. See Juicy J 2014.

Works Cited

Benjamin, Jeff. 2013. "Janelle Monáe Says 'Q.U.E.E.N.' is for the 'Ostracized and Marginalized.'" Fuse, September 18. http://www.fuse.tv/videos/2013/09/ardash-monae-queen-interview.

Beyoncé. 2013. "Grown Woman." Track 18 on disc 2 of *BEYONCÉ*. New York: Parkwood Entertainment/Columbia Records.

Callahan, Yesha. 2014. "Vogue Magazine Just Realized Big Butts Are a 'Thing' and Credits White People." *The Root*. September 10. https://thegrapevine.

theroot.com/vogue-magazine-just-realized-big-butts-are-a-thing-an-1790885701.

Carter, Kimora. 2013. "Juicy J. Scholarship | WORLDSTAR HIP HOP." YouTube. September 28. https://www.youtube.com/watch?v=qKwSg59XS4Y.

Cohen, Cathy J. 1997. "Punks, Bulldaggers, and Welfare Queens: The Radical Potential of Queer Politics?" *GLQ: A Journal of Lesbian and Gay Studies* 3 (4): 437–65.

Cooper, Carolyn. 1995. *Noises in the Blood: Orality, Gender, and the "Vulgar" Body in Jamaican Popular Culture.* Durham, NC: Duke University Press.

Creative Time. 2014. "Creative Time Presents Kara Walker." Accessed July 30, 2014. http://creativetime.org/projects/karawalker/inspiration.

Crunktastic [Brittney C. Cooper]. 2012. "Disrespectability Politics: On Jay-Z's Bitch, Beyoncé's 'Fly' Ass, and Black Girl Blue." Crunk Feminist Collective, January 19. http://www.crunkfeministcollective.com/2012/01/19/disrespectability-politics-on-jay-zs-bitch-beyonces-fly-ass-and-black-girl-blue.

Dines, Gail. 2014. "Nicki Minaj: Little More Than a Big Butt?" *Huffington Post*, July 29. http://www.huffingtonpost.co.uk/gail-dines/nicki-minaj_b_5629232.html.

Garcia, Patricia. 2014. "We're Officially in the Era of the Big Booty." *Vogue*, September 9. Accessed October 1, 2014. http://www.vogue.com/1342927/booty-in-pop-culture-jennifer-lopez-iggy-azalea (site discontinued).

Gaunt, Kyra. 2016. "A Time Signature of Black Bottom Lines (1936–2016): Compounding Gender Stratification on YouTube from Race Records to Rap Songs." Lecture delivered at the University at Albany, Albany, NY, December 5.

Gilman, Sander L. 1985. "Black Bodies, White Bodies: Toward an Iconography of Female Sexuality in Late Nineteenth-Century Art, Medicine, and Literature." *Critical Inquiry* 12 (1): 204–42.

Glenn, Pia. 2014. "You Can't Ignore the Degradation of Saartjie Baartman to Connect Her to Kim Kardashian. You Just Can't." *xoJane*, November 17. http://www.xojane.com/issues/saartjie-baartman-kim-kardashian.

Hull, Akasha (Gloria T.), Patricia Bell Scott, and Barbara Smith, eds. 1982. *All the Women Are White, All the Blacks Are Men, But Some of Us Are Brave: Black Women's Studies.* New York: The Feminist Press.

Juicy J. 2014. "Juicy J Selects the Winner of the $50,000 Scholarship Contest." YouTube, January 14. https://www.youtube.com/watch?v=p3xigZXd0o8.

Laster, Paul. 2014. "Kara Walker interview: 'The whole reason for refining sugar is to make it white.'" *TimeOut*, May 5. https://www.timeout.com/newyork/

art/kara-walker-interview-the-whole-reason-for-refining-sugar-is-to-make-it-white.

Miller-Young, Mireille. 2014. *A Taste for Brown Sugar: Black Women in Pornography*. Durham, NC: Duke University Press.

Minaj, Nicki. 2014. "Anaconda." Track 12 on *The Pinkprint*. New Orleans, LA and New York: Young Money/Cash Money/ Republic Records.

Monáe, Janelle. 2013. "Q.U.E.E.N." Track 3 on *The Electric Lady*. New York: Wondaland Arts Society/Bad Boy Records.

Newman, Vanessa. 2014. "'The Tragic Genius of Kara Walker's 'Sugar Baby' Exhibit." *Moodie Mills*, June 22. Accessed August 15, 2014. http:// moodiemills.com/2014/06/the-tragic-genius-of-kara-walkers-sugar-baby-exhibit (site discontinued).

Norris, John. 2017. "Miley Cyrus Breaks Silence on Rootsy New Music, Fiancé Liam Hemsworth, and America: 'Unity Is What We Need.'" *Billboard*, May 3. http://www.billboard.com/articles/news/magazine-feature/7783997/miley-cyrus-cover-story-new-music-malibu.

Oliveira, Cleuci de. 2014. "Saartjie Baartman: The Original Booty Queen." *Jezebel*, November 14. http://jezebel.com/saartje-baartman-the-original-booty-queen-1658569879.

Rose, Tricia. 1994. *Black Noise: Rap Music and Black Culture in Contemporary America*. Middletown, CT: Wesleyan University Press.

Spillers, Hortense. 1984. "Interstices: A Small Drama of Words." In *Pleasure and Danger: Exploring Female Sexuality*, edited by Carole S. Vance, 73–100. London: Pandora.

———. 1987. "Mama's Baby, Papa's Maybe: An American Grammar Book." *Diacritics* 17 (2): 65–81.

Van Meter, Jonathan. 2009. "Beyoncé: Fierce Creature." *Vogue*, April 1. http:// www.vogue.com/article/beyonc233-fierce-creature.

Wallace, Michele. 2003. "The Enigma of the Negress Kara Walker." In *Kara Walker: Narratives of a Negress*, edited by Ian Berry, Darby English, Vivian Patterson, and Mark Reinhardt, 175–79. Cambridge, MA: MIT Press.

Williams, Jennifer. 2014. "'The Booty Don't Lie': Beyoncé, Janelle Monáe, and New Black Feminism." Paper presented at the annual National Women's Studies Association Conference, San Juan, Puerto Rico, November 15.

Wilson, Samantha. 2015. "Nicki Minaj Is 'Flattered' by 'Rude' Pics with Her Madame Tussauds Wax Figure." *Hollywood Life* (blog), August 21. http://hollywoodlife.com/2015/08/21/nicki-minaj-wax-figure-inappropriate-madame-tussauds.

Putting a "Good Face on the Nation": Beauty, Memes, and the Gendered Rebranding of Global *Colombianidad*

María Elena Cepeda

Abstract: Via the discursive analysis of various memes, this essay inter-rogates the linkages between global *Colombianidad* and beauty in the #ItsColombiaNOTColumbia (#ICNC) social media campaign, and ex-amines the centrality of Colombians' digital labor in the production and circulation of media texts. It argues that in its efforts to contest the mas-culinist violence and political corruption permeating global scripts about Colombia, the #ICNC campaign ultimately reinforces the symbolic and material violence that has been waged against racialized, gendered bodies since the colonial era. **Keywords:** Colombia, diaspora, digital labor, gen-der, memes

On December 20, 2015, U.S. comedian and host Steve Harvey errone-ously crowned Colombia's Ariadna Gutiérrez-Arévalo Miss Universe on live television. Within minutes of his error—the winner was Pia Alonzo Wurtzbach of the Philippines—Harvey tweeted, "I want to apologize em-phatically to Miss Philippians [*sic*] and Miss Columbia [*sic*]. This was a terribly honest human mistake and I am so regretful." Twitter users quickly responded not only to Harvey's initial error but also his subsequent mis-spelling of Colombia; among them were Colombians around the world employing #ItsColombiaNOTColumbia (#ICNC). While this particular hashtag has been in circulation since 2013, Harvey's misspelled apology provoked a more vehement response than any other incident since its debut. Originally merely an effective means of righting an orthographic wrong, the meanings attached to #ICNC have multiplied, offering a vivid lens onto Colombians' mediated efforts to achieve cultural citizenship on the global stage. The hashtag's usage in conjunction with various memes

WSQ: Women's Studies Quarterly 46: 1 & 2 (Spring/Summer 2018) © 2018 by María Elena Cepeda.

121

proves symptomatic of an era defined by "hypermemetic logic," in which significant public events are marked, and measured in importance, by an outpouring of memes (Shifman 2014, 4). Within one day, #ICNC's creators had issued the following meme: "Dear Steve, You had the **courage** to accept a mistake. Wait, two mistakes in one night. Your apology is accepted. We welcome you to our country and invite you to spread the word: It's Colombia NOT Columbia" (emphasis in original). Superimposed over a transparent, turquoise image of a laughing Harvey and rendered "official" via the appearance of the square yellow #ICNC logo in the bottom corner, the meme assumes an intimate tone through its largely second-person directive. The bold red text, with the exception of the word "courage" offset in dark blue, grabs our attention visually. The reader is unquestionably reminded that the "you" who committed the multiple faux pas is Harvey, and that the "we" represents Colombians as an undifferentiated whole. Colombians are graceful losers, the meme professes—albeit losers still keenly interested in attracting the travel dollars of the Global North. More than merely a clever hashtag offering a flippant critique, #ICNC evinces an incisive digital tool for identifying and archiving the people, places, and things ostensibly worthy of collective Colombian pride.

The forceful responses to the Miss Universe incident and its centrality within the life of the #ICNC campaign underscore the longstanding importance of beauty pageants within transnational Colombian culture. Growing up in the United States, the Miss Universo pageant was the sole spectator sport my Colombian immigrant family watched together, and inevitably videotaped for later circulation among those not fortunate enough to view the event live. No other event provoked the same multigenerational enthusiasm from both male and female family members eagerly awaiting the first appearance of Miss Colombia, hopeful that she would make it to the competition's final rounds if not win. For Colombians around the globe, the pageant signals an opportunity to revel in the potential joy of a new Colombian Miss Universe, or a moment in which traditional media narratives about *Colombianidad* or Colombian-ness are momentarily upended. Such fleeting spectacles also provide diasporic subjects with more questionable claims to Colombianidad with a forum for engaging in socially sanctioned expressions of national belonging. Even more broadly, these dynamics exemplify the manner in which women's bodies, identities, and representations prove pivotal to the enactment of national narratives (Shome 2014, 21), and how a country's beauty queens offer a conduit for achieving and expressing worth among the community of nations. Within a space where national feminine identity is both performed and constrained, Miss Colombia is presented as an aspirational figure to Colombian women around the globe, and has historically been interpellated as a symbol for modernity and tradition (Banet-Weiser 1999, 130; Jha 2016, 2).

My discussion of the gendered memes associated with the #ICNC hashtag foregrounds beauty's function as a cultural mirror that enables us to trace the historical and cultural trajectory of a given society (Stanfield 2013, 1). Grounded in the discursive analysis of various memes, my consideration of the interlocking dynamics of global Colombianidad and beauty on social media acknowledges the increasing primacy of visual texts online, as well as the centrality of Colombians' digital labor in the production and circulation of said texts. Discourse analysis elucidates the manner in which "specific views or accounts are constructed as real or truthful or natural through particular regimes of truth" (Rose 2012, 196). It is with an eye toward interrogating the truth claims that unite the Colombian female body and the nation that I have selected the digital images herein. My analysis recognizes the representational weight of a normative strain of feminine beauty as a transnational, neoliberal project forged on and through the bodies of young women who bear the "'burden' of the national allegory" (Shohat and Stam 1994, 287). I posit that in its efforts to contest the masculinist violence and political corruption permeating global scripts about Colombia, the #ICNC campaign ultimately reinforces the symbolic and material violence that has been waged against racialized, gendered bodies since the colonial era. Therefore, the use of white/light-skinned, gendered bodies as representative of the nation in the Colombian context is nothing novel. However, its twenty-first-century deployment in neoliberal efforts at Colombian rebranding, and particularly its online role in building a specific brand culture, proves a newer development.

Michael Edward Stanfield posits Colombian beauty as a feminized construct juxtaposed against the "masculine beast," or the masculinist violence and structural inequities of the nation. Representing violence, poverty, the inept state, and racism, the "terror of the beast" reentrenches traditional gender roles that frame women as necessarily beautiful and men as inherently powerful (2013, 1–2). As the deployment of the Colombian beauty queen and other gendered memes connected to #ICNC demonstrates, this representational hardening also takes place beyond Colombia's borders, and reflects the multidirectional transnational flow of potent ide-ologies concerning gender, race, beauty, and power between Colombia and its diaspora. Media representations of Miss Colombia thereby denote "a site of contestation between a sense of the national . . . and the transna-tional" (Martín Barbero, quoted in Rutter-Jensen 2005, 15).

#ICNC is an ostensibly grassroots campaign quite literally designed to "put a good face on the nation" and refurbish Colombia's poor image on the world stage (Stanfield 2013, 3). Echoing much of the substance and spirit of the country's previous attempt at a neoliberal rebranding of the nation—the 2005-era Colombia Is Passion campaign (see Nasser 2012; Garbow 2016)—this recent rebranding attempt of #ICNC differs in its more marked reliance on the free digital labor of global Colombians. Significantly, the campaign's dependence on the efforts of a multitude of unemployed workers underscores the fact that labor does not necessarily equal employment. As Tiziana Terranova states, to acknowledge this is to comprehend how critical "free affective and cultural labor" proves to be on social media platforms such as Twitter and Facebook (2013, 45).

Centering the (White) Colombian Female Body

Michelle Rocío Nasser De La Torre contends that the body of the Colom-bian beauty queen is interpellated as both a *natural* resource and a *nation-al* resource—a product worthy of export. The exportation of beauty that #ICNC obliquely supports across multiple social media platforms results from the ongoing development of the nation's tourism industry and the historic popularity of the Miss Colombia beauty pageant. It is a particu-lar form of gendered exportation that has heightened in recent decades in order to combat the stigmatization of Colombia's drug exportation, and is ultimately meant to "redeem and replace" the masculinist images of drugs and violence that permeate media narratives about Colombia and to open the nation up to investment by multinationals (Nasser De La Torre 2013, 295, 306–7). #ICNC can thus be partially read as a move toward rescript-ing dominant representational paradigms for a post–civil war Colombia. It also equals a means of countering the ever-present Pablo Escobar narra-tive, a mediated rendering of the nation mired in the dramatically violent period during the 1980s and 1990s marked by the spectacular rise and fall of the infamous narcotics kingpin. Informed by the discursive stylings of a heavily commodified magical realism, the cultural industry built around the Escobar narrative constitutes a source of distress and resentment for many Colombians, yet the endless accumulation of tell-all books, films, and television series in this vein simultaneously provide a significant source of capital for many.

However, Colombia is no longer a space delineated by the war on drugs. Arguably, the nation's primary export product now is its women (Schaeffer 2012, 93). In Colombia as well as in the United States, beauty pageants are heavily linked to commerce. Colombian beauty queens therefore embody far more than just an idealized feminine aesthetic and dominant social mores; they are also political and economic powerhouses (Rutter-Jensen 2005, 12, 14). While the political economy of the beauty pageant is not denotative of any single culture or territory, the online interaction of global Colombians with its attendant imagery still rearticulates and enhances specific gendered and raced social mores. Accessible in real time and in multiple iterations by their fellow Colombians, the beauty queen memes exemplify the benefits of participatory culture (user-generated content and the circulation of mass media texts) as well as its downsides (the uncritical deployment of gendered bodies as stand-ins for the nation and as a gendered form of aspirational citizenship).

The light-skinned or white-passing physical appearance of the vast majority of Colombian pageant winners highlights the ongoing salience of *blanqueamiento* (whitening), or the racial ideology that embraces *mestizaje* (ethnoracial mixture), as part of popular and official discourses on Latin American identity provided the population steadily moves toward whiteness over time. The "myth of mestizaje" is virtually inseparable from the elitist discourse of blanqueamiento, which ultimately racializes (either implicitly and/or explicitly) the majority of the nation's citizens (Morgan 2005, 56). These hierarchies of race, class, and gender are on full display in the Miss Colombia competition in a reiteration of the "colonial hangover" (Stanfield 2013, 232). Indeed, the machinations of racial capital—a bodily resource attached to gradients of skin color and phenotype grounded in existing racial hierarchies—proves particularly potent in former European colonies and nations that experience a significant U.S. presence. Moreover, racial capital solely functions in societies in which the body is read as a commodity and potential source of individual advancement. Within this context, beauty pageants enact a form of gendered nationalism, in which young women embody particular national values, cultural norms, and racial pride (Hunter 2011, 143, 145; Jha 2016, 8). These dynamics coalesce

FIG. 1. Screenshot of an image of Miss Universe 2014 Paulina Vega Dieppa, posted on Facebook in 2015.

in the visual discourse of a meme featuring Miss Universe 2014 Paulina Vega Dieppa (fig. 1). In this simple photograph of the Colombian beauty queen with little editing beyond the insertion of the It's Colombia NOT Columbia logo, Vega Dieppa appears onstage in full regalia. She offers the obligatory winner's wave, with a hand artfully poised as if to signal the presence of the added logo and emphasize its message. A statuesque figure, Vega Dieppa occupies the center of the frame and our attention as the idealized embodiment of the "Latin look": dark hair, dark eyes, and light olive skin (but not too olive). In other words, she presents us with a visual narrative of difference that proves nonthreatening, as it echoes long-standing, transnational media representations of a gendered *Latinidad* firmly anchored in regional racial ideologies. The meme also underscores the manner in which Colombian society privileges white/ light-skinned women as the keepers of the "natural" racial and social order, tasking them with preserving their caste, and, by extension, the nation's reigning social hierarchies (Morgan 2005, 55).

Rebranding Colombia in the Age of Neoliberalism

The Colombian government is not alone in its reliance on the tools and strategies of corporate brand management in its attempt at shoring up the nation. Indeed, national branding has come to be perceived as a "necessary corrective" to the more porous national boundaries—and the potentially weaker national structures—provoked by globalization. An exercise in soft power, in recent decades commercial branding has been pursued by at least forty different countries as a means of rescripting the nation and addressing long-standing internal conflicts (Aronczyk 2013, 2–3, 16, 30). Rooted in the belief that national territory may be effectively harnessed as a "marketable and monetizable" asset, this latest iteration of national branding is designed to "articulate a more coherent and cohesive national identity, to animate the spirit of its citizens in the service of national priorities, and to maintain loyalty to the territory within its borders . . . the goal of nation branding is to make the nation *matter* in a world where borders and boundaries appear increasingly obsolete" (Aronczyk 2013, 3; emphasis in original).

Colombia's rebranding efforts also occur within a national and diasporic cultural milieu in which normative physical attractiveness has historically served as a commodity. For Colombian women, a reliance on beauty as a pathway toward upward mobility and social prestige has long constituted part of the hustle and flow of everyday life. It is akin to a type of survival aesthetics, or the gendered, classed, and racialized behavior many Latinas engage in while harboring an acute, or perhaps solely latent, awareness of the potential social risks uniting "modes of displaying the body and social response" (Cepeda 2008; Lewis 1990, 94). In the neoliberal context, these forces highlight the frictions that inevitably materialize "between the desire for visibility . . . and the economic, social, and cultural demands for the commodification of ethnic, racial, gender, and sexual Others" by media audiences (Molina-Guzmán 2012, 139).

Nation-making through neoliberal branding strives to rework the image of the nation through a repertoire of gendered aesthetic practices "staged in relation to history and, more specifically, the present transnational economy between Colombia and the United States" (Schaeffer 2012, 109). Deeply informed by neoliberal ideology, this approach to beauty reframes the individual female body as a vessel to be managed and (self-)cultivated as a means of ultimately achieving enhanced social mobility and realizing one's "productive worth" as a Colombian citizen. Couched within a neoliberal discourse of choice that implies that anything can be achieved if a woman simply makes the proper decisions, labors enough, and adopts the appropriate attitude, physical perfection emerges as a modality of constraint for Colombian women (Schaeffer 2012; Gill 2016, 624; McRobbie 2009, 19).

Colombia's two most recent presidents Álvaro Uribe (2002–2010) and Juan Manuel Santos (2010–present) have notably conceptualized the Colombian nation as a product, a national brand to be marketed and packaged with slogans and careful image management in order to "make-over" the nation. This logic rests on the assumption that the mere management or rebranding of Colombianidad is all that is required to rewrite its national identity. Modernization is the rhetorical cornerstone of the "new" Colombia, which has been rebranded as all that is beautiful, youthful, democratic, successful, and groundbreaking. However, the rhetoric of a new Colombia is not simply a case of Colombian presidential politics engaging in a makeover; rather, it indexes broader anxieties around what constitutes contemporary Colombian identity on the global stage. These anxieties are provoked by major political, socioeconomic, and social shifts, such as the aftermath of the 1991 Colombian Constitution and its implications for Colombian multiculturalism or the recent peace process. This impulse to reframe the nation has successfully shaped media coverage of Colombia in outlets as significant as the *New York Times*, which recently urged adventurous upscale travelers to head to Colombia and abandon "outdated ideas—like drug wars and gangsters—" about the nation (Wulfhart 2015).

Gendered Rebranding in the Virtual Realm

#ICNC emerged from an invitation (one that ironically misspelled "Colombia") extended to four Bogotá-based social media marketing professionals to attend New York's Social Media Week. Shortly thereafter in February 2013, the official "It's Colombia Not Columbia" Facebook page was launched by Emilio Pombo and Rodrigo Salazar of Compass Porter Novelli and Tatiana González and Carlos Pardo of Zemoga. While not explicitly presented as government-supported in the press (#ICNC is framed as a grassroots movement instead), the group was approached by the Colombian government's official brand Marca País with a request to use their New York presentation as a means of promoting Colombia (Castillo 2013). #ICNC is therefore best understood as a top-down, state-sponsored initiative, despite its alternative staging by its creators. Factors like the digital divide, the need for some degree of computer literacy, and English-language skills in order to fully participate enshrine the campaign as a platform for more privileged Colombians. This exemplifies the manner in which communication (and access to it) functions as a form of capital (Nixon 2015, 107). With a steadily growing presence on Facebook (with 30,494 followers at the time of writing) and Twitter (with 4,154 followers at the time of writing), #ICNC describes itself on Facebook as a "social movement that promotes the beginning of a change on the perception held abroad on Colombia. Our main goal is to share the current positive features and qualities of our Country, and let everyone know that today we are in the spotlight of big investors from around the globe, thanks to the economic, social and cultural growth we have had in the last 15 years" ("It's Colombia, NOT Columbia" n.d.). Notably, this discursive framework casts the project of nation-branding as a benign, benevolent solution to the communicative, developmental, and economic challenges confronting contemporary Colombia generally, and in particular the question of national visibility and legitimacy on the global stage. Here, the process of national branding illuminates how the discourse of nationhood is harnessed in a novel fashion by marketing experts, begetting a gendered, raced logic that shapes collective understandings of the nation and citizenship (Aronczyk 2013, 3–4). This point is of particular salience to the more than 4.7 million diasporic Colombians around the globe (approximately one out of every ten Colombian citizens) (Viventa 2016). It is a noteworthy figure, but fails to account for second generation Colombian transnationals, many of whom are eligible for dual citizenship and may also maintain vigorous affective, commercial, and political ties to the nation. Markedly geographically dispersed, the Colombian diaspora is uniquely suited to the virtual communal project that #ICNC proposes. As such, #ICNC inflects as well as reflects transnational conceptualizations of Colombianidad in a brand of "user-generated globalization" dictated by technology in addition to human forces (Shifman 2014, 55, 151, 155).

According to Emilio Pombo, #ICNC is aimed at encouraging travel to Colombia and generally educating others about the nation. For its creators, this social media campaign constitutes an attempt to shift media narratives of Colombia beyond the nation of recent decades, a narrative perhaps most persistently visible in the Global North. Indeed, the choice to utilize an English-language hashtag speaks not only to the primacy of English as the global language online but also to the socioeconomic and educational privilege of the campaign's authors. It gestures at a critical constituency within #ICNC's imaginary audience, and as such allows us to interpret the campaign as a contestatory gesture firmly leveled at the North.

#ICNC participants are encouraged to post material that spreads positive messages about Colombia and rebuke those who misspell the country's name. The content posted and spread is marked by user imitation and "remixing," both hallmarks of Web 2.0 participatory culture. In one such example, the filtered image of popstar Shakira featuring her bare midriff celebrates the white/light-skinned, gendered body as a symbol of global Colombianidad. The meme's text fuses #ICNC's themes with an intertextual song reference to Shakira's international hit "Hips Don't Lie," "Shakira, the woman who taught you that your hips don't lie is from Colombia, not Columbia!" With text and filtered imagery located at opposite ends of the meme, as readers we are visually obligated to absorb these disparate fragments of information and remix them for ourselves in order to formulate a coherent message. Stressing the gendered location of Colombian difference and deployed as evidence of Colombian worth, the arresting meme reinforces the frequent parallels drawn between the heavily commodified Latina body and hypersexuality, as well as the rigid mind/body distinction ostensibly dividing the Global North and South (Cepeda 2010, 75).

The overwhelming number of #ICNC Facebook posts and tweets are everyday misspellings of Colombia posted as a form of chastisement, along with endorsements for Colombian exports, celebrities, and travel to Colombia. It is a virtual display of white-washed, gendered nationalism obliquely endorsed by global Colombians that accrues "value by being global, where global is a sign of economic progress and Western cultural superiority" (Jha 2016, 71–72). Memes such as figure 2, which contains a crudely circled pageant banner draped across the body of Miss Universe 2016 first runner-up Ariadna Gutiérrez-Arévalo, also exemplify the manner in which participatory culture consistently blurs the boundary between media consumers and producers. All of these postings exemplify the gendered imagery that constitutes much of the #ICNC campaign's content, and that is embedded in the dualistic discourse that permeates Colombian ideologies about beauty. It is a binary that, on one hand, hypervalorizes whiteness, while on the other, debases nonwhite populations and fetishizes bodies of color as "dark objects of desire," if not erasing them entirely (Morgan 2005, 47). Such representations underscore the manner in which global Colombianidad is persistently filtered through gendered and sexualized imagery, and specifically via memes featuring female celebrities designed for maximum online exposure.

As Isabel Cristina Porras Contreras notes, not all female Colombian bodies are presented on equal terms. Rather, some are posited as more worthy "producers of value, not just for the self but in service of the

Nath Cardosi♡ @Natasha_Cardosi · 20 Dec 2015
@IAmSteveHarvey You had her right in front of you, it's COLOMBIA not Columbia 🇨🇴 😊

FIG. 2. A December 20, 2015, tweet by Natasha Cardosi of Adriana Gutiérrez-Arévalo referencing the infamous Harvey spelling error.

nation" (2016, 307). Colombian subjects around the globe are thus encouraged to generate value on behalf of the nation-state via the digital labor extracted by #ICNC. On one level, such labor endeavors to counter negative representations in a less tangible sense through online appeals to emotion and collective pride among Colombians. On yet another, it centers on generating capital via foreign investment and increased tourism through the Colombians around the globe who purchase T-shirts and baseball caps emblazoned with the campaign's logo. (Notably, while the campaign labels itself as "nonprofit" it has been generating approximately fifteen thousand dollars per month in merchandise sales for its creators [Zúñiga 2013; Wyss 2016].) The successful merchandising arm of #ICNC itself has in fact emerged as a sharp-edged commentary on North-South relations, as suggested by this recent Facebook headline, "These Two Guys Make $15,000 a Month Because Gringos Keep Misspelling Colombia" (Simón 2016).

Click and Post Labor: Global Colombians and Affective Online Engagement

Speaking of both #ICNC and Zemoga (the Bogotá digital agency that supports it), campaign cocreator Carlos Pardo states, "Our objective is to show as a company that you can change the image of a country, or improve the image, through social media. And what's happening to Colombia is not just happening here. There are many countries whose image abroad is incorrect or outdated so we want to set that example to say 'Take these social networks and use them as peaceful weapons' with which we can change the world" (Moreno 2013). The allusion to "peaceful weapons" proves a particularly potent and paradoxical reference in the transnational Colombian context, given the fact that the country is just now emerging from the longest civil war in the hemisphere following a protracted and contentious peace process. Within this discursive framework grounded in "playbour" or digital labor masked as play (Fuchs and Fisher 2015, 4), #ICNC thus expounds a utopian vision that adheres to the simplistic notion that the increased involvement of Colombians at the levels of media representation and production will somehow translate into more egalitarian, nuanced representational paradigms (Valdivia 2016).

The peaceful weapons of which Pardo speaks are thereby rooted in an affective engagement with the campaign by its participants that encourages a porous boundary between leisure and labor. Free digital labor is best understood as the moment when "knowledgeable consumption of culture is translated into excess productive activities that are pleasurably embraced and at the same time shamelessly exploited" (Terranova 2013, 37). Persistently framed as "weightless, unmaterial and sustainable" (Sandoval 2015, 44), digital culture frequently encourages affective engagement via tasks that actively extract affective labor and other forms of work while simultaneously promising empowering forms of play (Papacharissi 2015, 23). Within the #ICNC campaign, users are thus lightheartedly framed as "volunteer spellcheckers" whose digital labor is masked as benign virtual activism but is ultimately realized on behalf of the neoliberal state and corporations (Otis 2014). Per this perspective, the material dimensions of digital culture are elided and the relationship between technology and content is disarticulated, ultimately obscuring the manner in which widely held beliefs and ideas about Colombia "are themselves material forces" (Sandoval 2015, 53; Gramsci 2000, 215). Individually oriented and bound to gendered and raced assessments of normative, ostensibly self-achievable beauty, #ICNC acts as the perfect neoliberal, virtual counterpart to the material labor traditionally realized by transnational hometown associations.

According to Zizi Papacharissi, "Networked digital structures of expression and connection are overwhelmingly characterized by affect" (2015, 8). #ICNC emerges as the clear product of a strategic neoliberal deployment of affect, as the campaign's success largely lies in its reliance on playbour. As the popularity of #ICNC suggests, Colombians

around the globe feel disrespected, misunderstood, and silenced, resulting in an engagement with social-media-based rebranding marked by the
use of quasicontestatory memes featuring one of the nation's proudest
"exports": its beautiful women. However, #ICNC ultimately repackages
the nation as a glossy neoliberal haven, and in the process, reinvigorates
gendered, tropicalized aesthetic archetypes of Latin America in general
and Colombia in particular.

Conclusion

The networked Colombian publics discussed herein are generated and
maintained by sensations of community and solidarity, however imper-
manent they may be. In #ICNC, the narrative impulse of social media
platforms like Facebook and Twitter encourages diasporic Colombians to
plug into an "electronic elsewhere" (Papacharissi 2015, 4, 9; Berry, Kim,
and Spigel 2009) as a means of performing and validating their claims to
Colombiandad. In the multilayered imagery centered on a particular iteration of feminine beauty, normative aesthetics act as an affirmative tonic
for Colombians seeking respite from the political and institutional failures
of the nation-state (Stanfield 2013, 11). The gendered visual codes of
#ICNC thus belie a collective search for a national "makeover" that con-
fers symbolic and economic worth upon the nation. In this manner, "beautiful" white/light-skinned Colombian women are commodities wielded to
attract foreign capital. This is not to assert that a gender politic rooted in
personal aesthetics does hold transgressive potential, but this potential is
undermined when feminine beauty norms are stringently codified and deployed as a measure of individual worthiness for citizenship and belonging in popular media platforms where "relations of power are indeed made
and re-made within texts of enjoyment" (McRobbie 2009, 21).

   While shared on a micro basis, the impact of memes is felt on
the macro level, as they inform the mindset, behavior, and actions of
communities-in-the-making as well as project their social mores. They encourage the development of a specific brand of on- and offline solidarity
shaped by the public expression of emotion. Such emotions are married
to the indignation prompted by long-standing injustices (Shifman 2014,
18, 34; Pappachirissi 2015, 6), and are reflective of broader anxieties regarding the nature of Colombianidad. In the Colombian case, these are
the injustices provoked by long-standing media narratives that promote a

reductionist vision of Colombianidad. It is therefore perhaps even more critical that media about, for, and/or by Colombians does not trade one set of injustices for another under the guise of rebranding a nation barely entering the post–peace accord stage. Such a political aperture underscores the dualistic nature and, at times, antagonistic cross-purposes of the internet: while the web may provide the necessary framework for political subversion, it may also facilitate the reentrenchment of offline oppressions (Kido Lopez 2016, 183). In its present iteration, #ICNC demonstrates how corporate interests (so often inseparable from those of the state) may propagate narrow definitions of group identity online in such a fashion that global Colombians unwittingly promote the invisibility of most Colombian women juxtaposed against the hypervisibility of the few. In this way, the democratic and potentially liberatory impulses of participatory culture are reduced to a "façade of visibility, ownership, equality, and agency through . . . interactivity" (Kessler 2011, 141–42).

#ICNC has never been about a mere spelling error. Rather, it is always/already rooted in a set of small yet insistent public gestures aimed at reworking the nation, and rendering it more palatable, beautiful, and worthy in the eyes of the global populace. Grounded in *offline* conceptualizations of gender, race, diaspora, citizenship, and nation, #ICNC is a project that exploits the porous boundary between uncompensated digital labor, play, and the dictates of the neoliberal state in its assertion of global citizenship and gendered national worth. It ultimately leads us to question the idealistic belief in online participatory culture as a wholesale tool of democratic expression, given its structural underpinnings. As the memes analyzed here substantiate, the rapidly disseminated, remixed messages embedded in digital texts constitute a critical venue for illuminating the underlying cultural, political, and economic logics at play in the visual union of beauty, race, gender, and the Colombian nation.

Acknowledgments

Tantísimas gracias a Diane Garbow, A. J. Mejía, and Michelle Nasser for their insightful comments on earlier drafts of this essay. Many thanks as well to my anonymous reviewers and special issue editors Natalie Havlin and Jillian M. Báez.

María Elena Cepeda is professor of Latina/o Studies at Williams College. Her research focuses on the intersection of gender and race in transnational Latina/o media and popular culture. Email correspondence may be addressed to her at mcepeda@williams.edu.

Works Cited

Aronczyk, Melissa. 2013. *Branding the Nation: The Global Business of National Identity*. New York: Oxford University Press.

Banet-Weiser, Sarah. 1999. *The Most Beautiful Girl in the World: Beauty Pageants and National Identity*. Berkeley: University of California Press.

Berry, Chris, Soyoung Kim, and Lynn Spigel. 2009. "Introduction: Here, There, and Elsewhere." In *Electronic Elsewheres: Media, Technology, and the Experience of Social Space*, edited by Chris Berry, Soyoung Kim, and Lynn Spigel, vii–xvii. Minneapolis: University of Minnesota Press.

Castillo, Mariano. 2013. "Social Media Campaign Wants to Remind You: It's Colombia, Not Columbia." CNN, February 20. http://www.cnn.com/2013/02/20/world/americas/colombia-not-columbia/.

Cepeda, María Elena. 2010. *Musical ImagiNation: U.S.-Colombian Identity and the Latin Music Boom*. New York: NYU Press.

———. 2008. "Survival Aesthetics: U.S. Latinas and the Negotiation of Popular Media." In *Latina/o Communication Studies Today*, edited by Angharad N. Valdivia, 237–55. New York: Peter Lang.

Fuchs, Christian, and Eran Fisher. 2015. "Introduction: Value and Labour in the Digital Age." In *Reconsidering Value and Labour in the Digital Age*, edited by Christian Fuchs and Eran Fisher, 3–25. London: Palgrave Macmillan.

Garbow, Diane. 2016. "Crafting Colombianidad: The Politics of Race, Citizenship, and the Localization of Policy in Philadelphia." Dissertation, Temple University.

Gill, Rosalind. 2016. "Post-postfeminism? New Feminist Visibilities in Postfeminist Times." *Feminist Media Studies* 16 (4): 610–30.

Gramsci, Antonio. 2000. "Hegemony, Relations of Force, Historical Bloc." In *The Gramsci Reader: Selected Writings 1916–1935*, edited by David Forgacs, 189–221. New York: NYU Press.

Hunter, Margaret L. 2011. "Buying Racial Capital: Skin-Bleaching and Cosmetic Surgery in a Globalized World." *The Journal of Pan African Studies* 4 (4): 142–64.

"It's Colombia NOT Columbia." n.d. Facebook. Accessed December 21, 2017. https://www.facebook.com/itscolombianotcolumbia/.

Jha, Meeta Rani. 2016. *The Global Beauty Industry: Colorism, Racism, and the National Body*. New York: Routledge.

Kessler, Kelly. 2011. "Showtime Thinks, Therefore I Am: The Corporate Construction of 'The Lesbian' on sho.com's *The L Word* Site." *Television & New Media* 14 (2): 124–46.

Kido Lopez, Lori. 2016. *Asian American Media Activism: Fighting for Cultural Citizenship*. New York: NYU Press.

Lewis, Lisa A. 1990. *Gender Politics and MTV: Voicing the Difference*. Philadelphia, PA: Temple University Press.

McRobbie, Angela. 2009. *The Aftermath of Feminism: Gender, Culture and Social Change*. London: SAGE.

Molina-Guzmán, Isabel. 2012. "Salma Hayek's Celebrity Activism: Constructing Race, Ethnicity, and Gender as Mainstream Global Commodities." In *Commodity Activism: Cultural Resistance in Neoliberal Times*, edited by Roopali Mukherjee and Sarah Banet-Weiser, 134–53. New York: NYU Press.

Moreno, Carolina. 2013. "It's Colombia, NOT Columbia: Changing the Image of a Country Through Social Media." *Huffington Post*, February 22. https://www.huffingtonpost.com/2013/02/22/its-colombia-not-columbia-a-social-media-campaign-changing-the-image-of-a-country_n_2743909.html.

Morgan, Nick. 2005. "Ese oscuro objeto del deseo: raza, clase, género y la ideología de lo bello en Colombia." In *Pasarela paralela: escenarios de la estética y el poder en los reinados de belleza*, edited by Chloe Rutter-Jensen, 44–56. Bogotá, Colombia: Editorial Pontificia Universidad Javieriana.

Nasser, Michelle Rocío. 2012. "Feminized Topographies: Women, Nature, and Tourism in *Colombia Es Pasión*." *Revista de Estudios Colombianos* 40: 15–25.

Nasser De La Torre, Michelle Rocío. 2013. "*Bellas por naturaleza*: Mapping National Identity on Colombian Beauty Queens." *Latino Studies* 11 (3): 293–312.

Nixon, Brice. 2015. "The Exploitation of Audience Labour: A Missing Perspective on Communication and Capital in the Digital Era." In *Reconsidering Value and Labour in the Digital Age*, edited by Christian Fuchs and Eran Fisher, 99–114. London: Palgrave Macmillan.

Otis, John. 2014. "It's 'Colombia,' Not 'Columbia' – Get It Right." PRI, May 14. http://www.pri.org/stories/2014-05-14/its-colombia-not-columbia-get-it-right.

Papacharissi, Zizi. 2015. *Affective Publics: Sentiment, Technology, and Politics*. New York: Oxford University Press.

Porras Contreras, Isabel Cristina. 2016. "'Sofía Vergara Made Me Do It': On Beauty, Costeñismo, and Transnational Colombian Identity." In *The Routledge Companion to Latina/o Media*, edited by María Elena Cepeda and Dolores Inés Casillas, 307–19. New York: Routledge.

Rose, Gillian. 2012. *Visual Methodologies: An Introduction to Researching with Visual Materials*. 3rd ed. Los Angeles: SAGE.

Rutter-Jensen, Chloe. 2005. "Introducción." In *Pasarela paralela: escenarios de la estética y el poder en los reinados de belleza*, edited by Chloe Rutter-Jensen, 11–15. Bogotá, Colombia: Editorial Pontificia Universidad Javieriana.

Sandoval, Marisol. 2015. "The Hands and Brains of Digital Culture: Arguments for an Inclusive Approach to Cultural Labour." In *Reconsidering Value and Labour in the Digital Age*, edited by Christian Fuchs and Eran Fisher, 42–59. London: Palgrave Macmillan.

Schaeffer, Felicity Amaya. 2012. *Love & Empire: Cybermarriage and Citizenship Across the Americas*. New York: NYU Press.

Shifman, Limor. 2014. *Memes in Digital Culture*. Cambridge, MA: MIT Press.

Shohat, Ella, and Robert Stam. 1994. *Unthinking Eurocentrism: Multiculturalism and the Media*. London: Routledge.

Shome, Raka. 2014. *Diana and Beyond: White Femininity, National Identity, and Contemporary Media Culture*. Urbana: University of Illinois Press.

Simón, Yara. 2016. "These Two Guys Make $15,000 a Month Because Gringos Keep Misspelling Colombia." *Remezcla*, January 27. http://remezcla.com/lists/culture/its-colombia-not-columbia/.

Stanfield, Michael Edward. 2013. *Of Beasts and Beauty: Gender, Race, and Identity in Colombia*. Austin: University of Texas Press.

Terranova, Tiziana. 2013. "Free Labor." In *Digital Labor: The Internet as Playground and Factory*, edited by Trebor Scholz, 33–57. New York: Routledge.

Valdivia, Angharad N. 2016. "Implicit Utopias and Ambiguous Ethnics: Latinidad and the Representational Promised Land." In *The Routledge Companion to Latina/o Media*, edited by María Elena Cepeda and Dolores Inés Casillas, 55–71. New York: Routledge.

Viventa. 2016. "Colombianos en el exterior. ¿Cuántos somos y dónde vivimos?" February 25. Accessed July 15, 2016. http://viventa.co/colombianos-en-el-exterior-quienes-somos-cuantos-somos-y-en-donde-vivimos/.

Wulfhart, Nell McShane. 2015. "36 Hours in Bogotá, Colombia." *New York Times*, November 5. http://www.nytimes.com/interactive/2015/11/05/travel/what-to-do-in-36-hours-in-bogota-colombia.html?_r=0.

Wyss, Jim. 2016. "Colombia vs. Columbia: A nation scorned in spelling?" *Miami*

Herald, January 23. http://www.miamiherald.com/news/nation-world/world/americas/colombia/article56269340.html.

Zúñiga, Edgar. 2013. "It's Colombia, NOT Columbia!" NBC Latino, February 21. http://nbclatino.com/2013/02/21/its-colombia-not-columbia-media-campaign-hopes-to-correct-common-mistake-of-countrys-name/.

Beauty as an "act of political warfare": Feminist Makeup Tutorials and Masquerades on YouTube

Michele White

Abstract: Feminist makeup tutorial producers use cosmetic instructions as a means of interrogating gender norms and oppression. Their YouTube tutorials, reconfigured makeup names, and sly instructions indicate how feminism and beauty can be collaboratively deployed as a critical language. The producers thereby refute some feminists' assertions that makeup is inherently part of an objectifying system that normalizes women. Producers underscore how cosmetic applications are understood as masks and performances, and thus relate beauty practices to feminist analysis of the regulating and resistant aspects of masquerades. By deploying masquerades, feminist producers trouble women's position as image and establish a feminist beauty politics. **Keywords**: beauty, cosmetics, feminism, tutorial, online video

The light-skinned tadelesmith (2013) appears in red lipstick and playfully pretends to bite YouTube viewers in "Feminist Makeup Tutorial (PARODY)."[1] Her winks and knowing looks accompany such voiceover queries as, "Ever wanted to single-handedly dismantle the patriarchy?" By employing the melodious tones common to YouTube instructional videos along with indications of how women are oppressed, this video blogger, or vlogger, correlates feminism with beauty practices and products. Foundation is made "with the powdered ashes of Susan B. Anthony" and there is "*Lean In* mascara, courtesy of Sheryl Sandberg." tadelesmith thereby suggests that women are produced from their feminist foremothers and feminist critiques. In a related manner, Ariana Rodriguez (2015) engages with feminism and beauty in "Femme Power Make-Up Tutorial." Rodriguez, who is Latina, references Audre Lorde

WSQ: Women's Studies Quarterly **46**: 1 & 2 (Spring/Summer 2018) © 2018 by Michele White. All rights reserved.

(1988) when arguing that her cosmetic application and self-care "is not self-indulgence, it is self-preservation, and that is an act of political warfare." Rodriguez and tadelesmith combine makeup videos, beauty practices, feminism, and an attention to dismissed subjects. I argue that their feminist makeup tutorials, and the work of other vloggers addressed later in this article, figure a culture where women craft their appearance, and indicate how such cosmetic masquerades function as feminist and beauty languages.

tadelesmith applies foundation, moving the sponge across the varied parts of her face, and encourages viewers to "give every part of your face a fair and equal amount of representation, unlike the government and primetime television." She further foregrounds women's struggles for recognition when speaking about the glass ceiling and other institutional structures that oppress women. Rodriguez skillfully applies makeup as she deploys critical theory in the voiceover. Through such cosmetic applications and narratives, Rodriguez and tadelesmith invoke political strategies, including the need for self-care, in a society where such acts are dismissed as self-indulgent. As queer feminist theorist Sara Ahmed (2014) indicates in a blog post, "Self-indulgence tends to mean: being soft on one's self, but also can mean 'yielding to one's inclinations.'" Ahmed notes that feminism also is sometimes thought to be "too soft, too safe, too focused on individual suffering" and is "dismissed as a form of self-indulgence." Rodriguez and tadelesmith use YouTube beauty videos as a language and structure to interrogate cultural claims that feminism is too soft, excessive, and inequitable. Their employment of beauty tutorials and cosmetics is tactical as such practices have been used as evidence that women, and feminists who positively engage beauty culture, are frivolous and disengaged from politics. At the same time, makeup and related beauty procedures are expected of and seen as constituting women.

Rodriguez portrays makeup as an overt form of self-presentation and political combat. She states, "makeup is very in your face. It's not subtle." It is the "armor" she and "other Latinas and femmes of color, put on in the mornings to face the systems that work against" them (quoted in Reichard 2016). Rodriguez refutes the idea that cosmetic practices are placid and inwardly focused. tadelesmith also figures cosmetics as a shield, mask, and political method. She compares the process of priming "lids and lashes so your eye shadow and mascara stay strong" to "woman's spirit through millennia of misogyny." These YouTube producers suggest that resiliency is facilitated through cosmetics and masquerades, which foreground beauty practices and distance women from their positions as objects, images, and intense bodily presences.

Rodriguez and tadelesmith's videos are in dialogue with literature that considers how feminism can grapple with beauty norms, visual objectification, and women's pleasurable and artistic makeup practices. Their texts also underscore how cosmetics are understood as masks and performances, and thus are related to feminist analysis of the normalizing and resistant aspects of masquerades (Doane 1991; Briefel 2009). As a means of addressing these correlations, I will survey feminist academic texts about beauty that can be used to address and are evoked by these feminist video practices (Bordo 2003; Lorde 1988). I briefly mention women who refute makeup shaming, and then focus on a range of beauty producers who identify their videos as feminist, including a journey east (2015); Megan MacKay (2014a, 2014b, 2015); Rodriguez (2015); tadelesmith (2013); Theanne L (2015); and This Fashion Fiend (2015). I argue that these feminist vloggers show how feminism and beauty tutorials can function as a critical feminist language and thereby refute some feminists' assertions that cosmetics are inherently part of an objectifying system that structures and normalizes women. These vloggers deploy critical masquerades to disrupt women's position as image and support a beauty politics that is informed by feminist texts.

Feminism and Masquerade

Feminist Susan Brownmiller (1984) indicates that feminist resistance to women's objectification and recognition of women's reasons for wearing cosmetics have produced one of the most difficult to resolve conflicts in the women's movement. Feminists continue to be concerned about how women's bodies, emotional states, and careers are supposed to be best if made over. Cosmetic applications have been understood as regulating scripts, ways of negotiating cultural expectations, pleasurable creative practices, and shared experiences. According to feminist philosopher Susan Bordo, women spend a great deal of time anxiously working on and adjusting their bodies. Through these practices, women become "docile bodies" and are "habituated to external regulation, subjection, transformation, 'improvement'" (2003, 166). Women are trained to identify beauty as self-defining. As Tracey Owens Patton indicates in her work on

African American women's relationship to aesthetic norms, differences in "body image, skin color, and hair haunt the existence and psychology of Black women" and other women who diverge from mainstream standards (2006, 24). Margaret Hunter describes this as a "beauty queue" where women's beauty influences their status and lighter-skinned women garner more privilege (2016, 57). Sociologist Paula Black studies these regulatory practices in salons and then indicates how these spaces offer "pleasure, escapism, a means of 'coping,'" "sheer sensuality," and "social interactions in a feminized space" (2002, 16). All of this makes beauty practices a site of concern and significance for women.

Women use beauty practices to constitute themselves as feminine and female and to refute their relationship to these positions. Mary Ann Doane (1991) proposes that feminine masquerade, including beauty practices, can enable women to destabilize normative and binary distinctions between the object and subject positions that articulate women as passive. Much of the literature on women and masquerade references Joan Riviere (1929). She considers how some powerful women use feminine masquerade to make their intellectual competence and assertive positions less threatening to men. According to Doane, the "masquerade, in flaunting femininity, holds it at a distance. Womanliness is a mask which can be worn or removed." Masquerade allows women to employ and refuse essentialist gender categories. The "masquerade's resistance to patriarchal positioning would therefore lie in its denial of the production of femininity as closeness, as presence-to-itself, as, precisely, imagistic" (1991, 25).

Doane proposes this theory of masquerade, and the associated ways women renegotiate their position as object and bodily presence, in order to explain how women look at and are produced by texts. In doing this, she articulates active viewing positions for women rather than accepting Laura Mulvey's (1975) feminist psychoanalytic reading of how men are rendered as active and women as passive in classic Hollywood films. In Doane's analysis, women deploy and perform femininity rather than it being inherent. This foregrounds how cultural conceptions of "femininity as a closeness, a nearness, as present-to-itself, is not the definition of an essence but the delineation of a *place* culturally assigned to the woman" (1991, 31). The societal construction of women as objects can thus be highlighted and challenged through masquerades. There are, according to Kathleen Woodward's (1988–1989) outline of theories of masquerade, distinct ways self, and particularly women and femininity, are performed as a means of resistance.

There are also feminists who assert that masquerade is correlated with women's stabilization of and submission to cultural norms. As Aviva Briefel argues, "Riviere associates masquerade with the safety of a balanced heterosexual contract, and the absence or failure of masquerade with the violence that would ensue from a violation of that contract." According to this model, masquerade "solidifies male-female bonds and saves the woman from male retaliation"(2009, 466). It reassures men that women will seek their heterosexual interest and approval rather than dismissing hierarchical structures. In a critique of poststructuralism, Llewellyn Negrin argues that masquerades and the related literature do not challenge the "reduction of self-identity to image" (2000, 84). She indicates that cosmetic and other performances further commodify women. I understand masquerades as practices where women's resistance to being intimately tied to femininity and women's production of gender and sexual norms are cyclically enacted. Masquerades are the struggles and potential excesses that are produced when people highlight women's production of femininity and attempt to stabilize related societal norms.

Television makeover texts ordinarily discourage critical masquerades by recommending that people improve, or even find, their "authentic" self (Banet-Weiser and Portwood-Stacer 2006). Emma Maguire's study of YouTube celebrity Jenna Marbles suggests that the "typical beauty vlogger will begin with no make-up and gradually transform herself with cosmetics and beauty tools into a particular 'look' while giving how-to commentary" (2015, 75). Maguire emphasizes a singular look, but vloggers' overall practices forward difference and change because of the array of videos, applications, and products. In their production of looks and selves, vloggers reference feminine masquerades and women's distance from established representations. The women who produce feminist makeup tutorials further this deployment of videos and beauty practices as methods of changing cultural perceptions and the social position of women. Such feminist practices identify the varied ways beauty practices can be used as methods of change.

Feminist Makeup Tutorials and YouTube

Feminists have long interrogated the conflicting cultural expectations for women to manage their bodies and exist without intervention. On a women's blog, Mayura Iyer (2015) describes how women "are often shamed for wearing makeup, and are equally often shamed for not wearing makeup." Women are confused about how cosmetics fit into feminist practices, and if investments in beauty culture betray their commitments to feminism. Their concerns encourage interrogations of beauty production and masquerades rather than directives for individuals to be beautiful. Such issues are addressed in "#feminist-makeupping" posts and events. Morgan (2014) reports that "#feminist-makeupping is about makeup and how it relates to the politics of feminism: how we present our body and selves to the world, and how we engage with the beauty industry and patriarchy's ideals on gender presentation." Makeup has also been critically considered by beauty vloggers. For instance, NikkieTutorials's (2015) oft-cited "The Power of MAKEUP!" suggests that women are scorned for loving makeup because people believe cosmetics are used to attract men and are a sign of insecurity. As a counter to this, she proposes that "it would be cool to show you the power of makeup. A transformation. Because makeup . . . is FUN!" Thousands of beauty enthusiasts took Nikkie's video as a "challenge" and created their own response videos and social media posts in which they proposed that cosmetics enable pleasurable iterations of the self rather than improvement (White 2017).

Makeup tutorials, according to Andrew Tolson's research on this form, are a "major feature" of YouTube's "'How To & Style' category" (2010, 279). They include such common devices as vloggers centered onscreen and speaking directly to viewers, demonstrations of applications on producers' faces, itemizations of products and practices, and critical commentary on cosmetics, beauty, and society. Vloggers address cultural expectations about beauty as well as the possibilities and problems with envisioning empowerment through cosmetic practices. These issues are foregrounded by My Pale Skin (2015), a popular beauty vlogger who talks about her extremely light skin and acne problems. Her "YOU LOOK DISGUSTING" anti-bullying video allows her to share comments that were left on images of her face, including indications that she is "UGLY AS FUCK" and that viewers "CAN'T EVEN LOOK AT HER." My Pale Skin shares commentary about her face but she also suggests that commenters are writing on and trying to produce and deface her appearance and representations. She critiques cultural expectations about women's self-presentations and provides affirmative messages for women and other disenfranchised subjects. She argues that viewers "LOOK BEAUTIFUL," "ARE BEAUTIFUL," and should believe in themselves and never let anyone suggest anything else.

My Pale Skin's "YOU LOOK DISGUSTING" video (2015) and NikkieTutorials's "The Power of MAKEUP!" (2015) foster feminist empowerment and reconfigure women's engagement with beauty within a genre that is ordinarily associated with social control and beauty norms. Yet such texts risk reinscribing postfeminist celebrations of "choice" because they do not fully interrogate the cultural mandates that make it difficult for women to opt out of beauty culture. My Pale Skin directs viewers to ignore cultural dismissals and value themselves rather than fully addressing the politics of beauty and cultural expectations. tadelesmith (2013) also states, "physical beauty" is not related to "self worth." She assures viewers that they should "not have to follow this tutorial, nor any other makeup tutorial, in order to feel good about" themselves and "can put on all the makeup" they "want, or none." Yet tadelesmith suggests that individuals should watch her video in order to obtain information about cosmetic applications, women's relationship to beauty, and critical interventions into stereotyped conceptions of feminism and feminists. tadelesmith and other feminist vloggers redeploy online beauty tutorial conventions, including visually centering on vloggers, slow pacing, melodious voiceovers, and itemizing parts of the face and products, to engage beauty culture and feminist analysis.

Feminist Makeup Tutorial Parodies

tadelesmith's (2013) video is a "tongue-in-cheek parody" of "some of society's crazy stereotypes of feminists." tadelesmith uses the makeover as a method of cultural critique. She does not make fun of the makeover genre and the investments of beauty gurus. The video is also not a parody of feminism. Instead, tadelesmith creates a parody of misogynist and uninformed notions of feminism in order to reinforce the importance and politics of feminism. tadelesmith foregrounds tendencies to identify feminists as violent, power-hungry, man-haters with her absurd suggestion that women can rip out misogynists' jugulars with their teeth and "look fine as hell doing it" (2013). According to her, "people all too frequently misinterpret the concept of feminism" and "think of bra-burning, man-hating spinsters that rally in the streets calling for the destruction of the patriarchy—Straw

Feminists, which are a gross, fictional misinterpretation of the feminist movement" (quoted in Katy M 2013). She connects these misconceptions to misreadings of "Lipstick Feminists," who are "outwardly feminine and not burning their makeup in the fireplace" and are thus thought to be "settled into their roles within society." She "humorously mixed these two concepts of Lipstick and Straw Feminism together, forcing people to recognize not only the disparity between the two things but also the ridiculousness of feminist stereotypes in the first place." She also encourages people to see lipstick feminists as more resistant figures.

Megan MacKay, who is light-skinned and identifies as a Canadian comedian, also uses the makeup tutorial as a means of performing feminist critiques. MacKay (2016) foregrounds the commonality of this video strategy, stating that "people have done the makeup shtick before." Most of her tutorial videos use makeovers to address contemporary events and their larger implications for women, people of color, and LGBTQ folks. Her videos include "Ray Rice Inspired Makeup Tutorial" (2014b), and "Same-Sex Marriage Makeup Tutorial" (2015). MacKay argues that such "satire deconstructs and subverts oppression and the oppressors. It holds people in power accountable and points out the flaws in systems" (quoted in Schroeder 2014). Through her videos and comedic performances, MacKay addresses women's rights, domestic and child abuse, rape culture, and LGBTQ rights.

MacKay and tadelesmith's employment of feminist humor is designed to displace limited conceptions of feminism—including the idea that feminists have no sense of humor—and to address cultural inequities. In Limor Shifman and Dafna Lemish's research on humor, they argue that feminist humor opposes "gender inequalities and hegemonic stereotyping," is an expression of women's agency and right to critique social structures, focuses on gender issues, and requires a setting or medium through which to express these politics and the associated humor (2010, 873). Feminist humor, according to Mary Crawford's (2003) research, underscores producers' investments in using comedy to subvert normative and inflexible gender roles. MacKay and tadelesmith use feminist humor to foreground women's inability to attain prominent positions in many industries; women finding their access to contraceptives curtailed, as discussed in MacKay's Hobby Lobby video (2014a); and women and children having their experiences with sexual violence legally and culturally dismissed, as focused on in her Rice video (2014b).

tadelesmith (2013) amplifies feminist messages as a way of parodying presumptions that feminists are controlling. When applying eyeshadow, viewers are encouraged to "think of it like the glass ceiling: the thinner, the better" so that they can "shatter it more easily when the time comes for women to assume their rightful position as the dominant gender of the human race." While most of tadelesmith's video depicts her calmly putting on makeup, at times she gets close to the camera and contorts her face so that it looks like a mask. She humorously deploys cosmetics as a masquerade that enables women to access power through traditional femininity *and* as a performance that disturbs women's acceptable representations. tadelesmith exaggerates the common accusation that women are out to get men when she states that cosmetics will make everyone "know you're the head bitch in charge" able to deliver a "final kick to the balls" (2013). She parodies texts about feminists' aggressiveness, duplicity, and drive for power and combines these parodic critiques with references to makeover conventions. She uses the language of beauty vloggers in itemizing the facial features where cosmetics are applied, and cites these physiognomic features as a means of considering women's oppression and means of resistance.

MacKay and tadelesmith identify their humor as a form of parody. According to literary theorist Linda Hutcheon (1985), parodic reconstructions are reliant on clearly establishing the source text and alternating between similarities to and differences from this referenced text. As Amanda Nell Edgar argues in her study of YouTube parodies, familiarity with the "original" allows viewers to "get the joke" (2013, 12). Edgar identifies YouTube as a site where "fan-created parody videos" are related to and different from parodied producers (9). Feminist parodies and masquerades are connected through their citation of source texts and engagement in and disruption of feminine and female norms. MacKay and tadelesmith reference beauty videos through their titles and elaborate instructions about makeup application. They also shift the genre convention of listing products by inventing such names as "Smash the Patriarchy no. 2" lipstick (tadelesmith 2013) and "women are objects" eyeliner (MacKay 2014b). Here too, the possible relationship between cosmetics and objectification is referenced, and makeup is identified as a critical language that distances women from their images and position as objects.

Lipstick and other cosmetics, as suggested by media studies scholar Debra Merskin, are named after the product color or "food, beverages, sex, and romance." Women and femininity are articulated through cosmetic practices and the names manufacturers assign to products. By understanding the ways meaning is produced through makeup names, feminists can further analyze the "role of cosmetics in conflating femininity, self-esteem, and body image with the goals of patriarchal hegemony" (2007, 591). Lipstick and makeup names encourage women to become that named thing, to make themselves over, and to envision themselves through the associated frameworks. While makeup names that evoke demure femininity and other gender stereotypes suggest that women should regulate their bodies, the parody videos encourage women to see how cosmetics and related practices can be part of their feminist politics. These vloggers may seem to move away from the foci of beauty videos but MacKay and tadelesmith's applications of products and critiques of beauty norms are consonant with the source genre. Many beauty vloggers also address women's resistance to social norms, taking personal pleasure in crafting their image, artistic practices, and connections to other beauty gurus and viewers.

This Fashion Fiend (2017), a woman of color, comments on "Fashion, Beauty and all things Body Image!" This Fashion Fiend's (2015) "Date Night Makeup Tutorial (Parody)" critiques racist conceptions, heteronormativity, and the "male gaze." She references men's misogynistic beliefs that women are hiding things under their foundation. MacKay, My Pale Skin, Nikkie, and tadelesmith also critique related dismissals. This Fashion Fiend and these other vloggers interrogate the ways people reject cosmetics for being deceptive masks and masquerades. While MacKay, Nikkie, and tadelesmith do not focus on the hierarchical valuation of skin color, This Fashion Fiend critiques racial privilege and light-skinned beauty ideals. She chronicles "highlighter as white as the Eurocentric standards of beauty" (2015), women of color are expected to follow, and what Hunter (2016) describes as the beauty queue. Most women of color are continually informed that they do not meet Western skin-color and other standards and are culturally disenfranchised because of racist norms.

This Fashion Fiend also interrogates men's presumptions about women's heterosexuality. She directs viewers to use powder "in an effort to make your natural pigment almost as invisible as the representation of queer relationships." This Fashion Fiend (2015) names makeup "not too slutty intentions" and "mixed signals" in order to foreground the ways women are seen as too sexual and how they negotiate their sexual positions through masquerades. She disturbs sexual as well as gender narratives, including victim blaming, and the ways these perceptions are coupled with women and cosmetics.

Masquerade is overtly referenced when tadelesmith (2013) describes producing a "youthful and innocent appearance" with blush. By
highlighting discourses about seeming rather than being, as part of her
elaboration of makeup processes, tadelesmith describes how masquerades are produced and distances them from her "authentic" self. MacKay
poses her beauty practices as both distinct from and a commentary on
misogyny and intolerance. For instance, in "Ray Rice Inspired Makeup
Tutorial" MacKay (2014b) talks about the NFL's attempt to downplay
and excuse football player Rice's battering of his wife. She invents a foundation shade called the NFL. MacKay references the functions of such
beauty products, which are designed to conceal flaws and create an even
surface, as a means of arguing that the foundation and NFL will "cover
up anything just to save face." In doing this, she indicates how masquerades can stabilize cultural norms. The makeup that MacKay applies becomes a representation of such inequities and a practice where gender
norms are highlighted and refuted.

Reporters and viewers also assert that these videos demonstrate cosmetic applications and interrogate normative conceptions of feminism
and women's roles in society. For instance, Bridget March (2013) from
Cosmopolitan argues that the "new way to be a feminist" is to "Send up the
stereotypes on YouTube." March loves tutorials like tadelesmith's because
they "show real girls who are enhancing their natural beauty without a
team of stylists," and "we say more power to them." Tiffanie Petett (2017)
from Total Beauty asks, "Who said makeup isn't empowering?" She argues
that tadelesmith's video allows viewers to know what "feminist leaders are
thinking while they go about their beauty routine." Petett finds the "only
thing more compelling than the gorgeous look" tadelesmith creates to be
the "fact that she pulls it off while incorporating feminist language that
references the most compelling challenges facing women." Yet tadelesmith
also challenges proscribed beauty routines by making these practices into
comedic routines. Rather than extending postfeminist claims that cosmetics are inherently empowering, feminist vloggers show how makeup can
be part of a feminist language and that feminism can be part of a beauty
language. For instance, narratives about foundation allow feminist vloggers to consider what is hidden and parodic product names offer ways to
consider intolerance and objectification.

While many individuals have indicated their interest in MacKay and
tadelesmith's videos, there are people who express confusion about what is

being parodied. Due to such problems, tadelesmith added a "!!!!!!!!VERY IMPORTANT DISCLAIMER!!!!!!!!" to the video description and labeled the video with the term "PARODY." There are still risks that parodic approaches may seem to dismiss women's interests in beauty practices and feminist politics. Elinn Andersson (2017) finds humor in the confusion and writes in the comments section, "Some people actually think you're making fun of feminists" instead of "anti-feminists' stereotypes of feminists. Hilarious." Andersson underscores the divergent ways masquerades and performances of beauty stereotypes are read. MacKay and tadelesmith rely on these distinct conceptions of beauty and feminism as the base for their humor and critiques. It is thus not surprising that some of the people who are critiqued, do not get the joke. These issues encourage considerations of when feminist makeup parodies are useful and when one should use other techniques for facilitating critical engagements.

Feminist Makeup Tutorials and Politics without Parody

Some women produce feminist makeup tutorials as methods of articulating feminism and critiquing societal norms without employing parody. For instance, the vlogger a journey east (2015), who is a woman of color, discusses how feminism and beauty intersect. She identifies as a feminist who loves makeup and has an "entire YouTube channel focusing mainly on that topic." Her "Girl Talk: Feminists Don't Wear Makeup!" video, refutes societal beliefs that women only wear cosmetics as a means of pleasing men. Her practice is based on what she likes and wants to "play around with." a journey east asserts the importance of play to her production practice and personal motivations for using makeup. She declares, "Makeup can be a feminist thing." For her, this relates to the pleasures women beauty vloggers express when crafting their own images and deciding how to appear.

Ariana Rodriguez (2015) offers a "make up tutorial about feminism, femme of color power, and femmephobia." Rodriguez's descriptions, like the texts of other feminist makeup vloggers, indicate that makeup instructions and feminist teachings are enmeshed. She uses Nicki Minaj's 2014 song "Feeling Myself" as background music and critical framework. Viewers hear Minaj address Beyoncé, who appears throughout the referenced music video, and Minaj informs her, "they ready" for the performance and constitution of a community of color. In Rodriguez's "Femme Power" text, "they ready" also refers to the political actions of feminist and femmes of color. As Minaj repeats her refrain about feeling herself, Rodriguez touches her face with brushes, fingers, and makeup and feels herself. The hands caring for and crafting her image take on added resonance as Rodriguez cites Audre Lorde and asserts that self-care refuses the colonization of women of color's bodies and absorption of their images into white heteronormative viewing structures. Rodriguez insists throughout the video that beauty rituals are part of the self-care that women should afford themselves and are needed for comfortable and healthy lives.

In a related manner, Theanne L (2015) intermeshes beauty and feminism in her video. She offers "RED LIPS EVENING MAKEUP || for those who refuse to be silenced." As an Asian American and "avid subscriber to many Asian American beauty vloggers," Theanne watches videos as a form of "self-care" and because she adores makeup as "artistic expression" (Liu 2016). As media studies scholars Laurie Ouellette and Jacquelyn Arcy argue, "attending to and caring for oneself can become a strategy for coping with and managing a racist, sexist, and homophobic society and for fashioning and re-fashioning resilient selves for the *longue durée* of social change" (2015, 102). Theanne and other feminist makeup vloggers propose ways of using cosmetics to address power discrepancies and facilitate change. Theanne suggests that red lipstick can be part of this feminist politics. In a related manner, tadelesmith remakes the sexist link between glossy red lipstick and women "ball busters," who are imagined to improperly disturb the genital rights of men. tadelesmith encourages lipstick-wearing women to refuse normative cultural rules for their own interests.

Red is a color often identified as violent and sexual, and thus does not support proper and passive femininity. Feminist academic Alison Bartlett argues, "'painted' lips are a statement that claim attention." Women speak with their lips and of "course, they are not the only lips" women have (1993, 51). Bartlett references Luce Irigaray's (1985) correlation of facial and labial lips and Barbara Creed's (1993) evocation of "vagina dentata" as conveyors of erotic and dangerous women. Bartlett asserts, "Lips are definitely a subversive and potentially threatening symbol because of their potential—because of what women might do with them" (1993, 51). This is furthered because red lipstick is often associated with blood and therefore with women's menstrual cycle, through which women are understood as abject and too much. They are thought to be excessively dirty, leaky, and fluid. Women who use red lipstick map these purported differences between women and men onto their faces and assert the sexual features of feminine masquerades rather than remaining discreet and at the beckoning of men.

Rodriguez (2015) foregrounds the ways Latinas have been stereotyped as excessively sexual and how people understand her red-lipsticked masquerade as strutting. For Rodriguez, cosmetics act as a shield against the dismissals and violence directed at nonnormative people. Faced by such cultural violations and finding it difficult to get out of bed in the morning, she can pleasurably "think about" her "art." Rodriguez can plan the ways she will "contour, highlight, and blend everything together." Makeup is a method of change where the "possibilities are endless." Such possibilities advance feminist intersectional politics because fashion aesthetics, which include thick drawn eyebrows, afros, and black power berets, convey histories of resistance and political identification (Guzmán and Valdivia 2004; Davis 1994). To take the time to apply makeup and refuse to give this time up to others, according to Rodriguez, is "radical" and "political warfare." Rodriguez proposes that femmes of color use cosmetics to resist oppressive systems. Her practice is influenced by the work of Lorde (1988) on self-care and what Sara Ahmed (2014) describes as a "revolutionary, extraordinary sentence." Lorde's indication that self-care is a form of self-defense and political struggle, as Ahmed asserts, is a "much loved, much cited sentence. It is an arrow, which acquires its sharpness from its own direction." Rodriguez and tadelesmith's sentences and cosmetic practices, which are combined into a feminist language, point to the sharpness of women and their refusal to be rendered as objects in the service of others.

Rodriguez (2015) suggests that her strong femme position makes people uncomfortable and makes them want to challenge her self-representations. Her "eyeliner wing is so sharp," she "can cut any street harasser's heart out." Femme "is resistant because it ignores the male gaze, challenges racialized and gendered beauty standard forced upon femmes of color, and it questions the idea that a person can be surplus, excessive, and too much." tadelesmith also proposes that her eyeliner and other applications are forms of resistance. Rodriguez's makeup and "hyperfemininity" are feminine masks but their visual structures are strident rather than aligned with proper femininity. Rodriguez's cosmetic applications, like masquerades, reference gender and sexual norms and refuse femininity as closeness.

Conclusion: Tutorials and Cosmetics as Critical Tools

Feminist makeup tutorial parodies provide means of engaging cultural conceptions of feminism and varied forms of misogyny. They also suggest how cosmetics can be used as critical tools. MacKay and tadelesmith address broad and varied audiences in providing makeup tips, employing a feminist language about objectification and disempowerment, and wanting to engage men and women who have stereotyped views of feminism. Feminist makeup tutorials that assert the relationship between beauty practices and feminist politics, including videos by Rodriguez and Theanne L., more overtly describe how cosmetics work along with intersectional feminism and the ways makeup can be used to resist oppression. When viewed as a genre, these video practices and commentaries on feminism and cosmetics underscore how beauty can be a feminist masquerade and language.

Mary Ann Doane (1991) highlights the distancing features of masquerades, through which women renegotiate their position as objects and bodily presence. She posits how women perform as spectators and look at texts. Feminist makeup tutorials, and the women's everyday makeup tutorials upon which they are based, figure a culture where women can craft their appearance while demonstrating cosmetic and video production skills. This includes planning makeup applications and cosmetic and video descriptions, setting up lighting and cameras, editing and uploading videos, and communicating with viewers and other vloggers. Feminist makeup tutorial producers speak to a community of women who are interested in cosmetics, theorizing beauty, and considering the political work of feminism. Their masquerades figure feminists and beauty gurus as producing women who craft women's physiognomies, produce critical languages that address beauty and feminism, and interrogate gendered and racist beauty queues and other forms of oppression. The practices of feminist makeup vloggers suggest that research on masquerades should consider women's work and politics as well as their visual and viewing positions.

Michele White is professor of Internet studies in the Department of Communication at Tulane University. She is the author of *The Body and the Screen: Theories of Internet Spectatorship*, *Buy It Now: Lessons from eBay*, and *Producing Women: The Internet, Traditional Femininity, Queerness, and Creativity*. Her email is: mwhite@michelewhite. org.

Notes

1. Internet texts include unconventional member names, punctuation, spacing, spelling, and capitalization. I have retained these formatting features in quotations and references without qualifications.

Works Cited

a journey east. 2015. "Girl Talk: Feminists Don't Wear Makeup!" YouTube, March 25. https://www.youtube.com/watch?v=hso28T6b0HM

Ahmed, Sara. 2014. "Selfcare as Warfare." feministkilljoys, August 25. https://feministkilljoys.com/2014/08/25/selfcare-as-warfare/

Andersson, Elinn. 2017. "Feminist Makeup Tutorial (PARODY)." YouTube, February 9. https://www.youtube.com/watch?v=lET-WXTsSwc

Banet-Weiser, Sarah, and Laura Portwood-Stacer. 2006. "'I just want to be me again!' Beauty Pageants, Reality Television and Post-Feminism." *Feminist Theory* 7 (2): 255–72.

Bartlett, Alison. 1993. "Let's Talk About Lips." *LiNQ* 20 (2): 51–52.

Black, Paula. 2002. "'Ordinary People Come Through Here': Locating the Beauty Salon in Women's Lives." *Feminist Review* 71: 2–17.

Bordo, Susan. 2003. *Unbearable Weight: Feminism, Western Culture, and the Body.* Berkeley: University of California Press.

Briefel, Aviva. 2009. "Cosmetic Tragedies: Failed Masquerade in Wilkie Collins's *The Law and the Lady.*" *Victorian Literature and Culture* 37 (2): 463–81.

Brownmiller, Susan. 1984. *Femininity.* New York: Open Road.

Crawford, Mary. 2003. "Gender and Humor in Social Context." *Journal of Pragmatics* 35 (9): 1413–30.

Creed, Barbara. 1993. *The Monstrous-Feminine: Film, Feminism, Psychoanalysis.* London: Routledge.

Davis, Angela Y. 1994. "Afro Images: Politics, Fashion, and Nostalgia." *Critical Inquiry* 21 (1): 37–45.

Doane, Mary Ann. 1991. *Femmes Fatales: Feminism, Film Theory, Psychoanalysis.* New York: Routledge.

Edgar, Amanda Nell. 2013. "YouTube's 'Bad Romance': Exploring the Vernacular Rhetoric of Lady Gaga Parody Videos." *The Journal of Social Media in Society* 2 (1): 8–29.

Guzmán, Isabel Molina, and Anghard N. Valdivia. 2004. "Brain, Brow, and Booty: Latina Iconicity in U.S. Popular Culture." *The Communication Review* 7 (2): 205–21.

Hunter, Margaret. 2016. "Colorism in the Classroom: How Skin Tone Stratifies African American and Latina/o Students." *Theory Into Practice* 55 (1): 54–61.

Hutcheon, Linda. 1985. *A Theory of Parody: The Teachings of Twentieth-Century Art Forms*. New York: Methuen.

Irigaray, Luce. 1985. *This Sex Which Is Not One*. Ithaca, NY: Cornell University Press.

Iyer, Mayura. 2015. "Makeup, Beauty, and Being A 'Bad Feminist.'" Literally, Darling, July 16. http://www.literallydarling.com/blog/2015/07/16/makeup-beauty-and-being-a-bad-feminist/

Katy M. 2013. "Makeup 'Like a Feminist': An Interview with Taylor Adele Smith." WMC FBOMB, August 28. http://thefbomb.org/2013/08/makeup-like-a-feminist-an-interview-with-taylor-adele-smith/

Liu, Theanne. 2016. "Red Lips Evening Makeup Tutorial: for those who refuse to be silenced." Project Ava, February 5. https://projectava.org/2016/02/05/red-lips-evening-makeup-tutorial-for-those-who-refuse-to-be-silenced/

Lorde, Audre. 1988. *A Burst of Light: Essays by Audre Lorde*. Ithaca, NY: Firebrand Books.

MacKay, Megan. 2014a. "Hobby Lobby Makeup Tutorial." YouTube, July 11. https://www.youtube.com/watch?v=kNaVoibL0gw

———. 2014b. "Ray Rice Inspired Makeup Tutorial." YouTube, September 12. https://www.youtube.com/watch?v=zyNa9kqq8mk

———. 2015. "Same-Sex Marriage Makeup Tutorial." YouTube, June 30. https://www.youtube.com/watch?v=uc3SsHAkLPQ&feature=youtu.be

———. 2016. "RE: That Video that looks a LOT like Mine . . ." March 6. http://meganmackay.net/post/140564214463/re-that-video-that-looks-a-lot-like-mine

Maguire, Emma. 2015. "Self-branding, Hotness, and Girlhood in the Video Blogs of Jenna Marbles." *Biography* 38 (1): 72–86.

March, Bridget. 2013. "Introducing: The Feminist Makeup Tutorial." *Cosmopolitan*, June 21. http://www.cosmopolitan.co.uk/beauty-hair/news/a20677/the-feminist-makeup-tutorial/

Merskin, Debra. 2007. "Truly Toffee and Raisin Hell: A Textual Analysis of Lipstick Names." *Sex Roles* 56 (9/10): 591–600.

Morgan. 2014. "What Is #Feminist-Makeupping?" xoVain, October 30. https://www.xojane.com/beauty/makeup/what-is-feminist-makeupping

Mulvey, Laura. 1975. "Visual Pleasure and Narrative Cinema." *Screen* 16 (3): 6–18.

My Pale Skin. 2015. "YOU LOOK DISGUSTING." YouTube, July 1. https://www.youtube.com/watch?v=WWTRwj9t-vU

Negrin, Llewellyn. 2000. "Cosmetics and the Female Body: A Critical Appraisal of Poststructuralist Theories of Masquerade." *Cultural Studies* 3 (1): 83–101.

NikkieTutorials. 2015. "The Power of MAKEUP!" YouTube, May 10. https://www.youtube.com/watch?v=a4Ov8qvZ2_w

Ouellette, Laurie, and Jacquelyn Arcy. 2015. "'Live Through This': Feminist Care of the Self 2.0." *Frame* 28 (1): 95–114.

Patton, Tracey Owens. 2006. "Hey Girl, Am I More than My Hair? African American Women and Their Struggles with Beauty, Body Image, and Hair." *NWSA Journal* 18 (2): 24–51.

Petett, Tiffanie. 2017. "A Step-by-Step Feminist Makeup Tutorial." Total Beauty, February 26. http://www.totalbeauty.com/content/blog/stepbystep-feminist-makeup-tutorial

Reichard, Raquel. 2016. "This Empowering Feminist Makeup Tutorial Is for Every Femme of Color." *Latina*, July 11. http://www.latina.com/lifestyle/our-issues/empowering-feminist-makeup-tutorial-femme-color

Riviere, Joan. 1929. "Womanliness as Masquerade." *International Journal of Psychoanalysis* 10: 303–13.

Rodriguez, Ariana. 2015. "Femme Power Make-Up Tutorial." YouTube, June 12. https://www.youtube.com/watch?v=u3Qvooc91eQ

Schroeder, Audra. 2014. "How Megan MacKay turned YouTube makeup tutorials into a talking point." *Daily Dot*, October 16. http://www.dailydot.com/upstream/megan-mackay-youtube-makeup-tutorial/

Shifman, Limor, and Dafna Lemish. 2010. "Between Feminism and Fun(ny)mism: Analysing Gender in Popular Internet Humour." *Information, Communication & Society* 13 (6): 870–91.

tadelesmith. 2013. "Feminist Makeup Tutorial (PARODY)." YouTube, January 13. https://www.youtube.com/watch?v=lET-WXTsSwc

Theanne L. 2015. "RED LIPS EVENING MAKEUP || for those who refuse to be silenced." YouTube, December 12. https://www.youtube.com/watch?v=iOJIEd2u6No

This Fashion Fiend. 2015. "Date Night Makeup Tutorial (Parody)." YouTube, November 22. https://www.youtube.com/watch?v=1gYUqaTDE38

———. 2017. "About." YouTube, December 21. https://www.youtube.com/channel/UCSJ1eeTmGHqhU8YfDKi-b2w/about

Tolson, Andrew. 2010. "A New Authenticity? Communicative Practices on YouTube." *Critical Discourse Studies* 7 (4): 277–89.

Woodward, Kathleen. 1988–1989. "Youthfulness as a Masquerade." *Discourse* 11 (1) (Fall/Winter): 119–42.

White, Michele. 2017. "'There's nothing makeup cannot do': Women Beauty Vloggers' Self-Representations, Transformations, and #thepowerofmakeup." *Screen Bodies* 2 (1): 1–21.

A Fair Face

An excerpt from the novel-in-progress
"People We Trust"

Monica Macansantos

Their eyes rested on Paulette as she chased the other children across her parents' lawn, framing her within the limitations of a single word: *beautiful.* It was a term of endearment that could mean anything, but for her mother, *beautiful* meant clothes for her daughter that accentuated her creamy, freckled skin tone, dresses with little yellow flowers that brought out her natural glow as she marched past the tables of adoring relatives and family friends. *Beautiful* meant shoes with tiny heels that turned her walk into an assertive little strut, meant bobby pins that kept her curls shapely and full till evening. It meant fingernails that weren't chewed on, but were filed and painted once she was old enough to wear scoop-necked dresses and go on dates with boys who belonged to good families. It meant a willingness to smile, even when she wasn't asked to do so.

People were superficial; they drew conclusions based on what their eyes could see. Her beauty was her honor, rendering her untouchable. She came from a good family, and none of her parents' friends would dare harm her, for she was one of their own.

She was just like other girls in her circle of friends who were unafraid to use their beauty to their advantage. She would join them as they walked, arm in arm, down Session Road, flirting with boys from the public City High whom they had no intention of dating. They changed into their mini-skirts and bell bottoms and flashed their fake IDs at nightclub bouncers, knowing that a smile, or a pout, was enough to persuade these men with pockmarked faces and blank stares that they weren't troublemakers.

Their perfect smiles suggested an innate capacity to please when the situation called for it, and for their parents, this was more than enough to reassure them that their daughters would never stray from the path of

WSQ: Women's Studies Quarterly **46: 1 & 2 (Spring/Summer 2018)** © 2018 by Monica Macansantos.

good. Beauty's function was to provide physical proof of goodness. What the eye could see, the heart could easily accept.

It was impossible for her to know just how good or cruel she was, for people ceased to probe her as soon as their eyes fell on her face. *She has such fine bones*, people would tell her as she sat beside her mother. *She's so maputi*, they'd all say, *like an American girl with Spanish eyes*. They had no doubt that she had good genes: her mother was part-Spanish, her father a descendant of a German-American man from Wisconsin who came to Baguio and struck it rich in the mines. Beauty always came from distant lands, from the exotic and unreachable. *Don't stay out too long in the sun. You'll get too dark!* Her mother wouldn't allow her to lose her fairness, to become just another brown girl. Why would she want to become just as dark as everyone else, when her face was a source of light and joy? It was why eyes fell on her when she walked into a room with a darker-skinned friend, and it was why her teachers often asked her to lead the morning prayer in front of her classmates, believing that her voice, like her face, could guarantee salvation.

Paulette would look back upon her charmed youth with equal parts fondness and grief when she returned to Baguio, years later, to give birth. In her childhood room, she felt like a ghost revisiting the life of a dead girl whose shell of a body she had once inhabited. How she had hated that perfect little body, that reflexively ready smile. The dainty lace dresses that filled her closet no longer fit her, and her swollen feet could no longer slip into the pumps that had made her hips sway when she was a teenager. And yet she chose to return, believing that she could ease herself back into the innocence of her past life once she slipped into its physical space.

As she took her first bath in her parents' house, she eyed the porcelain doll with blond hair and blue eyes that stood on a wooden shelf, right beside a basket of fresh potpourri and a round silver clock that told the time with filigreed hands. The doll had been there since she was a child, and it hadn't changed its position on the shelf, as though it were waiting for her return. It was one of those sentinels of her childhood, like other knick-knacks her mother scattered around their house, guardians of pleasure that kept time still.

She was a child again, and the years she had spent away from her family had humbled her. She had questioned her parents' kindness when she was younger, but there was nothing more constant than their kindness.

There was a fresh cake of soap in a bamboo dish by the windowsill, and she reached for it, bringing it to her nose and breathing in. Her mother could conveniently classify emotions and desires according to scent, and although this was one of the reasons why she swore never to become her mother, Paulette found comfort in the thought that her mother had a citrusy, celebratory scent for this particular occasion.

When Paulette decided to return home, she was acting on a hunch; she was sure she had broken her mother's heart when she had disappeared from her dorm during her sophomore year in college, only writing to her parents when she had finally reached the safety of a rebel camp deep in the mountains and far away from their reach. But her mother was a generous woman, and although her love came with bourgeois trappings, she'd have to accept that it was the language her mother knew.

When Paulette was younger and water didn't flow from the tap at all hours, her mother would send Manang Rosing downstairs, to the water well, with an empty pail. As Paulette waited, shivering in her robe, for her bath, she'd look outside the bathroom window and watch as Manang Rosing pumped the well's heavy lever up and down, the veins in her neck swelling, her face unreadable, as though she neither enjoyed nor despised this task. As she rested her neck against the bathtub's lip, she thought of how she had once sought to embarrass her mother in front of Manang Rosing as payment for the old woman's physical subjugation, believing that if Manang Rosing was incapable of articulating her own situation through gesture, it was her duty to lend a voice to her plight. Years later, when Paulette was assigned to a barrio near the Sierra Madre to educate the peasants about the teachings of Chairman Mao, she would encounter the same blank face, the same inability to register anger or frustration.

It had been Manang Rosing who met her at her parents' gate, and as Paulette watched her emerge from the front door, approaching the front gate with timid steps and squinting through the grills to see who it was, she didn't expect the old woman to recognize her, much less open the gate for her. "Come in quick before the neighbors hear you," Manang Rosing whispered, taking her hand and pulling her inside. It wasn't such an unfamiliar sound, this gravelly hissing, urgent and forceful. Celeste waited at the threshold of the gate, her lips pursed as though too shy to bridge the divide between the outside world and Paulette's childhood home. She and Paulette had spent the entire day together in cramped, rickety buses, Celeste making sure that no one would recognize Paulette throughout their trip, ushering her away from crowds of men and shielding her from the blank gazes of soldiers who boarded their buses at odd, uninhabited stretches of highway. But before their exchange of looks could signal a final parting of ways, Manang Rosing waved Celeste in, as though she too were a child of this house whose life Manang Rosing was bound to protect. "It's ten minutes before curfew. Hurry up!" Manang Rosing whispered at Celeste, who stepped through the gate's open door and smiled at Paulette ruefully, as though to suppress a laugh. The windows of her childhood home's second floor blossomed into light, softly illuminating Manang Rosing's gray-streaked hair. Paulette smiled, afraid to speak lest the truth slip from her tongue: that she had regretted coming home the moment she saw Manang Rosing, believing that the old woman, a silent, fleeting ghost of her childhood, would turn her away.

Her parents stood at the foot of the stairs as Manang Rosing ushered her and Celeste inside. Sam, who had grown taller since she had last seen him, emerged, bleary-eyed, from the darkness of the second floor, rubbing his eyes beneath his glasses before peering over her father's head. Did he recognize her from long ago? Did her parents even talk about her in his presence? "Oh my God," her mother said, bringing her hands to her lips. Her mother's embrace was quick and urgent, pulling her into the warmth of their home, while her father's hands were gentle and firm as he lay them on her back, tears welling in his eyes as he said, "Anak, you're back."

As Manang Rosing closed the front door, her mother ushered them to the living room, glancing briefly at Paulette's stomach as though to acknowledge the other uncomfortable truth: that Paulette was pregnant. Whoever the father was, he was not with Paulette—instead, a stranger had accompanied her daughter to their home, her reticence telling a story to which they were not privy.

"If you didn't come home in your state, God knows what I'd do to you," her mother said. Manang Rosing stood by her mother's side, her wrinkled face lending its stillness to their gathering.

"And how did you get here?" her father asked.

"We took the bus from Isabela."

"*Dios mío*, all the way from Isabela, and in your state," her mother said, getting up. "Manang Rosing, if you could make her bed and fix up the guest room for her friend," she said, her eyes sweeping over Celeste as though her presence was unexpected, but not altogether unwelcome. "*Hija*, what's your name?"

"Celia," Celeste said, choosing to use her nom de guerre. Even in the safety of Paulette's house, she chose to remain anonymous, a soldier of the revolution.

"She's my friend," Paulette added.

"Well, both of you should shower before going to bed. *Dios ko*, all the way from Isabela. You must be covered in dust."

She found herself unable to sleep as she lay in her childhood room later that night, tucked underneath lavender-scented sheets and her floral childhood quilt. For the past four years she had fallen asleep to the sound of snores, crickets, and the airy cough of a forest creature that remained hidden from her sight throughout her time as a guerilla. She was not used to this clean-scented chill, to the heaviness of these blankets that engulfed her, to the enormity of her bed that she shared with no one else. She had never been afraid of the dark as a child, and although she did not believe in ghosts, the silence of her childhood room was unrelenting and unkind. For the past year she had slept on a rice sack stretched out on a bamboo frame and held aloft by wooden prongs; she and Carlos had faced each other as they lay in separate cots, telling each other stories about their hometown and their families before they took turns falling asleep. How was Carlos doing tonight, without her by his side? Would he wake the camp with his screams in the middle of the night, knowing, as he slept, that she was too far away to hear his calls for help? Would her own nightmares return to her in the silence of the night, now that Carlos could no longer rush to her aid?

She rose from her bed, pulled on the robe her mother left draped on a chair, and padded down the dark hall to the guest room. When she knocked, the sound of rustling sheets reassured her that Celeste was awake, just like she was. Celeste opened the door, and the frills of her borrowed nightgown made her appear, in the dark, like a child.

"Could you sleep in my room tonight?" Paulette asked.

A smile broke on Celeste's face. "I knew you'd ask that." Celeste took one last look at her narrow twin bed before shutting her door behind her. Paulette's bed was big enough for the two of them, and Celeste, who was unused to the chill of a Baguio evening, shivered as she snuggled beneath Paulette's sheets. "It's so cold here," she said, turning to Paulette as she propped her pillow beneath her head.

"I'm not used to it anymore either," Paulette said, giggling. "It's so quiet too."

"I don't think I could've gotten any sleep in that room."

"Does it feel weird?"

"A bit, but maybe it's just because I'm used to falling asleep with other people." Celeste pulled the covers to her chin. "It's really nice though, to be able to sleep in a real bed."

"I miss him already," Paulette said, feeling a sharp pain in her throat.

"He said he'd write, didn't he?"

"Yeah, he did," Paulette said, laughing. "I'm sorry, I'm so sentimental."

"That's all right. Must be a huge change for you."

"And for you."

Celeste laughed. "But your parents are going to take good care of you. I wanted to cry when they hugged you."

"I wish they were nicer to you, though."

"Let's not push our luck. It's enough that they welcomed you back and took you in, no questions asked."

"I don't know, I know they love me and all, but this is a huge change for me, having a room of my own, and having no one to keep me company at night."

"In a few months, you'll be so used to this that you might even have second thoughts about going back underground." Celeste took Paulette's hand. "Don't worry Paulie. I'll sleep here beside you tonight."

Celeste had enough sense to leave after breakfast, abandoning Paulette to this world in which few were welcome. At the breakfast table, Paulette realized that she had become more keenly aware of these little gestures she had taken for granted when she was younger, like the way Irene spoke to Paulette as though Celeste weren't in the same room. Paulette was sure that her mother would've been more polite if Celeste had been one of them, but she wasn't just a schoolmate who was bringing their strayed daughter home. In her mind, Celeste belonged to the group that had whisked their daughter away, and on top of that she didn't know how to hold a fork and knife. Perhaps it was this, or the way the Dutch clock chimed on the mantelpiece, announcing the time, that reminded Celeste that she did not belong in these unfamiliar surroundings, and that her job was done.

A look of amusement flickered across Celeste's face as she eyed the floral wallpaper of her guest room for one last time, and yet there was a quiet happiness in her smile, as though she were satisfied with the culmination of this trip. She did not belong here, but her friend, who had spent almost her entire life in these surroundings, would find protection in this beautiful, intimidating house.

"You will write, won't you?" Paulette said.

"I will. Now don't you worry, you're safe now." Celeste touched Paulette's arm, while Paulette hoped that this wasn't a final parting.

Paulette dipped the soap into the water, raised a wet arm, and lathered her wet skin. Carlos would've objected to these indulgences, but he loved the sight of her naked body and would've wanted to see her in this state. The mind may cling to an ideology, but the body surrenders itself to its own urges. She ran a soapy hand over her swollen belly, then lathered her thighs, allowing herself to sink into the water as her fingertips wandered between her legs. She closed her eyes as her fingers did their work before remembering that she was in her parents' house, and that her mother could easily barge in. She lifted her hand from the water, gripped the bathtub's curved lip, and lowered her head into the water as her legs floated upwards.

As the afternoon light traced its way across the water's surface, she thought of the silver charm bracelet Carlos had given her when they were both in high school, and wondered if she would find it in the drawers of her dresser if she looked. "You were so rich, and so beautiful," he had said, as they sat side by side on his hammock, watching other cadres assemble their cots at the leveled center of their camp. No one had called her *beautiful* in this camp, but it was because her beauty did not fulfill a particular necessity: it did not add flavor to their bland food, nor did it supply bullets for their guns.

"When I put that bracelet around your wrist, I couldn't keep my hands from shaking. Do you remember?" Carlos asked. In the darkness of the camp, his voice, disembodied from its source, belonged to a shy, skinny boy whose hands trembled as they fastened a bracelet's clasp around her wrist. How she had burned with shame as his friends cheered and he stepped back, waiting, perhaps, for her to fill the awkward silence that fell between them. A group of boys continued to hound her as she walked to her mother's car, and her ears burned as she slammed the car door at them, resolving to ignore this boy the next time she saw him after dismissal. Where did he get the nerve to humiliate her in front of both their schools? Their laughter continued to ring in her ears as she undressed in her room and put the bracelet away, in a cupboard, or maybe in a jewelry box, or perhaps in the porcelain cup where she kept old buttons and bobby pins. Why hadn't she given him a second thought years ago? Was it because of the darkness of his skin, the plainness of his looks, or the fact that they didn't move in the same circles?

"I saved up my allowance money for that bracelet," he said, blushing, as they sat on his hammock strung between two molave trees at the edge of the camp's clearing. "I didn't know where else to buy it, so I went to the shop your parents owned."

"And you still remember," Paulette said.

"I think that was the first and last time that I ever gave a girl an expensive gift. I was so embarrassed that I couldn't talk to you afterwards."

"You were just being brave, that's all," she said, chuckling. Their breaths mingled in the humid air, but they couldn't kiss, not in front of this group of new recruits who had gathered at this camp to train and become true soldiers of the revolution. She was their shooting instructor, while he, a former Army lieutenant, was the camp's most reliable source of information, depending on whether or not he was a spy. It was their duty to set a good example for these young, wide-eyed cadres, who had been lured from the universities of Manila with promises of adventure and possible heroism. How they envied these young people who didn't know what it was like to be captured by the enemy, how one could easily break after days of torture despite the fervency of one's faith in the revolution; how heroism entailed a willingness to be dehumanized, to receive an inheritance of bad dreams that preserved memories of physical pain. He took her hand, and in the dark they smiled. How tempting it was to seek comfort in physical contact, to remind each other that they weren't alone in facing their demons.

Monica Macansantos is currently pursuing her PhD in creative writing at the Victoria University of Wellington in New Zealand. Her dissertation partly consists of a novel-in-progress, from which this piece is excerpted, about the Marcos years in the Philippines. She can be reached at m.macansantos@utexas.edu.

PART IV. **RETHINKING BEAUTY IDEALS AND PRACTICES**

Toward a Phenomenological Analysis of Historicized Beauty Practices

Allison Vandenberg

Abstract: A great deal has been written about how beauty standards historically have placed pressure on women to engage in beauty practices in order to approximate a narrow, racialized, and unachievable beauty standard. This essay adds to that body of literature by engaging in a phenomenological analysis addressing the multiplicity of individuals' embodied experiences, focusing on how women felt as they engaged in a variety of beauty practices. I argue that the sensations and affects associated with these practices played an essential role in expanding historically shifting beauty standards to include a more racially diverse conceptualization and experience of feminine beauty. **Keywords**: phenomenology, embodiment, beauty, pageants

Public critiques of the unrealistic feminine beauty ideal exploded during the 1968 Miss America pageant. That year, the NAACP staged what the organization termed a "positive protest" against the whiteness of Miss America by organizing the first Miss Black America contest, which was held in Atlantic City just blocks away from the Miss America pageant. For two decades, the NAACP had fought for the inclusion of African Americans in beauty pageants, which had traditionally excluded nonwhites from participation. Some, like Miss America, officially barred women of color from participation, as illustrated through the organization's infamous rule number seven stipulating that contestants were "of the white race." Although the NAACP aimed to challenge racist beauty ideals by integrating pageants, Miss America wouldn't see its first African American contestant at the national level until Cheryl Browne represented Iowa in 1970.

WSQ: Women's Studies Quarterly **46**: 1 & 2 (Spring/Summer 2018) © 2018 by Allison Vandenberg.
All rights reserved.

However, integration was not the only strategy available for challenging the whiteness of beauty ideals. As the catchphrase Black Is Beautiful succinctly asserts, activists insisted on a valuation of beauty characteristics specifically associated with African heritage. Rather than urging conformity to or approximation of white characteristics such as long, straight hair, narrow lips and noses, pale skin, and light eyes, proponents of the Black Is Beautiful aesthetic encouraged black women to value their natural attributes (Craig 2002, 65–77). This included encouraging them to leave their hair in a natural or afro hairstyle rather than straightening their hair, as had been the dominant fashion for African American women until 1966. It comes as little surprise, then, that the first Miss Black America winner, Saundra Williams, wore her hair in a short, tightly curled, natural style.

While the Miss Black America pageant protested the pervasive whiteness of beauty pageants through a celebration of black women's beauty, a group of mostly white feminist protestors flocked to the boardwalk outside of the Atlantic City convention hall, where Miss America was being held. Women who participated in the protest of the pageant had a long list of objections to the ritual. Many believed that the pageant supported the objectification of women by parading them around as though they were animals, perpetuated a racist beauty ideal, encouraged woman to aspire to mediocrity, and forced women into an impossible balancing act by demanding that they simultaneously embody the virgin and the whore (New York Radical Women 1970, 70, 584–88; Echols 1989, 92–96).

In short, the pageant contestants epitomized the roles women were expected to play in society while the pageant itself replicated the worst aspects of gender socialization. The issues at the core of feminist objections to the Miss America pageant were captured by the manifesto that initiated the protest. Penned by members of the organization New York Radical Women, "No More Miss America" flatly condemned the pageant's participation in a culture of Orwellian surveillance. Presaging Michel Foucault's analysis of internalized social discipline in Jeremy Bentham's Panopticon, the group explicitly addressed social linkages between constructions of feminine beauty norms and ideals and perpetuation of gender inequality:

> The Pageant exercises Thought Control, attempts to sear the Image onto our minds, to further make women oppressed and men oppressors; to enslave us all the more in high-heeled, low-status roles; to inculcate false values in young girls; to use women as beasts of buying; to seduce us

to prostitute ourselves before our own oppression. (New York Radical Women 1970, 588)

Protestors hurled "instruments of torture to women" into a "freedom trashcan," including high-heeled shoes, copies of *Playboy* magazine, false eyelashes, curlers, and bras (Echols 1989, 93). As one woman held her girdle over the trashcan, she proclaimed, "No more girdles, no more pain. No more trying to hold the fat in vain" (Curtis 1968). These critiques not only condemned the pageant for its role in orienting women toward an unrealistic beauty ideal but also for the financial and physical duress that ideal perpetuated.

Although the main focus of the 1968 Miss America protest was a condemnation of social norms that enslaved women to unrealistic beauty standards and perpetuated sexism, the protestors' heterogeneity also resulted in the proliferation of mixed messages. Many of the protestors seemed to direct their hostility at pageant participants themselves by carrying signs with provocative slogans such as "Miss America Sells It" and "Up Against the Wall, Miss America." They also crowned a live sheep Miss America and paraded it around the boardwalk. Years later, feminists reflecting on the protest attributed the seemingly anti-woman sentiment to a lack of clarity in communicating that women were "forced to play the Miss America role" (Echols 1989, 92–96). The protest's objective was to reveal the artificiality of the beauty standards women were coerced into adhering to, not to blame them for having been led down the proverbial garden path. Their objections underscored the ways Miss America phenomenologically oriented women toward an iteration of female embodiment that prioritized their status as objects, rather than orienting them in such a way that they were encouraged to develop as self-aware and agentic embodied subjects. It also demonstrated the way that "beauty," which is normatively represented as a valuable attribute, was experienced as a violation, an affront, an incitement to rage, or even as a bad joke.

The Miss America pageant exemplified the assumption that women—or, rather, young, attractive, white women who adhered to conservatively middle-class notions of appropriate feminine comportment—enjoyed engaging in certain beauty practices, including wearing high heels and glamorous evening gowns, applying makeup, and maintaining long, carefully styled hair, among other things. It also assumed that the only people doing these things were cisgender women. These suppositions perpetuated a conflation of sex and gendered behaviors, and in the process, invalidated the femininity of those women who did not wear high heels and makeup and ignored the possibility that men may engage in these practices. The categorical exclusion of women of color from the beauty ideal was, as both protests had illuminated, an endorsement and perpetuation of a blatantly racist beauty standard.

As the 1968 protests surrounding the Miss America pageant demonstrate, the history of women's negotiations with beauty ideals and beauty practices illustrates the significance of beauty practices in daily life, both as an object of desire and an object of critique. This incident—one of many in American history—demonstrates that, far from being a trivial component of feminine existence, for many, engagement—or nonengagement—in beauty practices has played a crucial role in their embodied experience of femininity. While the 1968 Miss America protests have been discussed and analyzed as socially and historically significant moments that reflect the changing gender roles in the United States, they also offer insight regarding phenomenological experiences of beauty practices and how these experiences played a key role in the ongoing work of (re)defining femininity in the twentieth century.

Throughout the 1960s, constructions and performances of femininity and its associated acts were rapidly being critiqued and redefined by activists, scholars, and the general public. These multiple and fluctuating conceptualizations of femininity understandably affected notions of feminine beauty, which, in turn, affected engagement in beauty practices. Changes in women's social status were inextricably entangled with changes in their beauty practices. Knowing how engagement in beauty practices *felt* therefore informs our understanding of how it felt for women to change class status.

A phenomenologically oriented historical inquiry also allows us to ask different types of questions about what can be learned from archives and historically situated figures whose lived experiences of embodiment are too often thought to be entirely inaccessible to us. This approach to the study of beauty underscores the many ways intersectional aspects of women's identities affect their experiences of engaging in beauty practices, for the same act may be experienced in dramatically different ways by two or more individuals. Archival resources reflect this diversity of experience among woman-identified individuals, specifically paying attention to intersectional aspects of identity such as race, ethnicity, socioeconomic class, (dis)ability, sex, gender, sexual orientation, geographical location, education, age, marital status, nationality of origin, and so forth. These diverse perspectives often yielded disparate accounts of individuals' experiences engaging in the very same act, which in turn adds to the richness of our understanding of these experiences.

As situated practice, engagement in beautification is a productive site for theorizing gendered power dynamics. Yet rather than focusing on the ways beauty ideals and the engagement in beauty practices function as oppressive mechanisms, this essay elucidates the myriad of ways that the experience of beauty practices contribute to women's overall experience of themselves as embodied subjects. As such, it is necessary to consider inter- and intrapersonally diverse experiences of beauty practices, and to locate these experiences within a broader framework of a phenomenologically oriented examination of historically situated embodiment. Hence, in addition to the oppression and negative sensations beauty practices often entail, pleasure must also be considered, for beauty practices are quite frequently sources of enjoyment, sites of self-indulgence and relaxation, as well as means for self-expression. In other moments, the beauty practice itself is subject to greater or lesser degrees of social surveillance and discipline, therefore the practitioner's experience of engagement in this act should take the social context into consideration. Shaving body hair, for example, is something numerous women report disliking. However, many women comply in order to avoid critiques of their personal grooming.

Yet what is perhaps more significant to understanding the significance beauty practices hold in the lives of the subject are the myriad feelings that lie somewhere between and outside of the limited binary of pleasure and pain, as well as the ways in which feelings associated with beauty practices are so often at odds with one another. The acts we engage in on a regular basis not only shape what we can do as a result of repetition; they also affect our perceptions of ourselves. With regard to beauty practices, this is especially evident in notions of how people "should" look. This notion, which varies between individuals and changes over time, is strongly connected to our reiteration of acts; the same repetition that renders work invisible also has the capacity to alter the ways we see ourselves in everyday life.

Consider the example of false eyelashes, worn by legions of women in the 1960s and today, as attested to by the wide selection of false eyelashes at retailers ranging from drugstores to upscale beauty counters to websites.

The weight of false eyelashes can produce the feeling of droopy lids, heavy under the weight of the prosthetic lashes and adhesive, yet regular wearers of false eyelashes become accustomed to their burden, even ceasing to perceive it as such. Many habitual wearers eventually associate this practice with making their eyes appear larger, a desirable quality associated with hegemonic standards of feminine beauty. Thus the individual who regularly wears false lashes is likely to feel more beautiful while wearing them, and may even perceive her eyes as being smaller when she is not.

If someone's quotidian beauty practice includes full makeup, an elaborate hairstyle, and foundation garments, it is reasonable that, without these modifications, that person might experience a moment of misrecognition upon glimpsing her reflection in the mirror. She may feel herself to be "naked" or uncomfortably exposed in a way that would be utterly alien to women who do not regularly engage in these beauty practices.[1] Conversely, someone who generally wears very little makeup, whose hairstyle requires very little use of product, and whose clothing does not require complicated undergarments, may experience a similar moment of misrecognition if given a makeover with the techniques and products she does not ordinarily employ. She may feel weighed down—even suffocated—by the layers of makeup and hairspray, while support garments may pinch, poke, and squeeze portions of her anatomy, even interfering with her ability to breathe, sit, or consume liquids as she ordinarily would. For still other women, "normal" amounts of makeup may vary extensively depending on the occasion, season, or day of the week. In these cases, the varying quantities of makeup worn act as a visible signifier of the public and private selves more than as a marker of "realness" or artificiality.

Disparities between and among notions of normal are also historically contingent, and therefore should be evaluated with an eye toward changing fashions. For example, during the latter half of the 1960s, African American women regarded the practice of hair straightening quite differently depending on their generation, despite the fact that it was widely regarded as normal after 1920. For the thousands who became certified in hair treatment systems during the 1920s, 1930s, and 1940s, the increasingly popular process of hair straightening was a means of achieving financial independence; for their clients, many of whom worked as domestic servants, having their hair done at the end of the workweek demarcated the distinction between work and home (see Blackwelder 2003, Gill 2010, Rooks 1996, and Walker 2007). For civil rights activists like Anne Moody, who participated in sit-ins at Woolworth's, the combination of straightened hair and Sunday-best attire served as a protective shield, insulating her from the indignities of being covered in ketchup and mustard, while the physical space of the beauty parlor provided a respite afterwards, allowing her time to collect herself between the sit-in and returning to her college dormitory (Moody [1968] 1976, 268). Given this history, it is perhaps more understandable that the generations of women who reached adulthood prior to 1960 often reacted with horror when their daughters, nieces, and younger sisters deviated from the straightened hairstyles that they had come to regard as normal and began wearing natural hairstyles in the late 1960s. In contrast, many women of the younger generation felt their hair in its unaltered texture was a celebration of their beauty, and therefore arguably qualified as normal when compared to straightened hair.[2]

While I do not seek to refute or discount the capacity for beauty practices to act as a disciplinary force on the (female) body, I contend that this area of knowledge should be expanded and complicated through an examination of how beauty practices affect those who engage in them on a sensory level. This does, of course, necessitate an understanding of the Foucauldian power dynamics that contribute to the social and cultural milieu. Subjects' actions are situated within discourses on the body that encourage and facilitate women's experience of themselves as split subjects whose actions are not necessarily for the self, but are informed by *an other* (or set of others) who establish and maintain ideals of beauty, as well as the normative practices one is expected to engage in in order to meet beauty ideals, and the extent to which one's body and bodily practices fit within the hegemonic expectations for beauty and engagement in beauty practices. An examination of engagement in beauty practices as stemming solely from social pressures to conform to hegemonic beauty ideals, however, oversimplifies Foucault's assertions and runs the risk that the individual's agency may be considered to be subsumed by the pressure exerted through the disciplinary gaze. Such an interpretation overlooks the capacity of individuals and groups to resist, challenge, and expand beauty norms, as well as the potential for women to engage in beauty practices as part of an expression of selfhood and individual identity.[3]

Indeed, it is more accurate to conceive of the structural disciplining of gender norms as a subtle process influencing the subject's sense of self within a larger social context that also includes pressures exerted through social expectations and normative practices. The power dynamics at work do not function to force the individual subject to conform. Rather, they serve as a backdrop for the ongoing processes through which individuals develop an understanding of their bodies and encourage the development of an interior sense of self informed by split subjectivity, thereby influencing the subject in such a way that she may be predisposed to replicate many of these same expectations and understandings.

Clearly, engagement in beauty practices cannot be separated entirely from the discourses and ideologies that surround the practitioner. However, the pressures exerted on women are not the sole determinants of their actions. Rather, both the pressures of ideal beauty and normative expectations of feminine engagement in beauty practices contribute to the context in which these practices exist. Beauty practices are better understood as situated practices in that the choices exercised take place within the coercive context of these pressures. While many women have historically conformed to hegemonic expectations, resistance to and modification of these practices and norms is overwhelmingly evident, occurring not only among individuals but also manifesting as significant components of social movements, as the 1968 Miss America protests illustrate.

Sara Ahmed's work on affect suggests a way of using phenomenology to examine beauty practices, especially those that are repeated with regularity, without presupposing these acts' functions to be exclusively, or even primarily, disciplinary (2006). This, in turn, opens space for theorization of beauty practices in which pleasure, pain, and myriad other feelings are produced by the enactment of such practices. There is no doubt that many women, historically and contemporarily, regard beauty practices as compulsory aspects of gender performativity, deriving no pleasure and only varying degrees of discomfort and pain from their engagement in these rituals. However, I contend that in order to produce a comprehensive understanding of engagement in beauty practices, we must take into account the full range of sensory experiences that attend these practices, including those that defy classification as good or bad, positive or negative, or even as easily intelligible description.

In attending carefully to beauty practices as phenomenological experiences that are enacted on and through the body, we gain insight regarding how sensory perceptions, such as restricted movement in a sheath dress, the texture of a fabric as it comes into contact with the skin, the weight of a heavy shoe, or the shift in one's center of gravity resulting from wearing heels of varying heights, contribute to experiences of (gendered) embodiment. Focusing on this sensory perception allows for contradiction in experiences, which adds dimension to our understanding of embodiment and phenomenology by acknowledging and analyzing the disparate perceptual frameworks of felt beauty.[4]

Furthermore, Ahmed's observation that "what we 'do do' affects what we 'can do'" offers a strategy for conceptualizing beauty practices that require the subject to alter her corporeal movements (2006, 59). For example, when wearing nail polish, many individuals avoid certain movements, not because they will cause pain, but in an effort not to damage the polish. As a result, the freshly manicured tend to adapt their habits where their fingernails are concerned; for example, using tools to open containers when, if unpolished, fingernails would suffice. Sometimes the adaptive habits occur so quickly as to be almost unnoticeable, as when a woman attending a cocktail party or gallery opening licks her lower lip before drinking from a glass to minimize the transfer of lipstick to the edge of the glass—an act that simultaneously preserves the wearer's maquillage while avoiding staining one's stemware. Yet, when done "correctly," this maneuver *should* go unnoticed, as is the case with so many components of gendered beauty practices. The repetition of these practices renders them invisible, or at the very least imperceptible, which, as Judith Butler (1997) suggests, contributes to these practices being incorrectly perceived by an uncritical public as natural or innate skills associated with members of a gender category.

However, the alteration of one's range of motion that results from engagement in specific beauty practices is not uniformly characterized by restraint. Indeed, I suggest that while beauty practices may inhibit mobility in some respects, they can also foment an expansion in one's ordinary range of corporeal movements. For example, Miliann Kang finds, both in her own experience and that of the clients and employees with whom she interacts while researching Korean-owned nail salons, that a set of spectacularly varnished nails also induces many women to engage in behaviors that draw attention to the adorned fingernails, such as tapping on railings, tabletops, and other surfaces with their fingernails (2010, 28).

Beauty practices can indeed prompt individuals to restrict their range of motion or to alter corporeal habits, but these changes in behavior are not universally experienced in negative terms by all practitioners. Thus it is far more useful to consider beauty practices, not as falling into categories of "good" and "bad," but to evaluate them in terms of the extent to which such practices produce (or inhibit) phenomenological expansiveness.

Moreover, because of the inter- and intrapersonal variation of individuals' experiences, analyses of women's (or men's) engagement in gendered
beauty practices must take into consideration the multiplicity of phenomenological experiences that register for the individuals participating in any
category of acts, such as wearing makeup, donning high heels, or changing
one's hair color.

As individuals repeatedly engage in specific beauty practices, they develop skill sets and cultivate corporeal habits, forming a sedimented history of the body that accumulates and changes over time. This process is
readily apparent in the example of walking in high heels. For someone accustomed to wearing ballet flats, adapting to even a comparatively low heel
of two inches may require that the subject pay attention to how she positions her foot while walking. Even for someone accustomed to wearing a
two-inch wedge heel, adjusting to a stiletto heel—which is a minimum
of three inches high and extremely narrow (the size of a dime or less)—
would be difficult because that change not only shifts the wearer's center of
gravity but also requires that she balance on far less surface area than if she
were wearing a wedge, which has a significantly wider base. Wearers often
have to learn to walk in such shoes, first becoming accustomed to wearing stilettos while walking on flat, even, indoor surfaces, before learning to
navigate less predictable terrain, such as a brick or cobblestone pathway.
Softer surfaces, such as grass, can require that the wearer balance all of her
weight on the ball of the foot lest the heel sink.

While it may seem trivial to examine the implications of a woman's
ability to walk in high heels, comportment is a crucial aspect of how we
evaluate ourselves and others. And, for women who worked outside the
home in the 1960s, comporting oneself consistently with notions of feminine beauty (including the ability to walk well in high heels) was often
taken into consideration in ways we would consider inappropriate today.
For example, the occupation of airline stewardess was remarkable in that
they had immense opportunities for freedom of travel, education, social
interaction, and financial gain in an era when women could not get credit
cards issued in their own names. Yet in order to become a member of this
elite group, women had to undergo intensive interviewing, during which
they were acutely aware that every aspect of their grooming, speech, and
behavior was being analyzed at all times. In Joe Harding's documentary *I
Was a Jet Set Stewardess*, Diane Royce recalls being intensely aware of the
scrutiny directed at her every move during the interview process as a pro-

spective stewardess in 1965:

> I remember I had an initial interview with the senior stewardess. She was a bit like a sort of glamorous school mistress, and she said, "Take your coat off and hang it up." And you knew that you were being watched to see how your deportment was, what your poise was like, how you carried yourself, and so I was very careful about the way I removed that coat. (2014)

Royce was not alone in identifying the ability to move gracefully while attired in fashionable clothing and accessories as a pivotal challenge in the hiring process. In the same film, Barbara Anderson, who worked as a stewardess from 1957 to 1976, recounted her experience five decades later, saying,

> I always remember going in because the pile on the carpet was really deep, and in those days we were all wearing high stiletto heels. [I asked myself] "How am I going to walk without wobbling on this extremely deep pile carpet in my heels?" [Laughter] But I managed it obviously, so it was all right. (I Was a Jet Set Stewardess 2014)

While those who would go on to become stewardesses in the heyday of airline travel were evaluated on many criteria, the fact remains that they were not only expected to be young, thin, and beautiful—airlines hired single women aged age twenty-one to twenty-six with appearances "just below Hollywood standards"—they were also expected to be graceful and cultured (I Was a Jet Set Stewardess 2014). And while culture could be taught in the intensive training stewardesses received—which included an extensive knowledge of wine and cheese, among other things—prospective stewardesses could only achieve membership in the jet set if they met the airlines' standards for physical appearance and bodily comportment in their preliminary interviews. The prominence of these evaluative moments in former stewardesses' recollections underscores the importance they and their prospective employers placed on women's performance of feminine grace and contextualize them appropriately: successfully performing feminine beauty was, in this case, a prerequisite for professional success. Beauty practices could indeed effect real change in women's social and economic class status, and descriptions such as these tell us what this embodied social mobility felt like for women working outside the home in the 1960s.

As the 1968 Miss Black America pageant and the protest of the Miss America pageant the same year illustrate, beauty ideals and their itinerant practices may be experienced by individuals as oppressive, exclusionary, and damaging, particularly when those ideals are narrowly constructed to exclude certain individuals on the basis of race. However, beauty ideals and practices are not experienced as static cultural phenomena, nor do they dictate women's behaviors. Individuals and groups regularly challenge predominant notions of beauty, resulting in the revision or expansion of beauty ideals. The critiques of whiteness as a prerequisite for participation in pageantry reflected a widespread shift in social norms of beauty. The Black Is Beautiful movement and the Miss Black America pageant in particular encouraged African American women to *feel* beautiful without altering their hair texture and promoted women like Saundra Williams who wore their natural hair as representatives of ideal beauty. This expansion of beauty ideals facilitated an engagement in a broader range of beauty practices by greater numbers of women with more diverse intersectional identities. As I have argued in this essay, the cultural critiques of racially exclusive beauty norms encouraged an expansion of beauty ideals that included more diverse notion of physical beauty. This, in turn, encouraged women to engage in a wider variety of beauty practices, which increasingly included recognizing the beauty of nonwhite women. As these social norms of feminine beauty expanded and the types of beauty practices women engaged in multiplied, a more diverse group of women received encouragement to feel beautiful.

Acknowledgments

I thank Colin Johnson, Amrita Myers, Susan Stryker, and Brenda Weber for their comments. I also thank the editors of this issue and the two reviewers.

Allison Vandenberg is currently assistant professor of women's and gender studies in the Department of History, Languages, Critical Race, and Women's Studies at Minnesota State University Moorhead. Her research focuses on phenomenological experiences of gendered bodily practices and comportment. She can be reached at allison78v@gmail.com.

Notes

1. This moment is repeated in nearly every episode of Stacy London's makeover show *Love, Lust, or Run*. In standard makeover format, the makeover subjects (who are all women) must remove all vestiges of their former self, including makeup. The sight of their nude faces routinely prompts the subjects to comment that they don't recognize themselves, that they look ugly, "like a boy," or otherwise unfamiliar.
2. For further discussion of generational perspectives of, opinions on, and attitudes toward hair straightening and natural hairstyles, see Julia Kirk Blackwelder 2003, Tiffany M. Gill 2010, Noliwe M. Rooks 1996, and Suzannah Walker 2007.
3. For examples of ways that women express agency within a preexisting intersectional network of constraints, particularly with regard to beauty and beautification practices, see Kathy Davis 2003, Debra L. Gimlin 2002, and Miliann Kang 2010.
4. As Maurice Merleau-Ponty discusses in *Phenomenology of Perception* ([1962] 2003) and *The Primacy of Perception* (1964), a multiplicity of experiences do not invalidate one another through contradictory perceptions. Rather, these diverse experiences add nuance to our understanding of phenomenological perception.

Works Cited

Ahmed, Sara. 2006. *Queer Phenomenology: Orientations, Objects, Others*. Durham, NC: Duke University Press.

Blackwelder, Julia Kirk. 2003. *Styling Jim Crow: African American Beauty Training During Segregation*. College Station: Texas A&M University Press.

Butler, Judith. 1997. "Performative Acts and Gender Constitution: An Essay in Phenomenology and Feminist Theory." In *Writing on the Body: Female Embodiment and Feminist Theory*, edited by Katie Conboy, Nadia Medina, and Sarah Stanbury, 401–17. New York: Columbia University Press.

Craig, Maxine Leeds. 2002. *Ain't I a Beauty Queen? Black Women, Beauty, and the Politics of Race*. New York: Oxford University Press.

Curtis, Charlotte. 1968. "Miss America Pageant Is Picketed by 100 Women." *New York Times*, September 8. http://query.nytimes.com/mem/archive/pdf?res=9801E6D91539E63ABC4053DFBF668383679EDE.

Davis, Kathy. 2003. *Dubious Equalities and Embodied Differences: Cultural Studies on Cosmetic Surgery*. Lanham, MD: Rowman & Littlefield Publishers, Inc.

Echols, Alice. 1989. *Daring to Be Bad: Radical Feminism in America 1967–1975*. Minneapolis: University of Minnesota Press.

Gill, Tiffany M. 2010. *Beauty Shop Politics: African American Women's Activism in the Beauty Industry*. Urbana: University of Illinois Press.

Gimlin, Debra L. 2002. *Body Work: Beauty and Self-Image in American Culture.* Berkeley: University of California Press.

I Was a Jet Set Stewardess. 2014. Directed by Joe Harding. Washington, DC: Smithsonian Channel.

Kang, Miliann. 2010. *The Managed Hand: Race, Gender, and the Body in Beauty Service Work*. Berkeley: University of California Press.

Merleau-Ponty, Maurice. (1962) 2003. *Phenomenology of Perception*. Translated by Colin Smith. Reprint. London: Routledge.

———. 1964. *The Primacy of Perception, and Other Essays on Phenomenological Psychology, the Philosophy of Art, History and Politics*. Edited by James M. Edie. Evanston, IL: Northwestern University Press.

Moody, Anne. (1968) 1976. *Coming of Age in Mississippi*. Reprint. New York: Dell.

New York Radical Women. 1970. "No More Miss America." In *Sisterhood Is Powerful: An Anthology of Writings from the Women's Liberation Movement*, edited by Robin Morgan. New York: Vintage Books.

Rooks, Noliwe M. 1996. *Hair Raising: Beauty, Culture, and African American Women*. New Brunswick, NJ: Rutgers University Press.

Walker, Suzannah. 2007. *Style and Status: Selling Beauty to African American Women, 1920–1975*. Lexingtion: University Press of Kentucky.

The Soccer Tournament as Beauty Pageant: Eugenic Logics in Brazilian Women's *Futebol Feminino*

Cara Snyder

Abstract: This paper uses the case of a soccer tournament in São Paulo, Brazil to elucidate the salience of beauty in the context of commercial sports. Over the past two decades, as women's soccer has become more popular in Brazil, the physical appearance of soccer players has also changed. I focus on the selection practices of a major tournament in São Paulo to explore the dynamics of "beautification" in women's soccer. Namely, how does the whitening and feminization of Brazilian women's athletic bodies illustrate the racial logics that shape beauty? I draw on interviews with players, including the former national team captain, as well as an analysis of media coverage in order to investigate the tournament's exclusions and to make connections between the decisions of private soccer entrepreneurs and nationalist eugenic legacies. **Keywords**: beauty, feminization, whitening, women's soccer, Brazil

Two photographs of the Brazilian women's national soccer team, taken sixteen years apart, reveal an important shift in *futebol feminino*.[1] The first photo, taken in 1996 in Atlanta, Georgia, marks the debut appearance of women's soccer at the Olympics. In this image, six players stand in the back row, while in the front row, five players kneel on one knee in a pose common to men's soccer team photos. All but two players have dark, short, almost shaved, tightly curled hair. Nine of these eleven players would be identified as "Afro-Brazilian" by Brazilian census measures. Two players are smiling. The second photograph shows the 2012 Brazilian team at the London Olympics. Six players stand in the back, and five stand in front of them, slightly bent at the waist, with their hands on their knees in a more conventionally feminine pose. In contrast to the

WSQ: Women's Studies Quarterly 46: 1 & 2 (Spring/Summer 2018) © 2018 by Cara Snyder. All rights reserved.

first image, almost all the players (except two) have straightened hair and lighter skin. Very few appear Afro-Brazilian. Some are wearing makeup, and three, maybe four, are smiling.

The differences between these two pictures suggest that a regime of gender-conformist beautification has changed Brazilian women's soccer. By 2012 it has affected how not only how soccer players look and pose, but even the racial composition of the national team. Specifically, this regime of aestheticizing soccer has meant not only its feminization but also its whitening. Juxtaposing the two photos raises troubling questions about the racial underpinnings of beauty standards in this commercial sport, and these questions form the crux of this article. The cases I discuss below contribute to transnational feminist conversations about bodies and racialization by flagging the pervasive and supranational nature of Eurocentric beauty norms in a Global South context. Brazilian soccer is frequently held up to exemplify how the country celebrates racial mixing and blended identities; yet, my analysis demonstrates how whiteness shapes dominant standards of beauty in Brazilian women's soccer. Furthermore, sports arenas are presumed to be spaces where gender nonconformity is possible and practiced by women players, even if it is not always celebrated. I show how the pressure to conform to white heterosexy norms even determines career options for some soccer players.

My focus here is on a private regional tournament referred to as the Paulistana, which was intended to cultivate women's soccer in the country. This tournament has a specific place in the history of Brazilian women's soccer. Shortly after the 1996 picture was taken, the *seleção feminino* (national women's team) returned home to a country astonished by their Olympic success. The team, which had little financial support, had placed fourth. Even though Brazil was the first Latin American nation to have *futebol feminino* (women's soccer), few Brazilians could imagine "women" and "soccer" in the same sentence. The team's achievement awoke Brazilians to the potential of women's soccer. Hoping to capitalize on the team's success as well as new forms of television broadcasting, entrepreneurs invested in a women's soccer tournament, which they called the Paulistana, and staged it twice in São Paulo.

The first Paulistana took place in 1997, one year after the Olympic games. This hastily organized tournament was followed by a sequel in 2001 that executed a distinct plan to increase the popularity of women's soccer—by sexualizing it. In what the managers of the Federação Paulistana de Futebol (Football Federation of São Paulo, or FPF) referred to as the "solution" to women's soccer (Arruda 2001), selectors prioritized players' beauty over athletic ability (Matos 2001). In the sections below, I probe and dissect the logics that informed this tournament, and specifically what beauty meant in this context. The role of soccer in the development of Brazilian national identity through the twentieth century makes it an especially apposite site to understand the historical tensions in national identity formation; thus, I begin with a short sketch of historical context, focusing on the formation of the Brazilian nation and the place of soccer— particularly women's soccer—in it. Then, I draw from an archive of media coverage of the two Paulistanas, as well as interviews with soccer players (including those who tried out for this tournament and the former captain of the national team), to think through the apparent relationships between the "beautification" of athletic women's bodies and Brazil's eugenic legacy. The Paulistana's overt inclusions and exclusions, and its policing and managing of women's bodies, reveal a form of social engineering that is not uncommon in Brazilian history. For this reason, I close my analysis with a discussion of the legacy of eugenics in Brazil.

The case of the Brazilian women's soccer team I explore in this article can aid in understanding the production, performances, practices, and analysis of beauty today. In particular, as global interest in the presence of women in sports has increased, I suggest that we must be attentive to the underlying demands of femininity inherent in these discourses. My essay provides a critique of intertwined antiblack racism, gender, and sexuality norms in relation to capitalism and to state investments, which use sports as nationalist propaganda. While specific to Brazil, the racial ideologies at play in the national women's soccer team clarify how what might at first appear as a positive form of inclusion may still be beholden to capital and its attendant eugenic logics. Sports has frequently been upheld as a tool for empowering girls and women and helping them to develop bodily confidence, assertiveness, and leadership skills—see for instance, Nike's campaigns (Moeller 2014). I offer a less optimistic example of how commercial sports also work to pressure women to conform to bodily discipline or perform white beauty standards.

The Convergence of Gender, Race, and Nationalism in *O Pais de Futebol* (The Country of Football)

The history of Brazil's national sport is also a history of the social construction of race, gender, and class. Soccer arrived in Latin America in the late nineteenth century, a period when political and intellectual leaders began looking to Europe for models of modernity (Nadel 2014, 219).[2] The athleticism of the sport became bound with notions of national manhood (Mosse 1996, 7). Historian Joshua Nadel points to the Revolution of 1930 and the rise of President Getúlio Vargas as the moment when Brazilian men's soccer became explicitly racialized (2014, 65). The Vargas regime used the myth of racial democracy and universal "mixedness" as a distinguishing aspect of "Brazilian-ness." The state crowned football star Leônidas da Silva, the "Black Diamond," as a national symbol, just as it popularized Afro-Brazilian *samba* music and *capoeira* dance. Soccer increasingly drew from mixed race stereotypes that combined "the anti-modern, irrational nature of Africans . . . with European rationality and civilizing influence" (2014, 69). Even today, these racial clichés are viewed intermittently as strengths or weaknesses, depending on the needs of the state and its capitalist interests. When the men's national team loses, as it did in the "Mineiraço" of 2014, Brazil's racial inferiority is blamed, but when they win, like in the 1958 World Cup, certain racial traits are celebrated (Costa Vargas 2013, 470). While Brazilian soccer is undeniably unique, attributing this style to a racialized narrative of playfulness, thereby feeding the myth of an "inclusive" national identity, belies Brazil's persistent racial inequalities.

If *futebol* has a contentious relationship with race, its relationship with gender is also fraught. Brazil's political structure defined this "national sport" as purely masculine, thereby perpetuating the invisibility of female soccer players and indeed of Brazilian women more generally. Yet, Brazil was actually the first Latin American country to introduce an official women's soccer team (Rial 2012). Women's soccer tournaments, which took place in São Paulo and Rio as early as 1931, received accolades in local papers like *O imparcial* and *Jornal dos sports*. Fearing that women's desire to compete on the soccer field would threaten the "traditional order" of things, some government officials sought to exclude them from the national sport (Nadel 2014, 216).

The masculine coding of soccer happened alongside its weaving into

Brazil's national fabric. National policies drew on "medical justifications" that sports like soccer put female reproduction at risk and discouraged girls from playing soccer. They finally banned it altogether in 1940 (Rial 2012).[3] This thirty-nine-year ban was directed at middle- and upper-class women—the populations that nationalist, eugenic policies required for reproduction of "desirable" genres of Brazilian-ness. Thus, the medical industry, the sports industry, and government officials colluded to dampen the potential of women's soccer for decades.

Social barriers remained even after the state overturned the ban in the late 1970s (Nadel 2014, 234). The most significant barrier included the stigmatization of female masculinity and lesbian baiting (Fisher and Dennehy 2015). Attempts to counter these stereotypes, including the Paulistana, involved feminizing female athletes by promoting a hetero-sexy physical appearance. In effect, these attempts trivialized rather than valorized women's sports. After 1996, rather than white middle- and upper-class women, exclusions were targeted at black, poor, and gender nonconforming bodies. Even so, as the following sections will show, relationships between medicine, sports, and the nation still affect female athletes and nonathletes alike.

"Beauty Is Fundamental": From the Olympics to the Paulistanas

My opening discussion of the photos of the Brazilian national team hinted at the increasing sexualization and whitening of soccer players. These same processes can be tracked in more careful ways if we analyze media coverage of regional soccer clubs in the late 1990s,[4] when a concerted effort to recast women's soccer took place. At this more granular level, we can see how an effort to build a new culture of women's soccer in Brazil played out. Media articles in this period about professionalizing women's soccer all highlight the imperative of beautifying soccer players. Seven articles from popular sports, news, and fashion magazines, as well as newspapers based in the city of São Paulo, published between 1996 and 1997, introducing athletes from regional teams in Rio and São Paulo, contrast them visually with players from the 1996 Olympic team. The regional athletes are compared favorably as the "new" face of women's soccer. In a 1997 issue of *Marie Claire*, editors overlaid an image of the 1996 Olympic team on a team photo of Rio's Fulminense Club with the heading "The new generation picks up the ball on the sport [soccer]" (fig. 1). The cap-

FIG. 1. From "Elas Abrem O Jogo," *Marie Claire*, 1997, and the personal archive of Caitlin Fisher.

tion includes a reference to "models and actresses from the Globo [TV] network" who make up the Fulminense team (Camargo and Albuquerque 1997, 42). The implication here is that the new generation of athletes will perform like the older ones, but they will be conventionally beautiful. The images also suggest that the more beautiful "models and actresses" have lighter skin and longer hair than the Olympic players.

Seventeen-year-old Milene (fig. 2) offers further evidence of media emphasis on beauty. *Veja* magazine placed a full-page picture of the teenager next to a much smaller image of the Olympic team with the heading "Milene, of Corinthians, and the Olympic national team: beauty is fundamental to make visible the undertaking" (Cardoso 1996, 73). The "undertaking" here is the "professionalization" of women's soccer (74). The title "Flowers of the Field: middle class girls sign on to football, which now demands beauty in addition to talent" conflates class and beauty, and, implicitly, race. Popularizing the sport requires women's soccer players to be "beautiful," a concept narrowly defined through reference to Milene's features—middle class, white, and young, with long, straight, blond hair. In many respects, this reflects a modeling of women's soccer along U.S. lines, where it has been a heavily middle-class and white sport.

Perhaps the most striking example of these emphases is actress, model,

FIG. 2. From "Flores Do Campo: Meninas de Classe Média Aderem Ao Futebol, Que Agora Exige Beleza Além de Talento," *Veja*, October 1996, and the personal archive of Caitlin Fisher.

and *futebolista* Susana Werner, who became the poster child for Brazilian women's soccer in the late 1990s.[5] Posing for the soccer magazine *Placar*,[6] Werner embodies a similar whitened feminine aesthetic (fig. 3). The article and image highlight the new soccer generation's heightened femininity, celebrating the overturning of the supposedly negative stereotype of women athletes as masculine. Her suggestive pose and the absence of clothing reflect the sexualization of women soccer players.

Several articles about the Paulistana tournament define femininity in opposition to masculinity. Manuel Maria, then coach of the women's Santos

FIG. 3. From "Susana Werner: Acredite, ela joga bola!" *Placar*, September 1996.

team, specifies how "working with women is different. You must take care of certain things like menstrual cycles, respect the cramps, which men don't have. Besides female players are more sensitive, they can't do the stronger exercises" (Santos Futebol Clube 1997, 39). Drawing on a discourse of biological differences and associating femininity with sensitivity, weakness, and unpredictability, the comment reassures readers that women's soccer will not disrupt the gender binary. On the article's first page, Paulistana is described as a "show of grit, skill and . . . sensuality. The male fans applaud, the players respond with smiles" (36). Like the male players, women must have drive and talent, but, according to journalists, they must also be heterosexy in order to attract male audiences.

Soccer is also celebrated as a vehicle to cultivate beauty. In one article, a physical education professor claims that playing soccer burns calories and builds muscle, which is great for "women who like to have defined legs, buttocks, and stomachs. . . . In other words, women's soccer is not for macho-women" (Ramalho and Abrunhosa 1996, 80). Slim, fit bodies are feminine as long as muscle definition is confined to the lower body. Another article proclaims, "You're wrong if you think that football makes women more *masculine*" (*Cultura Inglesa* 1997, 9; emphasis in original). The images of fair-skinned, slim women with long, straightened hair that accompany the article make clear that soccer's feminine ideal is always already racialized as white.

The 2001 Paulistana received more funding than the 1997 tournament, attracted greater media coverage, and was more polemical about the place of women's soccer. The number of articles about the 2001 tournament was more than twice that of the 1997 tournament. Missing from the coverage, however, are in-depth interviews with the players themselves. To better understand perspectives of players, the following section offers analyses of interviews I conducted with three soccer players[7] in September 2015.

"More Feminine, More Beautiful":
The Selection Process for the 2001 Paulistana

In November 2015, I interviewed Cristiane[8]—a professional futebolista who played in both Paulistana tournaments. When I asked her about herself, Cristiane launched into a monologue about her remarkable career as a footballer. She described her birth in the state of São Paulo to working-class parents. Her father, a futebol fanatic without sons, encouraged his daughters to play "from the moment they could walk," which is unusual for Brazilian girls. When I asked her to describe her participation in the Paulistanas,[9] Cristiane said that the 2001 Paulistana tournament was unique. She had heard about the women's soccer league from a friend who advised her to register for tryouts at a gym in São Paulo. When she arrived, Cristiane noticed that promoters were using the image of a well-known actress wearing a tight, short uniform to advertise the tournament. Why, she wondered, would they publicize someone famous "for being beautiful" rather than for playing soccer. Oddly, the tryouts included many days of "tests," a departure from standard recruitment procedures. Cristiane and her teammates noticed that "any girls who played well but were sort of masculine" were cut by managers: "They didn't pass them. And the girls who were more beautiful but not very good, they were *aprovadas* (approved)."[10]

Media coverage confirms her observations. A reporter for the *Folha de São Paulo* wrote that the beautifying of athletes was among the "principal objectives" for the "success of the tournament" (Arruda 2001). The criteria included long hair, short shorts, and makeup that would "enhance the beauty and sensuality of the player to attract a male public." Eduardo José Farah, then president of the FPF, discussed the "necessity" of "trying to unite . . . soccer and femininity" (2001).

Media coverage indicates that, from the beginning, promoters imagined ideal Paulistana beauty as white and middle or upper class. Cristiane claimed that finalists were "more feminine, more delicate, they dressed differently. . . . They were more *vaidosa* (vain) . . . more beautiful girls, with long straight hair and more feminine" and that they were "more *cuidadas* (groomed) . . . they have more money." Most Brazilians would consider Cristiane racially white or *pardo*, brown. Phenotypically, she has brown eyes and long, straight, blond hair; by Brazilian standards, she is clearly not black, which she confirmed later in our conversation.

Cristiane's take on racial discrimination reveals dimensions of tournament "casting" omitted by the media:

Me: And how did race enter the tournament?
Cristiane: Because soccer is a sport, it's more dominated, even, by black Brazilians, by mixed race. It's the same [for men and women], *there's no prejudice in regards to race. It's that many girls who have . . . who had . . . that [masculine] appearance . . . normally they were black. I think just for the question of hair it's more difficult, no? Now it's easier to*

straighten, but at that time it wasn't so easy, there weren't as many products to make your hair "good" as people say here. (emphasis added)

Cristiane acknowledges here that characteristics like long straight hair are primarily white, phenotypically. According to Cristiane, white women advanced whether or not they demonstrated superior athletic skills. Afro-Brazilian players, many of whom had superior athletic skills but were read as masculine, didn't make the cut. Cristiane notes a correlation between masculinity, blackness and "bad" hair without quite acknowledging that such gendered tropes are racist.

Cristiane's stance on race in Brazil—that because the people are so mixed, racism doesn't exist—represents a widespread belief usually held by nonblack Brazilians. Afro-Brazilian activists, however, have long worked to dispel the myth of racial democracy and to expose how seemingly vague understandings of race dissolve when confronted with the realities of profiling. In the words of sociologist Djaci David de Oliveira:

> The Brazilian intellectual is no longer able to identify who the black people are in Brazil, but the police, the bosses, the media . . . in addition to other social groups and institutions, know how to identify black people the moment they physically and symbolically assault them, in the moment they deny them jobs they are qualified for. (Oliveira et al. 1999, 47)

According to Christen A. Smith, these "moments of racial contact" make evident and define racial subjectivities (2016, 11). The athletes who were disqualified from the Paulistana were, to use Oliveira's words, "symbolically assaulted"; they lost jobs and were deemed unfit in a racialized gender hierarchy. The moment of cutting them made clear not only who was black but also defined blackness as unfeminine and unattractive. It is such forms of inclusions and exclusions that have produced a racialized hyperfemininity in Brazilian women's soccer.

From Margins to Mainstream: The Longer View

Several kinds of feminists—postcolonial, transnational, intersectional, women of color—have long contended that categories of race, gender, class, and sexuality cannot be separated, and that they are formed "in and through relation to each other" (McClintock 1995, 4). Beauty as a category simultaneously expresses various kinds of social hierarchies. In Brazil, as in many other parts of the world, beauty is a constitutive element not only of sexism but also racism (Jarrín 2016, 536) and classism. As soccer moves from the margins of society into the mainstream, how do female athletes navigate the increased surveillance and disciplining that accompanies these shifts? How do bodies and surveillance interact with Brazil's legacy of eugenics? My 2015 interviews with athlete, activist, artist, and scholar Caitlin Fisher and Sissi do Amor, former Brazilian national team captain and current soccer coach of the San Francisco Stingrays, may help to answer these questions. (Sissi is, incidentally, the fourth player from the left in the front row in the 1996 Olympic photo.)

During my interview, Fisher insisted that mainstreaming women's soccer has pushed athletes to conform to dominant gender and beauty norms. Drawing on twenty years of research, first as a player and then as a scholar and activist, Fisher argues that players who are now in their thirties experienced a transition during the early 2000s, when soccer moved from the margins to the mainstream and players were suddenly expected to "go to the salon, put makeup on, wear short shorts." Some players adapted to this new regime, accepting the code switching if it meant earning more money. According to Fisher, however, the newer generation (ages seventeen and eighteen) has "internalized . . . the pressure [to be] heterosexy, hyperfeminine." Although many players might claim greater agency through their participation in beautification, Fisher notes that new generations of Brazilian soccer players have fewer options for their gender presentation, leading her to conclude that such agency is only meaningful in the presence of alternatives, a point she reiterates in her article "Body Projects: Making, Remaking, and Inhabiting the Woman's Futebol Body in Brazil" (Fisher and Dennehy 2015). Mainstreaming women's soccer and U.S. influence[11] factor into the hyperfeminization of women's appearance, but Fisher worries they can also lead to a decline in players' skills. Hyperfeminization shifts the discourse so that everyday people, including commentators and journalists, value appearance over athleticism.

Sissi do Amor confirmed this perception by drawing on her personal experience. Expressing frustration about the effects of mainstreaming soccer in Brazil, she commented:

> In Brazil, people were always criticizing my appearance . . . saying I wanted to look like a man. . . . *It made me indignant that my appearance was the*

constant object of criticism when I wanted to focus on what was happening on the field.

There is great prejudice about appearance in general, from the press, but also from society. Female players feel great pressure to be hyperfeminine.

I saw *changes in women's soccer after I left Brazil in 2000. Players before then were preoccupied with playing. Now I see much more preoccupation about how to satisfy the marketers and the press. If it were me, I still* wouldn't change at all. (emphasis added)

Like Fisher, Sissi perceives the 2000s as a turning point, where the mainstreaming of women's soccer shifted focus from athletic skill to aesthetics. The version of Brazilianness promoted through the Paulistana values a white, Eurocentric, feminine aesthetic. After 2000, evidence suggests that many women footballers have acquiesced to the industry's racialized, heterosexy standards.

The Paulistana works as a case study because it offers an unambiguous example of how Brazilian sports promoters and managers sought to recast Brazilian woman's bodies and skills. The 2001 tournament grabbed national attention precisely because it valorized aesthetic standards. Fisher and Sissi, however, suggest that discrimination was hidden in plain sight. In fact, their comments intimate that soccer's mainstreaming has encouraged both external and internal policing of women's bodies. Fisher and Sissi believe that the players *themselves* now do much of the policing. In fact, Fisher referred me to her conversation with a player named Thaisa who, due to harassment from family and teammates, "started taking on a more feminine image. It's a habit now" (Fisher and Dennehy 2015, 1000). Pointing to pressure from marketers and the press, Fisher and Sissi observed that players altered their behaviors. Paulistana beauty ideals, which largely excluded black and genderqueer bodies, seem to have seeped into Brazilian futebol feminino more generally,[12] culminating in the demographic shifts I observed in the juxtaposed images of the 1996 and 2012 Olympic teams.

Conclusions: A Transnational Feminist Critique of Conditional Inclusion

For many scholars of race in Brazil, it is clear that the maintenance of racial democracy as a national ideology exists alongside and in spite of eugenic practices. Amidst a superficial celebration of *miscigenação* (racial hybridity), national whitening is still enforced through the "spectacular and mundane repetition of state violence against the black body" (Smith 2016, 25), the biopolitics of beauty (Jarrín 2016, 535), and racialized regional narratives of progress (Weinstein 2015, 9).

The case of women's soccer exemplifies the convergence of these three factors. Cristiane's account confirms that official soccer leagues are pushing out Afro-Brazilian players; because of how much soccer is associated with national identity this can be likened to a eugenic project. The systematic erasing of Afro-Brazilian players as well as phenotypically Afro-Brazilian appearance (through requiring players to lengthen and straighten their hair and lighten their skin) depicts a different face of Brazilian women's soccer. More broadly, understanding the transnational manifestations of Eurocentric beauty norms and antiblackness requires centering the lived experiences of black people as well as locating how a continuum of blackness—in various transnational settings—functions as a category of abjection.

The Paulistana example can be generalized beyond a particular soccer tournament. If the 2001 championship marks a shift in the increasingly racialized sexualization of Brazilian women athletes, it also calls attention to shifting standards for deeming what is "beautiful" and "not beautiful." Women's soccer—and especially, but not exclusively the Paulistana— reveals the constraints placed on how Brazilian women perform femininity. Sissi, Cristiane, and Fisher all note the pressure players feel to achieve hyperfemininity and the physical appearance of the players on the 2012 Brazilian Olympic soccer team illustrates this impact. And because Brazil is a "soccer nation," as women's soccer becomes more mainstream, women's place on the football field begins to represent women more generally. For all of these reasons, I view the Paulistana as a critical turning point[13] in futebol feminino. The tournament captures the moment when women's soccer moved out of the margins and female athletes' bodies became subjected to new profit-oriented visual regimes. The dynamics of mainstreaming women's soccer described here offer persuasive evidence of antiblack racism within ongoing projects of beautification, and such dynamics warn against a superficial celebration of women's inclusion in sports.

Soccer has been coded in raced, gendered, and national terms in Brazil from its inception. Studying the effects of mainstreaming on women's soccer in Brazil, as mediated through eugenic policies, reveals the often-conflicting ways bodies are policed. In the mid-twentieth century, eugenic reasoning kept white, middle-class women off of the field, but as women's soccer becomes more mainstream, these once excluded bodies now appear to represent the desired athletic archetype. The 1940s ban on female athletics ostensibly applied to all women, but in fact, it kept middle-class white women at home bearing and rearing children. After 1996, however, the direction of racialized reproduction of Brazilian nationhood changed, now putting prototypically white and whitened bodies on the soccer field.[14] My case study suggests that the logic once used to exclude certain women from the soccer field is now being used to embrace them. Which bodies are showcased may be different, but Brazil's gendered and raced inclusions and exclusions persist as part of the nation's eugenic legacy. My essay offers insight into the ways antiblack racism, classism, and gender and sexuality norms manifest in women's sports through discourses of beauty, at the service of capitalist and nationalist agendas. Transnational feminist scholars must be attentive to such conditions for inclusion.

Acknowledgments

I am deeply grateful to Caitlin Fisher, Sissi do Amor, Lu Castro, folks at the Museu de Futebol in São Paulo, and the anonymous soccer players I had the pleasure of interviewing. I thank Ashwini Tambe, Catherine Schuler, Ivan Ramos, Dave Andrews, the anonymous WSQ reviewers, and the special issue editors for incisive suggestions and critique. Thanks also to Zita Nunes, Louisa Hill, Elizabeth Johnson, Britta Anderson, Sabrina Gonzalez, Victor Sang, Monica Ocasio, Jonathan Brower, Anna Storti, Jocelyn Coates, Sara Haq, Sina Lee, DB Bauer, Courtney Cook, and my querida familia—Lori, Will, Antonis, Julia, Nate, Avi, James—for their various forms of support and inspiration.

After living and working for two years in Brazil as a Fulbright teacher and professor at the Instituto Federal do Sertão Pernambucano, **Cara Snyder** joined the Department of Women's Studies at the University of Maryland, College Park, where she is currently pursuing a PhD. She can be reached at csnyder3@umd.edu.

Notes

1. I will use the terms soccer, football, and *futebol*, as well as women's soccer and *futebol feminino*, interchangeably. When referring to the Brazilian women's national/Olympic team, I will also use the Portuguese term *seleção*. For the

images I refer to of the Brazilian women's national team, see Bob Thomas 1996 and Matthew Ashton 2012.

2. Naturally, European models of whiteness had to be adapted to Brazil's racial *mestiçagem*, or mixing (Rodrigues 1938). Accounting for a population that would never be "white," Brazilian intellectuals proposed three racial categories—white, mulattos, and black—which could be identified not by genes but by appearance. Thirty years later, Gilberto Freyre (1975) argued that the uniquely Brazilian African, Amerindian, and European mixture constitutes a national treasure.

3. President Getúlio Vargas charged his minister of health to write a directive about the threat to Brazil's "future mothers" (Nadel 2014, 219). Decree 3199, article 54 included a list of sports that banned female participants because they were supposedly incompatible with women's nature.

4. All sources, seven articles about the 1997 Paulistana and fifteen from 2001, are from the personal archives of Caitlin Fisher.

5. Werner began playing just five years before the first Paulistana.

6. *Placar*, which has appeared monthly since the 1970s, is one of the most popular sports publications in Brazil.

7. I have interviewed a total of fifteen players, coaches, and marketers involved in the 2001 Paulistana, but have included the three (from 2015) that are most relevant my essay's arguments. I conducted the additional twelve interviews in 2017.

8. I was introduced to Cristiane (a pseudonym) through athlete, activist, artist, and scholar Caitlin Fisher. In September 2015, Caitlin put me in touch with several players, and Cristiane was the only one who responded to my emails.

9. Cristiane has played on numerous teams but never for the Olympic *seleção*.

10. I conducted this interview and my interview with Sissi do Amor, in Portuguese. All translations are my own.

11. Here I refer both to the influence of U.S. women athletes' physical appearances and to U.S. cultural, economic, and political power more generally. These impact Brazilian players who live and play in the United States—which is the largest importer of women soccer players—as well as Brazilian coaches and marketers who exchange ideas with executives in the U.S. women's leagues. See Rial 2014 for thoughts on the transnational migrations of Brazilian women athletes.

12. Although it may be unsettling to see how much aesthetic regimes affect athletics, anthropologists Alvaro Jarrín and Alexander Edmonds both demonstrate how aesthetic regimes shape everyday life in Brazil by specifically focusing on plastic surgery, and how it relates to racial hierarchies. One of Brazil's most popular surgeries, for instance, is rhinoplasty for the "correction

of a negroid nose" (Edmonds 2010, 134). Elaborating on the antiblackness inherent in beauty discourses, Jarrín contends that "Brazil's neo-Lamarckian eugenics movement was the first to craft beauty as an index of racial improvement within the nation," and that contemporary discourses of beautification showcase lingering eugenic ideologies (2016, 535). Eugenics in this context did not involve systematic extermination of racial others in the manner advocated by the Nazis. Rather, Brazil's state policies implemented a "positive" eugenics focused on expanding the numbers of the racially desirable population, such as "mandatory premarital certifications, increased sanitation, hygienic education, and fomenting white immigration from Europe" (538). Indeed, although the mechanisms for achieving it have changed, gradual whitening persists. Plastic surgery illuminates the ways race and beauty are implicated in social inclusion and exclusion (536). The gendered expressions of eugenics in the Paulistana corroborate Jarrín's and Edmonds's broader arguments about the racialization of beauty. If eugenics in Brazil can be understood as the racialized reproduction of the nation, and if mainstreaming women's soccer has brought women athletes into the purview of national representation, then the policing of women's bodies in this sporting arena has eugenic implications.

13. More data is needed to establish whether sexist practices were mainstreamed *because* of this tournament, or if the Paulistana merely captured what was happening in Brazilian women's soccer due to a combination of factors. In either case, this paper merely notes a correlation, rather than establishing causation.

14. Contributing factors include the advent of the television, which mainstreams women's soccer in the context of a globally connected world that links women's sports to "progress" and "modernity." For further reading on the ways middle-classification, aspirational whiteness, media awareness, and professionalization have contributed to the feminization of women's soccer see Hargreaves 1994, especially sections 2, 7, and 8. For further reading on sexuality and the disciplining of women's soccer see Fisher and Dennehy 2015 and Rial 2014.

Works Cited

Ashton, Matthew. 2012. "Olympic Summer Games - London 2012 - Womens Football - Group E - Cameroon v Brazil." Getty Images, July 25. www.gettyimages.com/detail/news-photo/brazil-women-team-group-during-the-olympic-summer-games-news-photo/525792716#brazil-women-team-group-during-the-olympic-summer-games-london-2012-picture-id525792716.

Arruda, Eduardo. 2001. "FPF insititui jogadora-objecto no paulista." *Folha de São Paulo*, September 16. http://www1.folha.uol.com.br/fsp/esporte/fk1609200119.htm.

Camargo, Denise, and Lina de Albuquerque. 1997. "Elas abrem o jogo." *Marie Claire*, February.

Cardoso, Maurício. 1996. "Flores do campo: meninas de classe média aderem ao futebol, que sgora exige beleza além de talento." *Veja*, October.

Costa Vargas, João H. 2013. "Always Already Excluded: The Gendered Facts of Anti-Blackness and Brazil's Male Seleção." In *A Companion to Sport*, edited by Dave L. Andrews and Ben Carrington, 465–80. Oxford: Wiley Blackwell.

Cultura Inglesa. 1997. "Sure-Footed Female Talent." May.

Edmonds, Alexander. 2010. *Pretty Modern: Beauty, Sex, and Plastic Surgery in Brazil.* Durham, NC: Duke University Press.

Fisher, Caitlin Davis, and Jane Dennehy. 2015. "Body Projects: Making, Remaking, and Inhabiting the Woman's Futebol Body in Brazil." *Sport in Society* 18 (8): 995–1008.

Freyre, Gilberto. 1975. *Casa-grande & senzala: formação da família Brasileira sob o regime da economia patriarcal.* 17th ed. Rio de Janeiro, Brazil: Livraria J. Olympio Editora.

Hargreaves, Jennifer. 1994. *Sporting Females: Critical Issues in the History and Sociology of Women's Sports.* London: Routledge.

Jarrín, Alvaro. 2016. "Towards a Biopolitics of Beauty: Eugenics, Aesthetic Hierarchies and Plastic Surgery in Brazil." *Journal of Latin American Cultural Studies* 24 (4): 535–52.

Matos, Marisela. 2001. "Beleza é fundamental?" *Lance!*, September 14.

McClintock, Anne. 1995. *Imperial Leather: Race, Gender, and Sexuality in the Colonial Contest.* New York: Routledge.

Moeller, Kathryn. 2014. "Searching for Adolescent Girls in Brazil: The Transnational Politics of Poverty in 'The Girl Effect.'" *Feminist Studies* 40 (3): 575–601.

Mosse, George L. 1996. *The Image of Man: The Creation of Modern Masculinity.* New York: Oxford University Press.

Nadel, Joshua H. 2014. *Fútbol! Why Soccer Matters in Latin America.* Gainesville: University Press of Florida.

Oliveira, Dijaci David de, Brasilmar Ferreira Nunes, and Movimento Nacional dos Direitos Humanos (Brazil). 1999. *50 anos depois: relações raciais e grupos socialmente segregados.* Goiânia, Brazil: Movimento Nacional de Direitos Humanos.

Ramalho, Cristiane, and Orlando Abrunhosa. 1996. "Futebol É Coisa de Moça." *Mancete*, December.

Rial, Carmen. 2012. "Women's Soccer in Brazil." *ReVista: Harvard Review of Latin America*, September 14. http://revista.drclas.harvard.edu/book/womens-soccer-brazil.

———. 2014. "New Frontiers: The Transnational Circulation of Brazil's Women Soccer Players." In *Women, Soccer and Transnational Migration*, edited by Sine Agergaard and Nina Clara Tiesler, 86–112. London: Routledge.

Rodrigues, Raymondo Nina. 1938. *As Raças Humanas E a Responsabilidade Penal No Brasil*. 3A. ed., feita sobre a 1a. de 1894 e prefaciada por Afranio Peixoto. Bibliotheca Pedagogica Brasileira. Ser. 5a.: Brasiliana, V. 110. S. Paulo: Companhia editora nacional.

Santos Futebol Clube. 1997. "As meninas da vila." *Revista Jovem Santos*, n.d.

Smith, Christen A. 2016. *Afro-Paradise: Blackness, Violence, and Performance in Brazil*. Champaign: University of Illinois Press.

Telles, Edward E. 2004. *Race in Another America: The Significance of Skin Color in Brazil*. Princeton, NJ: Princeton University Press.

Thomas, Bob. 1996. "1996 Olympic Games. Atlanta, USA. Sanford Stadium, Georgia. Women's Football. Semi Final. China 3 v Brazil 2. The Brazilian Team Pose for a Team Group Photograph." Getty Images, January 1. www.gettyimages.com/detail/news-photo/olympic-games-atlanta-usa-sanford-stadium-georgia-womens-news-photo/78986634#olympic-games-atlanta-usa-sanford-stadium-georgia-womens-football-picture-id78986634.

Weinstein, Barbara. 2015. *The Color of Modernity: São Paulo and the Making of Race and Nation in Brazil*. Durham, NC: Duke University Press.

Controlling Beauty Ideals: Caribbean Women, Thick Bodies, and White Supremacist Discourse[1]

Kamille Gentles-Peart

Abstract: This article explores the ways in which anti-black-woman body politics manifest themselves in the lives of Caribbean women living in the United States. Specifically, using the personal narratives of black Caribbean immigrant women, I examine these women's encounters with ideologies that marginalize them based on their bodies and preserve contemporary anti-black-woman ideologies in "post-racial" United States. This study addresses two areas that are typically understudied in body image research of black women: a critical understanding of how anti-black-woman sentiments manifest themselves in the everyday lives of black women and black women's own voices and reflections on their embodied social realities. **Keywords**: black women, body politics, white supremacy, Caribbean, immigrant

During the European colonial period, travel writers in Africa drew on and contributed to a European discourse of black womanhood that ascribed a big body to all black women and used it as a signifier of otherness, their inferior phenotype, and lesser culture and intelligence. The depiction of colonized black women in these writings represented them as having monstrous, "unwomanly" bodies that were not beautiful and admired as were the delicate bodies of their white counterparts. Perhaps the most iconic figure in this regard is that of Saartjie Baartman, the so-called "Hottentot Venus." Baartman, a South African slave, was brought to Europe in 1810 for the purposes of displaying her enlarged—by colonial standards—genitals and buttocks. Her body was exhibited across Europe as an example and model of all black women's bodies. The image of the voluptuous Hottentot Venus was harnessed to represent the hypersexuality and inferior intelligence of black women and justified their exploitation at the hands

WSQ: Women's Studies Quarterly 46: 1 & 2 (Spring/Summer 2018) © 2018 by Kamille Gentles-Peart.

of Europeans (Alexander 2014). This construction of the black female body as voluptuous and unwomanly—and thus built for functionality and labor—was employed to affirm the use of black women as slave labor in Europe (Morgan 1997). It helped to create what I refer to as the ideology of the "thick black woman," the notion that black women are naturally curvy and voluptuous (Gentles-Peart 2016).

On the other hand, many societies, such as those of the Afro-Caribbean, uphold the voluptuous body as a marker of desirable black femininity. In an effort to reject colonial (white) ontologies and cultivate notions of black empowerment (Bogues 2002; Meeks 2000), many independence movements in the Anglophone Caribbean idealized the image of the voluptuous black female body with ample derriere, hips, and thighs (the thick black woman idea). More than just a beauty ideal in black Caribbean societies, the idea of the curvy or thick woman has become a symbol of black identity and signifies resistance to whiteness, colonialism, and Eurocentric aesthetics. For example, Jenny Sharpe (2002) highlights how the only female in the pantheon of Jamaica's national heroes, Nanny of the Maroons, was credited with using her ample buttocks to catch bullets from the British in order to save her community, mythologizing her voluptuous body. Likewise, Bibi Bakare-Yusuf demonstrated how contemporary working-class and poor black women of the Caribbean celebrated "an unruly voluptuosity—the joy of being fat" to challenge the European upper-class morals that operated among black Caribbean elites (2006, 470).

The significance of the voluptuous black female body in Afro-Caribbean societies is also underscored by its prominence in Afro-Caribbean popular culture, particular that of the working class and poor (Cooper 2004; Bakare-Yusuf 2006; Hobson 2003). As Carolyn Cooper observes:

> The gender politics of the dancehall . . . can be read . . . as a glorious celebration of full-bodied female sexuality, particularly the substantial structure of the Black working-class woman whose body image is rarely validated in the middle-class Jamaican media, where eurocentric norms of delicate female face and figure are privileged. The recurring references in the DJs' lyrics to fleshy female body parts and oscillatory functions . . . signal the reclamation of active, adult female sexuality from the entrapping passivity of sexless Victorian virtue. (2004, 86)[2]

Celebrating the thick black female body in black communities does not automatically displace or erase white colonialist views of the voluptuous body and the dominance of white beauty standards. In spite of this reframing, the less favorable, anti-black-woman narrative surrounding the thick black woman persists in both black and white communities. The voluptuous black female body is still perceived as unattractive, ugly, and grotesque—the opposite of beautiful—when seen through the prism of white supremacy.[3] Largely driven by the proliferation of Eurocentric ideals of thinness in the postcolonial era, thick black bodies continue to be used in support of anti-black-woman agendas and to marginalize black women in general, not only in regard to beauty and femininity but also in relation to their participation in the global economy.

In this article, I explore the ways in which anti-black-woman body politics manifest themselves in the lives of Caribbean women living in the United States. Specifically, using the personal narratives of black Caribbean women, I examine these women's encounters with ideologies that marginalize them in the United States based on their bodies and that preserve contemporary anti-black-woman ideologies in a "post-racial" United States. This study addresses two areas that are typically understudied in body image research of black women: a critical understanding of how anti-black-woman sentiments manifest themselves in the everyday lives of black women and black women's own voices and reflections on their embodied social realities.

Color-Blind Racism and Social Stratification

According to Eduardo Bonilla-Silva (2006), systems of racial domination are not static, but shift based on internal and external societal pressures. Racialized systems within U.S. society experienced such a shift around the 1960s and 1970s when the civil rights movement challenged Jim Crow and the "racial apartheid" that existed for black people (Bonilla-Silva 2003, 272). This did not result in an end to racial stratification, however, as new strategies emerged to replace previous oppressions. Bonilla-Silva asserts that Jim Crow was replaced by a "'new racism'—a specific set of social arrangements and practices that produced and reproduced racial order" (272). Rather than based on discourses of overt biological inferiority, this new racism is based on more subtle, "softer" forms of racialized practices. The main ideological foundation of this new racial-stratification system is color blindness, which projects the idea that decisions and practices in society are not based on racial difference; therefore, inequality is not explained as a function or product of racism, but rather as the result of cultural and individual phenomena. This new hegemonic discourse better suits the post–civil rights era where overt racial insults and physical attacks are condemned. However, the results are the same: the new racism functions to maintain the contemporary racial structure and helps underscore white privilege without incriminating white people (Bonilla-Silva 2006).

Drawing on discourses of intersectionality (Crenshaw 1995), there is a gendered component to this new racism as well. Variations exist between color-blind strategies applied to black men and black women. Using the logic of Bonilla-Silva, all black people, regardless of their multiple positionalities (shaped, for example, by gender, sexuality, and class), are subordinated within the racial structure of the United States and are susceptible to any strategy employed to marginalize them. However, seen through the prism of intersectionality, gendered elements are evident. For example, the perception among whites that black people are welfare dependent is projected unto all black people, but is particularly applied to black women who have historically been deemed "welfare queens" (Lubiano 1992). Similarly, attributing superior athleticism to black people, a culturally racist means to undermine their intellectual and creative capabilities, has been specifically aimed at black men (Hoberman 1997). In addition, the notion that black people naturally make better domestic workers is specifically associated with black women, as exemplified by the mammy figure that I will discuss below. Therefore, color-blind strategies are mobilized differently against black men and black women.

Controlling Body Image and the New Racism

Historically, racialized gendered strategies targeting black women have predominantly focused on the body. That is, gendered racial inequalities have been upheld by constructing and normalizing ideologies about black women's bodies (Morgan 1997). The use of discourses of black women's bodies to promote and maintain gendered racial inequality has a long history in the United States. For example, Patricia Hill Collins (2000) writes about "controlling images" that have been mobilized throughout U.S. history. These are socially constructed conceptions of black women designed by white supremacists to justify the policing, controlling, and containment of black women. These images and tropes are designed to "make racism, sexism, and poverty appear to be natural, normal . . ." and disguise or mask social relations (Hill Collins 2000, 69).

Controlling images are used by white supremacist culture to construct and normalize expectations of black women's attitudes, temperament, sexuality, and bodies. In other words, these discourses are attached to and envisioned as being performed by certain body types; therefore, body size and shape are important to the conceptualization of these tropes. The most common embodied characteristic of these images is the big or voluptuous body. In this way, the most persistent controlling image and perennial strategy of the new (gendered) racism continues to be the ideology of the thick black woman. An infamous long-standing image is that of the mammy figure. This epitome of the faithful, obedient domestic servant was created to justify black women's exploitation as house slaves and restrict them to domestic service. The mammy's fat body significantly contributes to this construction of black femininity as her large body, dark skin, and round facial features create an image that poses no sexual threat to white women (Hill Collins 2000). Her body was used to mark her as docile and asexual. Another controlling image is that of the Jezebel, the sexually aggressive black woman that was (and still is) used to position all black women as sexually deviant and available, provide ideological justification for sexual assaults on their bodies, and feed discourses of high fertility. Unlike the mammy, the Jezebel is often presented as having a voluptuous body to signify the "wanton, libidinous black woman whose easy ways excused white men's abuse of their slaves as sexual 'partners' and bearers of mulatto offspring" (Austin 1995, 432).

There have been initiatives led by groups and individuals in black communities in the United States to create new, more positive narratives of black women's bodies, particularly those that are curvy, and these narratives have challenged the notion of the mammy and the Jezebel. They attempt to radically ascribe value to the ample black female physique, associating it with strength and power or the strong black woman (Beauboeuf-Lafontant 2003). In fact, the "large" black female body is now commonly accepted in African American communities as the ideal. As Cheryl Townsend Gilkes states,

> In spite of the high premium placed on culturally exalted images of white female beauty and the comedic exploitation that surrounds the large black woman, many African-American women know that the most

respected physical image of black women, within and outside of the community, is that of the large woman. (2001, 183)

Nevertheless, the image of the thick black woman continues to inform the racialized gendered marginalization of black women in the United States. Even as some in black communities work to counter or complicate the idea of black women as mammies or Jezebels, the parallel negative narrative of the voluptuous black female body still circulates and shapes black women's lives. In this sense then, the thick ideal for black women, upheld in both white and black spaces, can have deleterious effects for black women, as argued by Tamara Beauboeuf-Lafontant. In her reading of body image and black feminist literature, Beauboeuf-Lafontant found that while images of strength and deviance have historically been used to encourage black women to maintain larger bodies, their larger bodies have been used to mask black women's struggle with eating disorders and social problems and deny them protection from their communities and the state. Beauboeuf-Lafontant concludes that it is therefore "both disingenuous and premature to extol the strengths and freedom of black women with regard to their bodies," and in doing so, she says we are complicit in expecting black women to represent what racist discourses deem deviant womanhood (2003, 119). Moreover, promoting the ideology of the curvaceous black woman allows white supremacists to maintain and deepen gendered racial dichotomies while absolving themselves of racism. With this in mind, I explore Afro-Caribbean women's experiences with and responses to the ways their voluptuous bodies are mobilized for the agenda of white supremacy in a post-racial U.S. society.

The analysis that follows is based on information gathered from focus groups and interviews conducted between 2006 and 2014 with thirty-seven first- and second-generation English-speaking Caribbean women in the United States (twenty-three of the first generation and fourteen of the second generation). The participants are based in New York City, which houses one of the largest black Caribbean diasporic communities in the world. Both first- and second-generation participants are working- and middle-class women between the ages of nineteen and fifty-five. Many of them migrated from or have heritage in Jamaica (which is not surprising, since Jamaicans comprise the largest group of black Caribbeans in New York City [United States Census Bureau 2010]), but there are also women from other islands, including Antigua, Trinidad and Tobago, St. Vincent, and Barbados. All have completed high school, and some have completed or are pursuing college degrees and technical or professional training. All the participants are culturally situated (because of skin tone, hair texture, etc.) and self-identify as black women.

The narratives from the participants are contextualized by my own experiences within the English-speaking Caribbean community in New York City. As an immigrant black woman from Jamaica, I spent over fifteen continuous years in a major black Caribbean enclave where I interacted with and observed black Caribbean family members, friends, and colleagues at social gatherings, hair salons, restaurants, and in classrooms. While being of black Caribbean heritage and living within the community does not automatically make me an authority on this group, my cultural position provides knowledge of and experience with the community and facilitates the opportunity for long-term informal observations of and interactions with cultural traditions and texts.

The Things White Women Say

Black women's size and skin color are often used to physically remove and distinguish them from the ideals of true (white) womanhood (Townsend Gilkes 2001; Shaw 2005; Beauboeuf-Lafontant 2003). One of the ways in which this anti-black-woman discourse manifests itself in the lives of the participants is through interactions with white women who position them as exceptional because of their curvy bodies. One respondent said,

> I had a conversation with a girl in school. She was a white girl and if there were two girls standing side by side, both were size twelve, one white, one black, she wouldn't see the black woman as overweight, but she would see the white woman as overweight. She said, "I don't really see any women of color that is overweight to me." Because in her eyes, she just sees that as the norm, but when she sees a white woman that's a little bigger she says, "Wow! She looks sloppy." And I thought that was so interesting because you can have two women that are the exact same size and just their color [is different] . . . and this was coming from a white girl.

Similarly, another participant said,

> I have a friend of mine that her and I are pretty much the same size, and we were working out together, jogging, and I am like, "I have to lose my

thighs and my butt," and she is like, "You don't need to lose weight; you are perfect the way you are. I don't even know why you are working out with me." One day, I finally said to her, "We have the same body type; we wear the same size!"

As black women from the Caribbean, they ascribe to and desire voluptuous bodies, even in the context of the United States (Gentles-Peart 2016). On the surface, the comments and feedback they received from white women with regard to their bodies seem to validate their differential body ideals. However, the statements also reveal the implicit othering of black women; they position black women's bodies as different from those of white women. More precisely, their bodies are opposites: what is unacceptable for white women (bigness or "sloppiness") is the norm for black women. The white women referenced here clearly suggest that it is not only acceptable, but expected that black women do not pay as much attention to their bodies as white women because their bodies do not have to be thin—which signifies beauty in mainstream U.S. society. The white women's judgements of the participants' bodies as outside of thinness reinforce the idea that black women are less delicate, less fragile, less dainty, and therefore more masculine than white women. In this sense then, the white women's comments help to maintain structures of gendered racism without explicitly using skin color.

The comments by white women also trivialize and ignore the weight and body image issues that black women may face, overtly discouraging body care that the participants pursue (as when the white woman said her black friend did not need to workout). This dismissal and denial of the participants' struggles with weight promotes the strong black woman ideology that is prolific both in- and outside of black communities (Beauboeuf-Lafontant 2003). It is a modern-day example of the attribution of strength based on the women's body size, implying that, because their desired bodies are not thin (and delicate), black women have overcome struggles with body image. It also reinforces the notion that concerns with the body and beauty are domains of middle-class white women of the Global North, suggesting that black women, particularly those in the Global South, should not have the body anxieties of their white counterparts. This reflects and upholds the exotic nature of "third world" black women who are perceived as unnatural and existing outside of the bounds of normalcy, meaning whiteness and thinness.

The participants themselves do not accept to this idea. They are aware of the implications of these white women's statements, but they recall these remarks with some humor, incredulity, and cynicism. During the sessions when these statements came up, the women generally chuckled and exhibited expressions that indicate their rejection of the implied message, such as rolling their eyes and sucking their teeth. This is not to say that the women do not believe their preferred body type is different from that of their white counterparts—because they do; rather, they resist the implications about their womanhood embedded in the comments. In addition to their immediate reactions to the comments, the women register their resistance by engaging in many body modification projects to get and maintain a voluptuous body. They share their strategies to improve stomachs, arms, and thighs that are deemed unacceptable, their frustrations with working to be not too big and not too skinny, and the dietary supplements that help create a bigger buttocks, such as the "chicken pill," a growth hormone allegedly given to chickens that can make humans plump.

These body sculpting practices indicate that the voluptuous ideal produces as much anxiety and questionable habits as the thin one. These women embraced the thick body type, but in spite of its endorsement of larger, seemingly healthier aesthetics, it is still a patriarchal normalizing mechanism that can engender self-contempt and undermine their body image. Furthermore, their focus on their bodies demonstrates that they themselves have not evaded the dominant norms of female behavior; they place emphasis on their bodies, thus reinforcing, rather than disrupting, the body's significance in Western conceptions of femininity. On the other hand, by taking the time to sculpt their bodies, especially to fit an aesthetic that is not thin, the women demonstrate defiance of the white supremacist construction of womanhood. They do not necessarily challenge the association between femininity and the body, but certainly question the prominence of the thin body as the only representation of femininity.

No Clothes for the Thick

Anti-black-woman ideologies also manifest themselves in the participants' lives through clothing. One woman said, "It's hard to find clothes that fit. Now I feel like I have to lose weight, because I want to fit in. I had two friends, one was a size zero, the other a size two. When we went shopping together they had an easy time finding deals and I couldn't find anything. It was hard then."

This limit on available sizes is felt most acutely by women who work in corporate culture who have difficulty finding business clothing for their bodies. A woman shared her frustration:

> I try to get rid of my butt because I don't fit into clothes. I work in corporate America and I buy clothes that all the white people make—Calvin Klein, Tahari—and I don't fit into [their pants] for anything. I always buy two sizes up and get the [waist] tailored. It's so annoying, so I tried to get rid of my butt. . . . When I go to work, I don't want to look all hoochie and [my clothes] too tight. . . . So where I am it's a bunch of white guys and they don't pay attention to me anyhow, but when I leave the office and I am walking down Wall Street . . . I get very self-conscious. There are no designers that cater to curvy women. . . . Clothes don't fit my body type; my body doesn't fit the clothes. So I am just trying to assimilate to be able to fit into my clothes.

Another woman similarly said,

> When I go to buy my clothes, with my suits, whenever I go to the register, I pray to God they don't look at the sizes . . . [because] I switch [them]. I have to get a size two blazer and like a size six pants. I am always at the register saying, "Dear God, please don't let them look at the tags so they see the different sizes." I am sorry, but I have to do that. When I buy dresses it's really difficult; I wear a size six dress, but then the top is really big for me so then I have to pin it up or take it in.

Both statements exemplify the women's frustration with and negotiations of mainstream business attire that seem to systematically exclude their bodies. Their challenges with clothing are not only related to fashion but also have to do with the larger implications for job opportunities and social mobility that come with not being able to find professional-style clothing. Women's bodies are generally policed and disciplined at white-collar workplaces with regard to dress, appearance, comportment, and image. This is particularly true for black women since notions of professionalism for women is closely related to middle-class status, thinness, and whiteness; and thus is inextricably connected to particular types of embodied and performative femininity. Specifically, the most successful and desired body for women in the corporate workplace is that of a "fit" (meaning slender), white body that signifies self-control and discipline (Trethewey 1999). In other words, business settings have historically excluded black women, particularly those who do not have thin bodies.

The participants' implied that they experience this anti-black-woman sentiment in corporate spaces through their clothing choices or the lack thereof. Black women who prefer voluptuous bodies are already systematically marginalized in corporate spaces (because of their race and their body size), but clothing helps to deepen (and justify) this marginalization by promoting anti-black-woman practices. In the larger social context, black women are expected to be curvy or thick, but the mainstream clothing industry does not provide them much choice in regard to dressing that body for corporate spaces. The lack of professional clothing serves to embarrass and marginalize voluptuous black women in these spaces, as one participant highlighted in her comment. When thick black women have to make do with the clothing choices they have, the result may be ill-fitting, tight clothes that make them self-conscious and discourage them from participating in these spaces. More importantly, restricting the availability of business clothing for thick bodies becomes a passive-aggressive way to further constrain black women's participation in professional spaces. Without access to clothes that is acceptable within dominant corporate culture, voluptuous black women can be excluded from these spheres on the grounds that their comportment does not fit corporate environments.

These and other statements by the women also indicate that, while they are aware of the limitations placed on their bodies in corporate spaces, they also actively negotiate these limitations. For example, they defy the fashion industry (and the sales policies of clothing stores) by size switching, as indicated in one of the statements above. By mixing the sizes of available clothing, putting bigger bottoms with smaller tops, these women are able to create outfits that better suit their voluptuous bodies. In this way, the women challenge established ideas about what the ideal body should look like, as dictated by the way sets are put together in stores and how clothing is sized by mainstream designers and manufacturers. Furthermore, by manipulating the fashion industry to create their own professional clothing and dress themselves in ways that are acceptable to the business world, black women are able to negotiate their marginalization and defy anti-black-woman oppressions.

The women's attempts to fit into mainstream business clothing include "mimicry" of racist discourses of body politics. According to Homi K.

Bhabha (1994), this mimicry is ambivalent. It resembles the colonizer's culture, and thus at least partially reinscribes it, but when enacted by "in-appropriate," othered bodies, it also creates a mocking and threatening presence—a "menace"—that disrupts the authority of the imperial power. By seeking to mimic the dominant dress code of U.S. corporate culture, the women reinscribe Western and white supremacist notions of profes-sionalism, but they also engage in self-directed meaning making; they un-dermine the place of their oppression and marginalization. Their bodies become sites of intervention that challenge, though do not dismantle, axes of legitimacy.

The Butt Revolution

Anti-black-woman ideologies also manifest themselves in the interview-ees' lives through current mainstream white discourses around the but-tocks. As one woman said, "Here comes J.Lo and Kim Kardashian with their big butts [and they are considered 'hot'] and women way out of Afri-ca had some [big butts] . . . and then they would call you fat. . . . They call Mrs. Obama fat because she has a big backside." This woman and others in the study recognized that the current popularization of the voluptuous body, specifically the butt, by women who do not identify as black is not a celebration of the voluptuous black female body; rather, it is an appropria-tion of a body image that black women have long embraced.

The participants responded to this development in the United States with some despondency, but also anger. They are very proprietary of the butt, as it gives black women (and Latinas) a body image that is theirs and allows them to exist outside the confines of white beauty ideals. By now including it in mainstream white beauty discourses, U.S. white beauty sys-tems co-opt and neutralize the resistive potential of the derriere for black women. In addition, given the prerequisite of whiteness to participate in this celebration of bigger buttocks, this recent obsession with bigger butts actually reinforces the marginalization of thick black women. Since black women can never be white, their bigger bodies are perennially excluded from these positive readings and acceptance of the voluptuous body. On the other hand, the women also use this appropriation of the butt—and other body parts deemed "black," such as thick lips—as evidence of the importance of black women's bodies in white beauty discourses. Seeing women with their bodies, even if they are white women, validates their own buttocks and encourages them to celebrate their "deviant" body parts. For them the question becomes, if black women's bodies are so repulsive, why do white women and white culture continue to imitate and embody them or parts of them?

Conclusion

The voluptuous black female body is a way to speak back to Eurocentrism and challenge the normalcy of thinness. In this way, "a particular brand of whiteness is disrupted" as both "ideal beauty and sexual desirability are mapped onto the curvaceous, ethnically marked female body" (Durham 2012, 37). However, there are real, material consequences to pursuing this ideal. Durham says that black women who style their hair in ways associated with the working class willfully put themselves in harm's way. Similarly, black women who embody voluptuousness run the risk of further marginalization because of how they are perceived in dominant white spaces. Therefore, it is worth recognizing and interrogating the ways in which the thick black woman ideology is mobilized in white-supremacist societies to justify the devaluation of black women in modern spaces.[4] Given the continued use of voluptuous bodies to promote anti-black-woman ideologies and practices, our work should be to not only create an alternative to thinness but also to encourage the *queering* of body politics. According to Kimberly Springer, "Queerness . . . is not an identity, but a position. We can use 'queer' as a verb instead of a noun. Queer is not someone or something to be treated. Queer is something that we can *do*" (2012; emphasis in original).

The queering of body politics means recognizing that body politics is a sociopolitical system that cannot be dismantled solely through personal affirmations and individual empowerment; it requires a collective ontological shift. The queering of body politics also means realizing that beauty ideals and constructions can be modern means of racial stratification. Body image and beauty discourses are subtle ways of maintaining the racial structures that foster the marginalization of black women in economic, social, and political spaces. Therefore, we cannot challenge old and new racism without simultaneously confronting the role of beauty politics in these systems. In other words, normative body aesthetics of black women can help to prop up white supremacy and need to become a more significant part of the work of black feminisms. Finally, to queer black women's body politics is to resist creating and perpetuating a singular idea of beauty. We have to collectively move toward thinking about black women's bodies on a continuum rather than in exclusive categories; we must dismantle all forms of normative body standards and promote inclusion of and equity for all body types.

Notes

1. Adapted from *Romance with Voluptuousness: Caribbean Women and Thick Bodies in the United States* by Kamille Gentles-Peart by permission of the University of Nebraska Press. Copyright 2016 by the Board of Regents of the University of Nebraska.

2. It is important to recognize that not all voluptuous black female bodies are celebrated in the Caribbean. For example, black women of low socioeconomic status with voluptuous bodies—such as the higglers in Kingston, Jamaica (Brown-Glaude 2011), the dancehall queens (Cooper 2004), or the big women who revel in Trinidad's carnival (Barnes 2000)—are viewed negatively in middle-class black Caribbean societies. In addition, fat and dark-skinned black women continue to be marginalized (Shaw 2005; Charles 2010; Hope 2011).

3. I use variations of the terms "white supremacy" and "anti-black-woman" to focus attention on a particular ideology and its practices—rather than specific locations and groups—which can exist and manifest in any community. This helps to avoid the perception of a singular black and a singular white community.

4. While not directly engaged in this paper, we should also note that this ideology and its corollaries are not only racist but also heterosexist as they racialize black women and assume their heterosexuality.

Kamille Gentles-Peart is an interdisciplinary cultural scholar whose scholarship engages and contributes to critical discourses of race, gender, and the African diaspora. Her work interrogates the manifold ways in which power manifests itself in the lived realities of black women and how black women make meaning in the context of race and gender hegemonies. Her research specifically focuses on black Caribbean immigrant women in the United States and their negotiations of various systems of power. She can be reached at kgentles-peart@rwu.edu.

Works Cited

Alexander, Simone A. James. 2014. *African Diasporic Women's Narratives: Politics of Resistance, Survival, and Citizenship*. Gainesville: University Press of Florida.

Austin, Regina. 1995. "Sapphire Bound!" In *Critical Race Theory: The Key Writings That Formed the Movement*, edited by Kimberlé Crenshaw, Neil Gotanda, Gary Peller, and Kendall Thomas, 426–37. New York: New Press.

Bakare-Yusuf, Bibi. 2006. "Fabricating Identities: Survival and the Imagination in Jamaican Dancehall Culture." *Fashion Theory: The Journal of Dress, Body and Culture* 10 (4): 461–83.

Barnes, Natasha. 2000. "Body Talk: Notes on Women and Spectacle in Contemporary Carnival." *Small Axe* 4 (1): 93–105.

Beauboeuf-Lafontant, Tamara. 2003. "Strong and Large Black Women? Exploring Relationships Between Deviant Womanhood and Weight." *Gender and Society* 17 (1): 111–21.

Bhabha, Homi K. 1994. *The Location of Culture*. New York: Routledge.

Bogues, Anthony. 2002. "Politics, Nation and PostColony: Caribbean Inflections." *Small Axe* 6 (1): 1–30.

Bonilla-Silva, Eduardo. 2006. *Racism without Racists: Color-Blind Racism and the Persistence of Racial Inequality in America*. Lanham, MD: Rowman & Littlefield.

———. 2003. "'New Racism,' Color-Blind Racism and the Future of Whiteness in America." In *White Out: The Continuing Significance of Racism*, edited by Ashley "Woody" Doane and Eduardo Bonilla-Silva, 271–84. New York: Routledge.

Brown-Glaude, Winnifred. 2011. *Higglers in Kingston: Women's Informal Work in Jamaica*. Nashville, TN: Vanderbilt University Press.

Charles, Christopher A. D. 2010. "Skin Bleaching in Jamaica: Self-Esteem, Racial Self-Esteem, and Black Identity Transactions." *Caribbean Journal of Psychology* 3 (1): 25–39.

Cooper, Carolyn. 2004. *Sound Clash: Jamaican Dancehall Culture At Large*. New York: Palgrave Macmillan.

Crenshaw, Kimberlé Williams. 1995. "Mapping the Margins: Intersectionality, Identity Politics, and Violence Against Women of Color." In *Critical Race Theory: The Key Writings That Formed the Movement*, edited by Kimberlé Crenshaw, Neil Gotanda, Gary Peller, and Kendall Thomas, 426–37. New York: New Press.

Durham, Aisha. 2012. "'Check On It' Beyoncé, Southern Booty, and Black Femininities in Music Video." *Feminist Media Studies* 12 (1): 35–49.

Gentles-Peart, Kamille. 2016. *Romance with Voluptuousness: Caribbean Women and Thick Bodies in the United States*. Lincoln: University of Nebraska Press.

Hill Collins, Patricia. 2000. *Black Feminist Thought: Knowledge, Consciousness, and the Politics of Empowerment*. New York: Routledge.

Hoberman, John. 1997. *Darwin's Athletes: How Sports Has Damaged Black America and Preserved the Myth of Race*. Boston: Mariner Books.

Hobson, Janell. 2003. "The 'Batty' Politic: Toward an Aesthetic of the Black Female Body." *Hypatia* 18 (4): 87–105.

Hope, Donna P. 2011. "From *Browning* to *Cake Soap*: Popular Debates on Skin Bleaching in the Jamaican Dancehall." *Journal of Pan African Studies* 4 (4): 165–94.

Lubiano, Wahneema. 1992. "Black Ladies, Welfare Queens, and State Minstrels: Ideological War by Narrative Means." In *Race-ing Justice, En-Gendering Power*, edited by Toni Morrison, 323–63. New York: Pantheon.

Meeks, Brian. 2000. *Narratives of Resistance: Jamaica, Trinidad, the Caribbean*. Kingston, Jamaica: University of the West Indies Press.

Morgan, Jennifer L. 1997. "'Some Could Suckle over Their Shoulder': Male Travelers, Female Bodies, and the Gendering of Racial Ideology, 1500–1770." *The William and Mary Quarterly* 54 (1): 167–92.

Sharpe, Jenny. 2002. *Ghosts of Slavery: A Literary Archaeology of Black Women's Lives*. Minneapolis: University of Minnesota Press.

Shaw, Andrea Elizabeth. 2005. *The Embodiment of Disobedience: Fat Black Women's Unruly Political Bodies*. Oxford: Lexington Books.

Springer, Kimberly. 2012. "Queering Black Female Sexuality." In *Women's Voices, Feminist Visions*, edited by Susan Shaw and Janet Lee, 207–10. New York: McGraw-Hill.

Townsend Gilkes, Cheryl. 2001. *If It Wasn't for the Women . . . Black Women's Experience and Womanist Culture in Church and Community*. Maryknoll, NY: Orbis Books.

Trethewey, Angela. 1999. "Disciplined Bodies: Women's Embodied Identities at Work." *Organization Studies* 20 (3): 423–50.

United States Census Bureau. 2010. "Place of Birth for Foreign-Born Population in the United States." Accessed December 28, 2017. http://metrolina.org/wp/wp-content/uploads/2012/07/Place-of-Birth-for-Foreign-Born-Population-in-Charlotte.pdf.

Subject/Object/Body: Recent Perspectives on Beauty and Aesthetics in Gender Studies

Uri McMillan's *Embodied Avatars: Genealogies of Black Feminist Art and Performance*, New York: NYU Press, 2015

Sherri Irvin's *Body Aesthetics*, Oxford: Oxford University Press, 2016

Meeta Rani Jha's *The Global Beauty Industry: Colorism, Racism, and the National Body*, New York: Routledge, 2016

Freda Fair

In their 1977 black feminist statement, the Combahee River Collective calls attention to beauty as a regime of regulation that disciplines belonging. The Collective offers the formulation "smart-ugly" to articulate recognition and marginality as deeply racialized, gendered, and sexualized (2000, 268). Taking the body as central to social interpretation from the standpoint of black lesbian positionality, smart-ugly serves as an instructive point from which to highlight the contributions of three recent books that advance theories of beauty and aesthetics with a primary focus on the body: Uri McMillan's *Embodied Avatars: Genealogies of Black Feminist Art and Performance*, *Body Aesthetics* edited by Sherri Irvin, and *The Global Beauty Industry: Colorism, Racism, and the National Body* by Meeta Rani Jha. Like the Combahee River Collective's statement, all three books interrogate the cultural capital attributed to beauty and aesthetics sutured to the body. Working through performance studies, visual cultural studies, affect studies, women of color feminism, transnational feminism, critiques of capitalism and neoliberalism, sports studies, and food studies among other approaches, the authors recast the body as pliable subject and object. Readers seeking nuanced interdisciplinary approaches to the study of embodiment will value the diverse perspectives each book offers.

The body itself is elaborated as a primary site of economic, cultural, and political inquiry as the authors mobilize formulations such as "performing objecthood" to index the bodily risks taken by black women performers (McMillan, 7), "subject and object of the gaze" to refer to the aesthetic

WSQ: Women's Studies Quarterly **46**: 1 & 2 (Spring/Summer 2018)

assessment of the body (Irvin, 1), and "beauty capital" signaling the distribution of contradictory social rewards assigned to the body as it circulates within the exchange relations of transnational capitalism (Jha, 4). In this review, I trace the body as it takes shape in each book to examine how the relationship between subject and object is reworked toward varying ends. Feminist thought has distinguished subject and object positions in part to challenge biological determinism and sexual objectification. The positionality of the body with respect to the subject-object relation undergirds the theories of aesthetics and the critiques of beauty put forth by McMillan, Irvin and the other contributors in *Body Aesthetics*, and Jha.[1] McMillan argues for the body as a site for black women to literally transform the body into object for the purpose of challenging social and political exclusion. Jha addresses object status by attending to individual and institutional practices of objectification that govern access to the contradictory rewards of neoliberal beauty markets. While Irvin's introduction accounts for object status less as a measure of performative capacity and more with respect to questions of bodily assessment.

The authors labor in the vein of what Samantha Frost, referencing Anne Fausto-Sterling, describes as the challenge to the "unidirectional model of causation" that signals the living body's implication in its own construction (2011, 69–70). For example, Jha, drawing on Inderpal Grewal, points to the "white-savior narrative" as oppressive while highlighting that it primarily operates by assigning object status to women in the Global South. Jha attends to white-savior objectification as it disarms women of color while securing an agential subjectivity for white Western liberal feminists: "Feminine whiteness is valorized at the cost of objectifying women from developing nations as passive" (55). While Jha's critique demonstrates the politically fraught dynamics of objectified bodily passivity in the transnational beauty economies that condition subjective potentiality, McMillan ardently argues for objecthood as a liberatory pathway toward subjectivity for black women performers particularly Joice Heth, Ellen Craft, Adrian Piper, Howardena Pindell, and Nicki Minaj. *Embodied Avatars* advances a sharp and skillful retelling of the history of black embodiment as one dependent on artful practices of escape and disappearance vis-à-vis object status.

McMillan invites us to consider embodied self-alienation as a strategy to fashion self-determination. For McMillan object status is made meaningful through the act of "performing objecthood"—a strategy of resistance deployed by black women cultural workers who mobilize "the tactics and aesthetics of the avatar" (11). The avatar registers black women's disarticulation from normative femaleness, what Hortense Spillers has previously theorized as the distinction between "body" and "flesh" (1987, 67). Black women performers utilize the body as performative material that integrates form and content, further destabilizing the distinction between subject and object. The body is staged as a series of actions referencing Craft's "utilitarian bodily acts" performed to secure freedom from slavery during the nineteenth century, while Piper's performances articulate "aesthetics" as a lens that accounts for questions of "style and form" that have been problematically understood as distinct from ideological concerns even as they reflect Piper's desire to "escape aesthetic and identity strictures" while emphasizing "concept over material" (104–7).

Published in the Routledge series "Framing Twenty-First Century Social Issues," *The Global Beauty Industry* is written accessibly and offers an interdisciplinary approach to the study of beauty as a site of economic and social power. Jha traces beauty politics through the Black Is Beautiful movement in the United States, the popularization of skin-lighting products and beauty pageants in India, and cosmetic surgery economies and beauty media in China to illuminate the ways in which women of color exercise subjectivity through both resistance to and incorporation into Western beauty norms. Jha's transnational feminist approach details the processes by which "beauty can be converted into forms of social, economic, and symbolic power that devalue . . . some physical features while idealizing and privileging others." Further, beauty serves as a "marker of cultural and moral superiority in a hierarchy of racialized difference" where whiteness is hegemonic (5). As Jha describes, beauty "consumption offers women the means to commodify and consume femininity to gain status, validation, and identity" (2). Jha accounts for the complex ways in which beauty practices might be embraced toward social advancement, resistance to dominant ideology, or to experience pleasure in social rituals. Similar to *Body Aesthetics*, Jha demonstrates the ways in which beauty judgement bolsters superiority hierarchies that function simultaneously as ontological and moral.

Body Aesthetics—organized into four parts: Representation, Look, Performance, and Practice—interrogates beauty as "moral comportment" and "aesthetic judgement" as it theorizes the body as a valid category of philosophical inquiry. Irvin's introduction highlights Yuriko Saito's essay

"Body Aesthetics and the Cultivation of Moral Virtues" to articulate aesthetics as "the style and manner with which we act" that "consists of the perceptible qualities of our actions, including how they look, feel, and sound" (7). Irvin explains that in "practices of bodily movement and performance" morality and aesthetics intersect. "The moral quality of our actions lies not just in what we do, but in how we do it—or, to put it differently, how we do something is part of what we do, not separable from it" (7). In *Body Aesthetics* questions of "style and manner" extend to uncommon bodily domains such as the act of eating in the essay "Somaesthetics and the Fine Art of Eating" by Richard Shusterman and to questions of representation as Maria del Guadalupe Davidson examines in "Black Silhouettes on White Walls: Kara Walker's Magic Lantern."

While considerations related to the style and manner of actions surface in *The Global Beauty Industry*, beauty as a lens instead orients the how and what of bodily interpretation. Beauty is theorized by Jha as the institutionalization of Eurocentric appearance norms, and as "the commodification of women's bodies" which essentializes and accentuates "their sexual differences" (2). Jha highlights the example of the 2004 Miss Artificial Beauty Pageant in China, the first beauty pageant to base contestant eligibility on plastic surgery procurement. The pageant's evaluation of beauty hinged primarily on the logic of appearance as commodity rather than the idea that beauty "radiates" outward from a natural internal place as is interrogated by Irvin. The explicit investment in artifice over "realness" further complicates subject and object entanglements with regard to embodied beauty. Whereas in *Embodied Avatars* questions of emanating beauty lose traction as primary evaluative criteria for performances that fuse art, life, and survival. The authors' perspectives coalesce around subject, object, and body as subject and object relations are reworked to argue for self-determination through objecthood, to posit embodiment as a legitimate site of philosophical attention, and to interrogate neoliberal beauty politics.

Freda Fair is assistant professor of gender studies at Indiana University, Bloomington. Freda's research centers on questions of U.S. black gender and sexual difference, labor, regionality, and queer cultural production. Freda can be reached at ffair@iu.edu.

Notes

1. While in conversation, the authors address the convergence of race, sexuality, gender, and other categories of difference in related but distinct ways. For instance, while some of the essays in the *Body Aesthetics* collection engage women of color feminism through explicit attention to intersectionality, Jha positions difference feminisms and black feminism in the "third-wave" alongside "postfeminism":

   > Second-wave feminism from the 1960s to the mid 80s focused on women's bodies as a site of patriarchal control; and third-wave feminism challenges second-wave feminism's universal category of "woman," extending a feminism of difference combined with the dissolution of sex-gender distinctions. Third-wave feminism has also been theorized as postfeminism, which includes multiple kinds of feminist ideas such as black feminism, postcolonial and Third World feminisms, feminist cultural and media critiques, and queer and transgender feminisms. (16)

   By contrast, McMillan's discussion of black women artists engages a genealogy of women of color feminism that is in conversation with Becky Thompson (2002), Roderick Ferguson (2004), and Grace Kyungwon Hong (2006) and resists and recasts the waves paradigm to unsettle the periodization of the second wave by insisting on a focus on women of color and multiracial feminisms throughout the 1960s, 1970s, and the 1980s. Although noting this delineation of the second wave, Jha more closely aligns the emergence of multiaxis critique—what in the early 1990s Kimberlé Crenshaw termed intersectionality—with the third wave (19–21).

Works Cited

Combahee River Collective. 2000. "The Combahee River Collective Statement." In *Home Girls: A Black Feminist Anthology*, edited by Barbara Smith, 264–74. New Brunswick, NJ: Rutgers University Press.

Crenshaw, Kimberlé. 1991. "Mapping the Margins: Intersectionality, Identity Politics, and Violence against Women of Color." *Stanford Law Review* 43 (6): 1241–99.

Ferguson, Roderick. 2004. *Aberrations in Black: Toward a Queer of Color Critique.* Minneapolis: University of Minnesota Press.

Frost, Samantha. 2011. "The Implications of the New Materialisms for Feminist Epistemology." In *Feminist Epistemology and Philosophy of Science: Power in Knowledge*, edited by Heidi E. Grasswick, 69–83. New York: Springer.

Hong, Grace Kyungwon. 2006. *The Ruptures of American Capital: Women of Color Feminism and the Culture of Immigrant Labor.* Minneapolis: University of Minnesota Press.

Spillers, Hortense. 1987. "Mama's Baby, Papa's Maybe: An American Grammar Book." *Diacritics* 17 (2): 64–81.

Thompson, Becky. 2002. "Multiracial Feminism: Recasting the Chronology of Second Wave Feminism." *Feminist Studies* 28 (2): 337–60.

A Brief History of Beauty

Nina Sharma

"Don't tell anyone, but the boys in school tease me for my mustache," said my nine-year-old niece.

"I'm sorry. You know that just means they are insecure."

"Oh. Well then I feel bad for them."

"Did you tell your parents?"

"If I tell them, they will say wax it. I don't want to. Did it ever happen to you?"

"Yes, boys and girls. And you know what, those same boys would ask me out on dates years later."

"Did you go?"

"No."

"That's good."

I lied. Those boys didn't ask me out. Long after the blond girl stopped taunting "Amazon woman" at my eleven-year-old hairy legs, thick pubic, armpit, and upper-lip hair in the shower after gym, long after I started going to the waxing lady working out of the back of a sari shop and then to the many others waxers and waxing parlors that cropped up in my town afterwards, the boys didn't ask me out.

I lived the kind of life I imagined I was supposed to live. Not the life of the ugly, but of the not-as-beautiful. I was the funny one. The thinker. The one generous with money, time, and patience, infinite patience for white suburban teens especially.

At home, my father would twist his face so it lost all symmetry. The lips a disheveled pout, one eyebrow slanting up and the other down, head cocked to the side. He put on a gruff voice.

This was my mother. This was how he saw his wife.

WSQ: Women's Studies Quarterly 46: 1 & 2 (Spring/Summer 2018) © 2018 by Nina Sharma. All rights reserved.

Sometimes there was no twisted face. There was just him watching some movie with a pretty woman saying, "I should have married a woman like that, not you."

I would let out a laugh—a full-throated "Julia Roberts in *Pretty Woman*" type of cackle, an unabashed laugh, a sexy laugh, a laugh like my life depended on it.

When I was a toddler, my older sisters lined me up with stuffed animals, placing me in the center. "We'd pretend you were our doll."

At twelve I began to go to a child psychiatrist, I was worried about what was real and what was a picture—scared of movie monsters in particular. I just wanted to cry. My father drove me home. "You are like the story of the ugly duckling," he said to comfort me.

For my thirteenth birthday, the blond girl who called me "Amazon woman" bought me lingerie, a see-through maroon Calvin Klein bra-and-panty set. She demanded to know which boy I liked.

I was reluctant to tell her about the boy. It was not a secret as much as it was an issue of permission. *Am I allowed to be that kind of girl? The one with a romance life, with a body?*

That blond girl would grow all of her hair out, dye her hair blue, and begin to ardently follow white-boy-hippie-bands like Phish.

I wore a low-cut dress from a vintage shop to junior prom. I loved myself in it. Next year, the white girls would take me shopping at Macy's, where they'd find me a "proper gown," as they put it.

A white boy reluctantly took me to senior prom. I was going to go alone; our friends suggested we pair up. We dated through my first year of college.

"Who do you love more, him or me?" my father demanded once over the phone. I burst into tears; he just yelled the question louder. "Who do you love more, him or me?"

At the start of my sophomore year, I had a manic break. I walked around campus for twenty-four hours straight asking questions and expressing worries to any passing stranger. My mom drove me back to New Jersey from Rhode Island. "Where are we going?" I asked when I saw her turning off of the expected route. We were going to the salon. I had not slept in days and the last shower I took was before I went in-patient. "I can't have you looking like this if I want to introduce to suitable boys."

When Babita raked a thread across me, my whiskers came undone from their roots.

That night I cut my long curly hair short with a pair of desk scissors. My mother came into the room and cried.

Waking up in a hospital bed after the first time I tried to kill myself, with pills, I saw my mother with a hairbrush in her hand.

Felt the tug of the hairbrush trying to make a part out of my curly hair.

Felt the sting of the hair-straightening formaldehyde trying to deaden the curls.

Felt the crack and thaw of a burn scar on the lip when the wax was too hot.

Felt the thread string like an incessant paper cut, as grating as the woman who would make conversation saying, "You are Punjabi? Aren't Punjabis cheap?"

I gained forty pounds on one medication, acne on another, lost my appetite on one more—around that time I straightened my hair.

My Dad's macho friend said, "Wow, what beautiful eyebrows on this girl."

A friend's mother said, "You are beautiful but you do not know it yet."

My oldest sister said, "I wish I could take an eraser to your face, to your acne marks."

When I returned to school, another school, I wore my hair long and straight and spent two hours every few weeks in a waxing parlor and nail salon getting dehaired and shiny-fingered. After a night out, I tried to hail a cab with two white women. "Caroline should do it, she's prettier," Lisa said to me.

In my thirties, I text this new guy I started dating:

"I'll go with you. I'll be that something nice on your arm."

"Someone," he texted back, "You'll be that someone beautiful with me."

On the eve of my wedding to this man, my oldest sister asks me, "Nina, if he's black, then why is his skin so light?" I begin to cry. "Does he have Europeans in his blood?" I cry louder. "I'm only asking how he has Europeans in his blood, geez." My middle sister comes in running, scolding our elder sister: "Don't talk to her like that! Hello! Bipolar disorder!" she says without looking at my face.

Nina Sharma's work has appeared in publications such as the *Asian American Literary Review*, *Blueshift Journal*, *Longreads*, and the *Margins*. She currently writes, teaches, and does improv in New York City. She can be reached at sharma.nina@gmail.com.

PART V. **"AN UNSHAMED CLAIM TO BEAUTY IN THE FACE OF INVISIBILITY": REVISITING SINS INVALID**

Ten Principles of Disability Justice[1]

Patricia Berne
With the support of Aurora Levins Morales and David Langstaff,
and on behalf of Sins Invalid

From within Sins Invalid, where we incubate both the framework and practice of Disability Justice, this burgeoning framework has ten (10) principles, each offering new opportunities for movement builders:

1. Intersectionality. We know that each person has multiple identities, and that each identity can be a site of privilege or oppression. The mechanical workings of oppression and how they output shift depending upon the characteristics of any given institutional or interpersonal interaction; the very experience of disability itself is being shaped by race, gender, class, gender expression, historical moment, relationship to colonization, and more.

2. Leadership of Those Most Impacted. We know ableism exists in the context of other historical systemic oppressions. We know to truly have liberation we must be led by those who know the most about these systems and how they work.

3. Anti-Capitalist Politic. We are anti-capitalist as the very nature of our body/minds resist conforming to a capitalist "normative" level of production. We don't believe human worth is dependent on what and how much a person can produce. We critique a concept of "labor" as defined by able-bodied supremacy, white supremacy, and gender normativity. We understand capitalism to be a system that promotes private wealth accumulation for some at the expense of others.

4. Cross-Movement Solidarity. Necessarily cross-movement, Disability Justice shifts how social justice movements understand disability and

WSQ: Women's Studies Quarterly 46: 1 & 2 (Spring/Summer 2018) © 2018 by Patricia Berne, David Langstaff, and Aurora Levins Morales, on behalf of Sins Invalid. All rights reserved.

contextualize ableism, lending itself toward a united front politic.

5. Recognizing Wholeness. We value our people as they are, for who they are, and understand that people have inherent worth outside of capitalist notions of productivity. Each person is full of history and life experience. Each person has an internal experience composed of their own thoughts, sensations, emotions, fantasies, perceptions, and idiosyncrasies. Disabled people are whole people.

6. Sustainability. We pace ourselves, individually and collectively, to be sustained long-term. We value the teachings of our lives and bodies. We understand that our embodied experience is a critical guide and reference pointing us toward justice and liberation.

7. Commitment to Cross-Disability Solidarity. We value and honor the insights and participation of all of our community members. We are committed to breaking down ableist/patriarchal/racist/classed isolation between people with physical impairments, people who identify as "sick" or are chronically ill, "psych" survivors, and those who identify as "crazy," neurodiverse people, people with cognitive impairments, and people who are of a sensory minority, as we understand that isolation ultimately undermines collective liberation.

8. Interdependence. Before the massive colonial project of Western European expansion, we understood the nature of interdependence within our communities. We see the liberation of all living systems and the land as integral to the liberation of our own communities, as we all share one planet. We attempt to meet each other's needs as we build toward liberation, without always reaching for state solutions which can readily extend its control further over our lives.

9. Collective Access. As brown/black and queer crips, we bring flexibility and creative nuance to engage with each other. We create and explore new ways of doing things that go beyond able-bodied/minded normativity. Access needs aren't shameful—we all have various capacities which function differently in various environments. Access needs can be articulated within a community and met privately or through a collective, depending upon an individual's needs, desires, and the capacity of the group. We can share responsibility for our access needs, we can ask that our needs be met without compromising our integrity, we can balance autonomy while being in community, we can be unafraid of our vulnerabilities knowing our strengths are respected.

10. Collective Liberation. How do we move together as people with mixed abilities, multiracial, multi-gendered, mixed class, across the orientation spectrum—where no body/mind is left behind?

This is Disability Justice, an honoring of the longstanding legacies of resilience and resistance which are the inheritance of all of us whose bodies or minds will not conform. Disability Justice is not yet a broad-based popular movement. Disability Justice is a vision and practice of a *yet-to-be*, a map that we create with our ancestors and our great grandchildren onward, in the width and depth of our multiplicities and histories, a movement towards a world in which every body and mind is known as beautiful.

Patricia Berne is cofounder and executive director of Sins Invalid, and has a professional background in mental health support to survivors of violence. A Japanese Haitian queer disabled woman, she sees her work to create "liberated zones" for marginalized voices. She can be reached at pattyberne@sinsinvalid.org.

David Langstaff is a Detroit-based writer, radical organizer, coproducer of Rustbelt Abolition Radio, and former program manager of Sins Invalid. He has been published in *Interface, Abolition, Counterpunch*, and *The Palestine Chronicle*. He can be reached at undercommoner@gmail.com.

Aurora Levins Morales is an internationally known Puerto Rican Jewish feminist writer and audio artist living with multiple disabilities. She is the author of six books, including *Kindling: Writings on the Body*. She lives in a chemically accessible tiny house on wheels in Northern California. She can be reached at aurora@historica.us.

Sins Invalid is a performance project on disability and sexuality that incubates and celebrates artists with disabilities, centralizing artists of color and queer and gendervariant artists as communities who have been historically marginalized from social discourse. Visit http://www.sinsinvalid.org/ or email at info@sinsinvalid.org.

Notes

1. Reprinted from *Skin, Tooth and Bone: The Basis for Movement Is Our People, a Disability Justice Primer* (2016).

FIG. 1. Micah Bazant with Sins Invalid, *This Is Disability Justice*. Courtesy of Micah Bazant and Sins Invalid.

Reclaiming and Honoring:
Sins Invalid's Cultivation of Crip Beauty

Shayda Kafai

Beauty can be expansive and rhythmic. Its standards can shift, stretching outward to include and honor all of our "bodyminds." I stress *can* here because beauty is still imbued with overwhelming power and privilege. Despite our current feminist landscape of plurality and intersectionality, for most of us, beauty is still a place of restricted access and pain. There are so many people, myself included, who struggle to actively rewrite the toxic hold beauty has own our own lives. At the same time, this struggle is supported by our communities who work in earnest to help us unlearn the connotations of heteropatriarchy and whiteness that rigidly define and discipline beauty's borders. The collective work of the body positivity and fat liberation movements, particularly in communities of color, has helped to expand the meanings of beauty beyond the normative image of thinness and whiteness.[1]

Feminism has continued this work by exploring the sexist, racist, colonized, and sizest aspects of beauty; however, more recently, disability studies has intersected with feminism and has offered an additional lens through which we can view beauty: ableism. As an intersecting system of oppressions, ableism reinforces the idea that the nondisabled bodymind is "natural" and "normal" and that any deviation from the standard of nondisability is "abnormal" and needs to be fixed or cured.

Ableism reinforces beauty in the most perversely subtle ways. The normatively beautiful body, we are taught, has two arms and two legs. It is proportioned, balanced, and, if anything, is hyper-nondisabled in its appearance and mannerisms. In fact, disabled models and mannequins have just recently begun to enter into our visual lexicon of what beauty can look

WSQ: Women's Studies Quarterly 46: 1 & 2 (Spring/Summer 2018) © 2018 by Shayda Kafai. All rights reserved.

like and although they are most necessary, they too, at times, still replicate normative depictions of what our Western culture deems beautiful.[2]

Crip[3] artists and activists, along with disability studies scholars, have dedicated themselves to rewriting what beauty means in disability culture. Within the last eleven years, the San Francisco Bay Area–based performance project Sins Invalid, in particular, has guided and transformed the conversations surrounding crip beauty. As a performance project that holds space for queer and gender nonconforming, crip folks of color to make art and activism since 2006, Sins Invalid has birthed a definition of beauty that embraces the rolling, drooling, stimming, signing, mad magic of all our bodyminds.

The most unique aspect of Sins Invalid's community, for me, is how they move us beyond the traditional, limiting rhetoric of beauty. They instead create crip beauty, an expression of the communal honoring of crip bodyminds.[4] Crip beauty fractures the ableist assumption that beauty is reserved for the nondisabled bodymind. It urges that there is pleasure and eroticism in bearing witness to disability, in cultivating a space where bodyminds that are traditionally forced into invisibility can gather together. Sins Invalid's fostering of crip beauty challenges the long and painful history of the institutionalization of disabled folks. Their tagline, "An unshamed claim to beauty in the face of invisibility," references this history, reinforcing the fact that disabled folks will no longer exist in isolation or in invisibility. The visibility and public nature of crip beauty reminds us that disability is something to celebrate and not something to hide.

Throughout their twelve years of disability justice activism,[5] evenings of performance art, and community workshops, Sins Invalid has created a discursive bodymind that liberates beauty from the isolating and painful restrictions of ableism, heterosexism, patriarchy, and racism. In speaking about beauty, Sins Invalid cofounder Patty Berne shares that "part of [our work] is to liberate [the] idea of beauty from . . . a vision that's rooted in profit-driven motive[s]. Beauty is much more sacred than what it's been reduced to. . . . One of the catch phrases we [in Sins Invalid] have is that beauty always, always recognizes itself" (Allen 2013). In spaces of collectivity and activist art-making, Sins Invalid cultivates an environment where queer, crip folks of color can be made visible again in their beauty. Here, we can *crip* beauty, an action that empowers communities who previously were unable to access beauty to reclaim and augment its parameters, rendering beauty fluid and malleable for all of our bodyminds. In this way, crip beauty becomes a self-made and resilient political expression.

Many of Sins Invalid's performance artists create work that makes them once again visible to and aware of the inherent beauty of their own bodyminds. They carry with them the realization that the intersectional oppressions of beauty can be undone at their root. Holding onto Berne's reading of beauty as sacred and that which has the potential to recognize itself outside of normativity, Sins Invalid's manifestation of crip beauty is rebellious and assertive; it is presence and acceptance. Crip beauty says, you are here despite the violence of eugenics and patriarchy, despite all the institutions that say you should not own this word: *beauty*.

Crip beauty is queer, fat, amputee musician Nomy Lamm (2016) performing against a background of bright fuchsia. She is naked and sitting behind a rectangular piece of beige lace that she sways back and forth. Repeatedly she sings, "Stay open, open to the world." She concludes her piece reminding us to "fee[d] all who come near the most vibrant, brightest, undeniable truths." For Lamm, crip beauty communicates the disabled bodymind as luscious, open, vulnerable, and unafraid. At the end of her song, Lamm drops the lace and reveals her body to the audience, full-figured and nude, her arms reaching skyward. There is no room for body shaming here, for normative guidelines. Lamm teaches us that crip beauty embraces what we are taught to hide.

For Maria Palacios (2008), a crip Latina poet whose performances reposition crip women of color beyond ableism's norms, crip beauty is an empowered embodiment of crip femininity. As her performance begins, Maria sits in her wheelchair. She wears a long, black skirt with a flowing shirt that exposes her left shoulder. Looking toward the audience, she says, "I used to hate my body, cringe at the thought of a mirror, deformities staring at me." Her performance acknowledges the emotional riptide that accompanies the conflation of beauty and nondisability. With the unlearning Palacios guides us through as she sits facing the mirror, she moves toward a full-hearted ownership of her crip body. For Palacios, crip beauty is a verb, a radical reclaiming of the self.

Crip beauty is Lateef McLeod (2016), a black crip poet and activist, walking on stage supported by a man who stands behind him. McLeod wears a white suit and walks with rigidity. As he points, smiles, and shifts his body weight, the narrator reads his poem: "My children, you are beautifully and wonderfully made. . . . Don't be fooled . . . you were not a mistake. I molded and crafted your bodies as masterpieces." McLeod's steps are quietly echoed by a conga drum. His performance of crip beauty is one of interdependence and support, visibility of a disabled body of color whose bodymind exists not in error, but just exactly as it should.

These moments are brief excerpts from Sins Invalid's performances. They express a range of what crip beauty looks like and how it shifts normative framings of beauty. As an audience member, these performances urge me toward radical bodymind love, reminding me that crip beauty is political and self-crafted, that it is about more than just appearance. Most critically, Sins Invalid's works extend feminism's call to decenter and disrupt the normative narratives that rigidly define beauty. Sins Invalid serves as a reminder, as an intervention, that demands feminism acknowledge disability as an identity, as a part of its plurality. To claim stake to crip beauty, here, becomes a rising of unheard voices: deliberate, present, and always, always unshamed.

Shayda Kafai is currently a lecturer in the Ethnic and Women's Studies Department at California State University, Pomona. As a queer, disabled woman of color, she is committed to exploring the numerous ways we can reclaim our bodies from intersecting systems of oppression. Her email is skafai@cpp.edu.

Notes

1. Many, often intersecting, communities are involved with reshaping the beauty ideals in the United States. The body positivity movement, the Health at Every Size Movement, and fat studies in general have all worked together to expand the dialogue surrounding beauty. Campaigns by feminists of color like Nalgona Positivity Pride and the online disability campaign This Is What Disability Looks Like, created by Bethany Stevens, are intersecting examples.

2. The disability organization Pro Infirmis created and displayed mannequins based on the bodies of folks with physical disabilities in Zurich in 2013. Although beauty and access to beauty culture is equally important for disabled and nondisabled folks, the culture of normative beauty negatively affects disabled folks. For example, while physically disabled folks did appear on the runway at the 2015 New York Fashion Week, they reinforced normative beauty standards of thinness and attractiveness.

3. Some folks in the disability community are choosing to define as "crip" instead of "disabled" because disabled, for some, reaffirms a medicalized origin while crip "describes more of the politics and the culture where a lived experience of disability is centered" ("Interview with Sins Invalid on Disability Justice" n.p.). A shortened version of the derogatory term "crippled," crip is an appropriated, empowered term. It also serves to strongly push against gender normativity, as it addresses the centering of queerness within the disability community. For this reason, many of the folks involved with Sins Invalid identify as crip as opposed to disabled. In this piece, I use the terms "crip" and "disability" interchangeably.

4. This is a term I have created to explore how Sins Invalid negotiates and expands the meanings of beauty from a disability justice context.

5. Disability justice is considered by some to be the second wave of the disability rights movement. Created in 2005 by queer, crip people of color—particularly Patty Berne, Stacey Milbern, and Mia Mingus—this framework calls for the intersectionality of disability activism.

Works Cited

Allen, D. 2013. "Liberating Beauty: A Conversation with Sins Invalid's Patty Berne." *The Body Connected* (blog), October 6. Accessed July 5, 2017. https://thebodyconnected.com/2013/10/06/liberating-beauty-a-conversation-with-sins-invalids-patty-berne/.

"Interview with Sins Invalid on Disability Justice Theory & Praxis." *Feminist and Queer Disability Politics* (blog), April 25. Accessed July 5, 2017.

Lamm, Nomy. 2016. *Birthing, Dying, Becoming Crip Wisdom*. ODC Theater, San Francisco. October 15, 2017.

McLeod, Lateef. 2016. *Birthing, Dying, Becoming Crip Wisdom*. ODC Theater, San Francisco. October 15, 2017.

Palacios, Maria. 2008. *Testimony*. Sins Invalid. Brava Theater, San Francisco. September 5, 2008.

FIG. 1. Neve Be(ast) and Antoine Hunter perform in Sins Invalid, 2016. Photo by Richard Downing. Courtesy of Richard Downing and Sins Invalid.

Disability Justice and Beauty as a Liberatory Practice

Mordecai Cohen Ettinger

I have a firm and persistent belief—perhaps it is even a conviction, rooted in and in alignment with my vision for collective liberation—that all people hold the capacity to conceive of and experience beauty in a manner that *well* transcends that which we are conditioned into recognizing as beautiful by normative, twenty-first-century, United States societal standards. I posit that there exists a type of phenomenological overlay or precursor to the highly disciplined and disciplining modes of beauty that operate to glorify and legitimize the institutionalization and embodiment of white christian supremacist, ableist, heteropatriarchal, settler-colonial capitalism. This phenomenological process is "beauty as a thing in and of itself," an affect state and experience that even as it is always already socially, culturally, and historically conditioned and constructed—often as a means of control, conquest, and submission—is also something enduringly subjective and connected to expansive and positive states and possibilities.

The development of my own aesthetic and phenomenological sense of beauty, not unlike the development of my vision and analysis of collective liberation, have necessarily and indelibly been informed by the social movements of which I am a part. Through the works curated by Sins Invalid's annual performances featuring disabled artists and the grounding principles of disability justice that is masterfully conveyed in their 2016 disability justice primer, *Skin Teeth and Bone: The Basis of Movement Is Our People*, the extended Sins Invalid community—led by the founding executive director Patricia Berne, and many other staff and performers—have played a tremendous role in this development. I interpret and experience Sins Invalid's body of work and their incubation of the disability justice

WSQ: Women's Studies Quarterly 46: 1 & 2 (Spring/Summer 2018) © 2018 by Mordecai Cohen Ettinger.

movement as opening up a field of knowing, witnessing, and reclaiming beauty that is in and of itself a liberatory practice.

This type of beauty—intrinsically relational—is lived, breathed, shared, and cocreated. It can be accessed through communion with the vastness of our living breathing planet and nonhuman beings, the unique and irreplaceable intimacy of friends, lovers, family, and chosen kin, or through art. When collectively experiencing works of art like those in the annual curated Sins Invalid performances, liberatory beauty emerges adjacent to and entangled within normalizing and coercive performances of beauty. Yet these experiences live and breathe in resistance to them and are in close kinship with "truth," "awe," and "wonder." Here, I introduce truth, awe, and wonder, as phenomenologically lived and experienced, and perhaps, as such, they can only be fully known and understood through the practice of a lived and contemplated life supported by opportunities to touch in liberated zones/prefigurative worlds, like those generated through Sins Invalid's performances. Since time is so constrained and enclosed upon in late capitalism, especially for people with disabilities, I configure beauty as this contemplation and communion that also involves the liberation of time. This requires reclaiming interior space and imagination, in and of itself an act of beauty, sometimes subtle, sometimes silent, sometimes bold decolonization.

Capitalism and the matrices of oppression that support and enable it, inure us against the experience of beauty in and of itself, ultimately marginalizing and rendering "ugly"—worthy only of derision, rejection, abuse, (mis)use, and death—all who fail to service the perpetuation of white christian supremacist, heteropatriarchal, ableist capital, and often reduces beauty to a hypercommodified means to an end: domination. Following the analysis of Black feminist thought as articulated by Kimberlé Crenshaw, Sins Invalid envisions disability justice as centering intersectionality. Ableism is inherently always already white supremacist and heteropatriarchal. To undo ableism, we must see our collective liberation as inextricably connected. In disability justice, as proposed by Sins Invalid, movement towards conjoined liberation, a process which necessarily exposes and challenges ableism, transforms that which is ugly into beauty. No one and nothing is disposable.

From this lens, practices and performances that witness, know, encourage the recognition of one's own (nonnormative) crip beauty, and engage in what Sins Invalid announces pithy organizational description as an "unshamed claim to [that] beauty" constitute rebellion if not revolution. For if, as disabled people, our existence is resistance, then our insistence on our inherent beauty is always already liberation.

Sins Invalid reminds us that reclaiming beauty as a liberatory practice and acknowledging liberatory practices as constituting a unique and transformative beauty (re)instills in oppressed people the capacity to know and experience beauty within ourselves and one another freely; that is, to live in beauty unfettered from the obstacles, noise, and false conceptions of beauty foisted upon us to perpetuate settler-colonial capitalism. Excavating from our internal worlds all the space that internalized oppression has occupied—not merely in our psyches, but in our viscera, our veins, our sinew, and our nervous systems—brings with it a new sense of realness, a renewed sense of power to know our bodies as our own. Our shared crip communities are spaces in which we can see our beauty reflected back to us and magnify a spectrum of human ability and potential, all completely and utterly invaluable. Where shame and isolation once were, the beauty of interconnection, interdependency, and mutual recognition takes shape. From this emergent beautiful liberatory space, the grounds of collective justice and its possibility emerge.

Mordecai Cohen Ettinger is adjunct faculty at the California Institute of Integral Studies, where he teaches critical science, technology, and medicine studies. His research focuses on the neurobiology of the social nervous, trauma, historical trauma, and resilience. He is the author of the forthcoming book *We All Hold Up the Sky: Lessons in Health Justice for the 21st Century*. He can be reached at mettinger@ciis.edu.

Works Cited

Berne, Patricia, and Sins Invalid. 2016. *Skin, Tooth and Bone: The Basis for Movement Is Our People, a Disability Justice Primer*. Oakland, CA: Sins Invalid.

FIG. 1. Juba Kalamka and Leroy Moore perform in Sins Invalid, 2011. Photo by Richard Downing. Courtesy of Richard Downing and Sins Invalid.

"Beauty Always Recognizes Itself": A Roundtable on Sins Invalid

Patricia Berne, Jamal T. Lewis, Stacey Milbern, Malcolm Shanks, Alok Vaid-Menon, and Alice Wong

In August 2017, Natalie Havlin and Jillian M. Báez, coeditors of *WSQ: Beauty*, talked with Patricia Berne, Jamal T. Lewis, Stacey Milbern, Malcolm Shanks, Alok Vaid-Menon, and Alice Wong about the work of Sins Invalid and the relationship of beauty to disability justice. Since 2005, Sins Invalid has presented multidisciplinary performances by artists of color and queer and gender-variant artists with disabilities in the San Francisco Bay Area.

Natalie Havlin (NH): We are excited to host a discussion about Sins Invalid's approach to beauty and justice. Thank you for joining us. To start, we are interested in hearing how Sins Invalid's approach to storytelling as a way to create a collective vision of beauty and liberation has influenced your own work and thinking

Patricia Berne (PB): Sins Invalid intervenes into cultural landscapes engaging disability, gender, race, and sexuality, contextualizing beauty in *our* bodies and communities while debunking myths of beauty within ableist, white-supremacist, cispatriarchy. As marginalized peoples, we've been positioned to be in conflict with our bodies. I think we must decolonize ourselves, play large, know our fabulousness, our worth, our power in the face of being told that our beauty could not be. And when I say beauty, I mean a beauty based in our integrity, our lineages, our aesthetics, in self-possession of our sexualities and being desirable to ourselves; a beauty that radiates from our hearts, not from symmetrical bone structure. I believe liberation is intimately tied to the experience of being human, to every cell of our beings saturated in love—self-love and love of others—liberated from the shaming enforced by ableism

WSQ: Women's Studies Quarterly 46: 1 & 2 (Spring/Summer 2018) © 2018 by Patricia Berne, Jamal T. Lewis, Stacey Milbern, Malcolm Shanks, Alok Vaid-Menon, and Alice Wong. All rights reserved.

and other systems of oppression. And liberated *to* be responsible for creating a culture, a world, which values all communities. A liberatory experience can't happen only at an individual level; there's a collectivity that is part of what creates us as individuals. So, if liberation is self-love, and our identities are comprised of our community relationships, liberation is also loving our people.

Alok Vaid-Menon (AVM): I think we are all in a constant state of transformation. The ways that we are able to transform are totally linked to the conversations and people we have access to. Encountering the work of Sins Invalid has been foundational not just to my thinking about these questions, but my embodiment of them. As a gender nonconforming, transfeminine person, I am often told that I am ugly. Sins Invalid has created the space in me and in the world to challenge that, to find power in what they call despicable, and to rally in solidarity with all who are disenfranchised by normative beauty and ability.

Stacey Milbern (SM): I've been a long-time fan and friend of Patty and the organization, and I have worked with the Sins Invalid program team. I have also participated in disability justice work, particularly around working with youth. One of the things I really like that Sins Invalid says is the idea that beauty always recognizes itself. I think when you're talking about liberation for people with disabilities, specifically people of color with disabilities, we're talking about unraveling ableism, racism, and all of these systems of oppression that have told us to think certain ways. People have all of these unspoken ways of thinking about disability. We can look at pop culture and see that how many characters who are the villains are people with disabilities or we could read all of those statistics about dating apps and the people who are not going to be selected as dates. All that is shaped by race and disability. Or we can think of the legacy of freakery and circus shows. All of these show how afraid people are of disabled bodies. In order to unravel ableism, racism, and these frameworks, people need access to imagery that contests those images. That is one thing I really value about the work of Sins Invalid and Patty, specifically introducing a new narrative around what disability means. So I think if we want to imagine liberation for people with disabilities, we have to think about the beauty that we all have as humans. I really appreciate how spiritual Sins Invalid's work is for myself and for a lot of people. I'd be curious later, Patty, if you could speak to that element of spirituality, too.

Alice Wong (AW): I am the founder of the Disability Visibility Project, an online community that creates, shares, and amplifies disability media and culture. There is power in storytelling. Before I can even tell you a story, you need to really love and praise yourself. You need to say that "I do have a story, that I do matter." These are all intimately linked with the ideas of beauty and liberation and disability justice. It's a lot about giving us space and also reveling in who we are, being open, and sharing that with the world. That to me is part of the labor of creation. Each act of storytelling is not just an individual thing, but it's definitely a collective effort. It's really about bridging out to the world and sharing who we are and our stories with the world. All of these things add up to a larger purpose and I think I see that with Sins Invalid's work.

AVM: The world has so many stories that it tells about us and the people we love without our consent. Storytelling is political because it's about reclaiming our narrative. What I've found in my art practice is that even to tell my own story I need the support of the people around me. The world that we live in often forcibly separates us from the things that are most dear and urgent to us. Through connecting, collaborating with other people, I am able to experience myself more fully. It's not a con- tradiction—it's a recognition that, at a basic and fundamental level, we need each other to get free.

Jamal T. Lewis (JTL): Sins Invalid has been an invaluable resource to my thinking. This is where I've always looked toward when thinking of disability justice. It gave me a framework to not only think from but to also approach organizing and healing. It changed me for the better. Storytelling provides us a blueprint through which to work out these things. For myself, I'm using film to do this with *No Fats, No Femmes*, a feature length documentary about desire, body image, and discrimi- nation in the gay community. I think of beauty and liberation through my artistic work, disrupting narratives that create hierarchies of beauty that label one particular kind of body as beautiful or worthy of adu- lation over others that may fail constructed notions of beauty. Every time I have the opportunity, I remind people that beauty is deeply in- formed, distorted, and manipulated by capitalism. I also link to beauty through the space of vulnerability and confession: writing through my own struggles with my fat, black, femme body and approaching ugli- ness as a space to explore and revisit, not as a contrast to beauty but an otherwise possibility. I divest from constructed notions of beauty that tell me my body must look like this or that to access a thing I'm denied. There is magnificence in failing it.

Malcolm Shanks (MS): I came across Sins Invalid's work in 2012, about six years after they were founded. As a political educator, I realized that it is impossible to talk about race and gender without using a disability justice lens, which has since impacted me greatly. Though I come to this conversation from the vantage point of someone with able-bodied privilege, I also feel affirmed by Sins's paradigm. My later interaction with Sins Invalid's brilliance has been through the spiritual elements that Stacey mentioned: ancestors, reproduction, and legacy. While looking for ancestors who reflect me, I was only finding evidence of black, trans ancestors in court records and institutional clinical documents. I realized that colonialism has a logic that ranks people by our usefulness to capitalism. Those who are more easily exploited outside of wage labor are considered useless or monstrous, accusations that are consistently hurled at people with disabilities. Racism, transphobia, and ableism all believe that our bodies aren't shaped correctly or that we aren't using them correctly. This is all part of a body-reasoning that steals our agency to find beauty in our own experiences and in our own bodies; it even takes away a community's abilities to recognize that beauty.

AW: I appreciate what Malcolm said. Pathologization is definitely a frustrated action of white supremacy—it's in all oppression. Believing our own beauty depathologizes our bodies, our spirits, and our souls. This is what art does, and particular[ly] what Sins Invalid does.

AVM: Liberation is about being liberated from "beauty" and, in turn, approaching beauty with our own terms. Beauty can be a violent system: one which sanctions whose lives matter and whose do not, one which justifies, and indeed glorifies, brutality in the name of a greater good. But I believe it is possible to reclaim beauty for ourselves, by which I mean finding ways of relating to each other outside of what we've been taught to desire.

In terms of liberation and beauty as collectively produced and performed through storytelling, the world has so many stories it tells about us and the people we love without our consent. Storytelling is political because it's about flipping the script and reclaiming our narrative. What I've found in my art practice is that even to tell my own story I need the support of the people around me. Living in the world that we do often forcibly separates us from the things that are most dear and urgent to us. Through connecting, collaborating with other people, I am able to experience myself more fully. It's not a contradiction, it's a recognition that at a basic and fundamental level we need each other to get free.

NH: One of Sins Invalid's many artistic and political interventions is centering the erotic experiences and sexual desires of queer, trans, and gender nonconforming people of color with disabilities in order to forward a disability justice politics. How and why does an inclusive vision of sexuality and gender inform your disability justice framework?

JTL: An inclusive vision of sexuality and gender colors how I approach my thinking and organizing. My politic is grounded in the following affirmations: One, all bodies deserve self-autonomy and agency to define gender and sexuality on their own terms; two, all bodies deserve pleasure; and three, all bodies are deserving of experiencing the affect and power of intimacy and touch. That's actually one of the most important to me. Touch is transformative. An inclusive vision must also include possibility. That binaries and limitation inhibits our potential to experience otherwise freedoms.

PB: We can't engage a feminist understanding of sexuality without simultaneously addressing ableism, white supremacy, cis-heteropatriarchy, and constructions of nationalism, right? If there is an underlying politic, one that moves others forward, it would have to be or resonate with disability justice (DJ), because DJ at its core, is about folks' beloved bodyminds, an embodied resistance to the oppression of our bodyminds.

AVM: Liberalism has confined the demands we are allowed to make. We are granted superficial recognition, and rarely permitted our entirety. When we ambition beyond and have the audacity to assert our full personhood, we are punished for it. Desire is often one of the first aspects of ourselves we are made to give up. Sins Invalid has profoundly shifted the terms of engagement for both disability justice movements and queer and trans movements (and where they intersect). The goal is not just about inclusion, it's about desire. Do we just want to be acknowledged or do we want to be desired?

AW: Yes, I think that when we talk about beauty and art, it's not this superficial thing, right? Creating art can be a struggle and a lot of work to get to that place. It is an unfortunate thing that people think artists magically create for ourselves, and I think that is really from the outsider's perspective. They see all these people are well-adjusted or people who love themselves. Loving yourself takes so much work and I think that's a real evolution. However, the work and process of coming to love yourself is invisibilized in our communities. We talk about beauty and we talk about self-love and us being unapologetic; those aren't buzzwords. Pride comes out of your identities and getting there takes a lot of work. I think that's what's misunderstood by a lot of people when they're outside looking within our own communities.

AVM: So often work around beauty gets dismissed as superficial, but I think activism at the level of aesthetics is incredibly important. Beauty is part of the way that these foundational systems reproduce themselves. We are taught to desire the very things that destroy us, and we are taught to fear the very things that have the potential to set us free. Finding beauty in that which we have been told is abject and disposable has profound implications. It's about challenging the core logics and hierarchies that underpin, well, everything.

JTL: Sins Invalid's call is linked directly to the everyday ways disabled, queer, and trans people use technology and creative collective power to display their own beauty, which serves as counternarratives to manipulated notions of beauty presented by mainstream media through magazine covers, billboards, television, and infomercials that seek to make people feel bad about themselves in order to buy in to products and enhancements for instant gratification.

PB: We perpetuate violence against ourselves by thinking that we are not beautiful. Sins Invalid uses the phrase "Beauty always, always recognizes itself," and self-love is a really hard-learned lesson for many of us. When we experience threats that we may be institutionalized, sterilized, deported, disowned, constantly told that we should be grateful for any quality of life, as people with disabilities, as women of color, as trans and gender nonconforming folks, as immigrants, as people incarcerated—we're told "You're not being killed, so be grateful!" So, if Sins can create a space where someone is bathed in their own beauty, and they can use that in times when their beauty and existence are being threatened by the violence of oppression, then we are doing our jobs as disability-justice-based artists.

NH: How do you see Sins Invalid's call for an "unshamed claim to beauty" linked to everyday social change? How might claiming beauty challenge social structures such as racism, colonialism, and capitalism?

MS: As Alice mentioned, people often have negative reactions to pride. It's a moment where we get to say, "Actually, fuck everybody and everything that has made it impossible to recognize this divinity in ourselves and others." At the same time as I'm actively problack, I also plot against whiteness for consistently treating blackness as a threat. One of the things about Sin's Invalid's work that excites me is the double-sided "unshamed claim to beauty." There is the intervention that "we celebrate our own beauty and power" and "we name and shame those who harm us." Building community and shifting culture are both large and interrelated projects, and the combination of those is part of what makes pride an important tool for the survival of our people.

AW: There's something that's so magical about live performance and witnessing art as it unfolds in front of you. It feels like a spiritual experience. It feels like there is a coming together of the audience with the artist and really sharing this moment. That, to me, is sacred. Sins Invalid's performance in 2016 had such an amazing lineup of different artists. I feel this deep sense of gratitude for the people who I've been connected with because they give me strength, and I give them strength, and we're all bound together in this struggle. And that to me is a revolution, right? Liberation happens when we all recognize each other and try to work together towards that goal however we can.

SM: To what Alice just said, for people with disabilities it feels like survival every day is just about proving your humanity. We could do all of our activism and still have work to do. One thing that is really cool is that Sins Invalid's work is asking a higher question about what Patty mentioned earlier, divinity. I really think that at the end of the day the work that we're doing is examining or investigating what we've been told to understand is brokenness and then discovering that's not the case. Then we learn more about why we were told those things and what purpose these narratives serve. I feel like that is deeply political work.

AW: Returning to what Patty said earlier about spirituality, we are all whole and perfect to people already when we come into this world. It's just once we jump into the world, forces are upon us to reshape us, change us, and strip away our powers. Sins Invalid's call is a reaffirmation that we've always had this power, we've always been perfect, and we've always been whole despite what we've learned and we hear every day.

PB: Do you know Don Cherry or Charles Lloyd, both musicians, or the poetry of Aurora Levins Morales? Exquisite artistic work brings me to connect with myself, and also to connect with something greater. That openness and joy is a spiritual experience, a site of love. I think that oppressive forces are not trying to cocreate this experience! I think people feel a deep love, a mirroring experience at a Sins Invalid performance. There's a synergy between the audience and the performers, the backstage crew and performers are casting a love-net out to the audience, envisioning and cocreating this liberated zone, loving the shit out of our crip lives and bodies and trying to hold everyone in that. That's what I can only imagine what liberation is like, so sign me up! It's worth this struggle.

NH: Patty, I really love what you just said about Sins Invalid's intervention as producing the experience of what liberation and joy could be like every day if we could make the changes that we want. How do you see the spiritual as well as collective and personal intervention in beauty and divinity relating to our current political moment as you define it?

AVM: In times of crisis we are compelled to do work that has "immediate impact." Resources for art get slashed for the sake of "urgency" and cultural workers constantly get dismissed as idealistic and impractical. This is such a tragedy because it is precisely in moments like these that we need art more than ever. Political art, like that of Sins Invalid, gives us refuge, gives us permission to imagine beyond the present, gives us a template of what the world could look like, gives us confidence to challenge the shame and fear that hold us back

MS: I feel that addressing our current political moment requires deciding what time scale we even operate in. I hear a lot that I'm apparently in a post-Charlottesville moment. One of the things that I find really interesting is that it's only when white people are in crisis that they start to approach political time in the same way that people of color often have to. To name a moment in time after a place is also interesting to me because both white and able-bodied people are often unwilling to admit that how we/they think and move through time is contingent on the space that they/we inhabit. Am I to understand Charlottesville or the United States differently after this incidence of white supremacists terrorizing black and brown people to preserve their precarious sense of self?

I think spiritual and embodied communion with ancestors is essential right now. They have resisted transitions of capitalism and white supremacy in other time-spaces. It is essential that our practice be one that accounts for recognizing beauty in ourselves, otherwise we may not be open to knowledge and blessings from the ancestors who need us and whom we need most.

AW: I've always been looking and hungry for this kind of art. I think now more than ever, or perhaps it's always been this way, that art like this keeps me going. Art has a role in keeping us alive, keeping us full of joy, and reminding us what's good. I think that's really what's powerful and so needed by groups like Sins Invalid. Marginalized folks have always been resisting and with more people interested in "resistance," this might [be] an opportunity, right? It could be an entry point for more people to come in and learn about disability justice. I'm trying to see the good things out of this rather than just feeling cynical about it. But I feel, for so many folks, we've always been here and always [been] doing that work. And I think it's really unfortunate that it's driven us to these extremes and suddenly we realize, "Oh shit, this has been happening and that we should give a damn and we should pay attention." History is relevant within these time periods, as Malcolm has said.

SM: I think that this political moment feels like we are really being tested and having to develop a lot of different strategies. We already have been working to create a radical imagination, that is the work that Sins Invalid does, and now people are also starting to have very real conversations about "How are you going to show up for me? How are we going to survive this? If infrastructure like health care goes away, how are we going to keep ourselves alive?" Those conversations have always been happening. At the same time, I feel like there's more and it seems like the need for political education is amped up now as well. I can just see all the movement work that has to happen, the strategies that we're going to need to use and the relationships that are going be critical right now.

PB: In terms of this political moment, there are so many openings right now politically. My concern is that there's a clock ticking. I live in the Bay Area and Berkeley is supposed to get over 110 degrees over the weekend. I grew up in San Francisco, and I know this climate and it is out of sorts. With the floods in Houston, the late winter [in] the Midwest, the tsunamis, the fires, the earthquakes—there is a clock ticking. We have to see each the human ecosystem and the body of the earth as part of this beloved "we." As we move toward a liberatory moment or vision, we must "each one bring one." This moment can and needs to be that moment to allow us to survive.

Patricia Berne is cofounder and executive director of Sins Invalid and has a professional background in mental health support to survivors of violence. A Japanese Haitian queer disabled woman, she sees her work to create "liberated zones" for marginalized voices. She can be reached at pattyberne@sinsinvalid.org.

Jamal T. Lewis is an emerging multidisciplinary artist, writer, and activist living in Bed-stuy, Brooklyn, hailing from Atlanta, Georgia. Lewis produces work around the body, specifically exploring and interrogating identity formation, race, gender, sexuality, de-sire, beauty, and ugliness. Contact Jamal at jamalterron@gmail.com.

Stacey Milbern is a disability justice community builder with over twelve years of expe-rience working in disability communities, particularly at the intersections of race and queerness. She can be reached at stacey.milbern@gmail.com.

Malcolm Shanks educates to build decolonial knowledge and movement. Malcolm works at Race Forward providing training and coaching on racial equity. They are cocre-ator of the zine *Decolonizing Gender: A Curriculum*. They can be reached at malcolm.shanks@gmail.com.

Alok Vaid-Menon is a nonbinary writer and performance artist. Their work grapples with themes of intimacy, alienation, and transmisogyny. Contact Alok at info@alokvmenon.com.

Alice Wong is a media maker, research consultant, and disability activist based in San Francisco, California. She is the founder of the *Disability Visibility Project*, a com-munity partnership with StoryCorps and an online community dedicated to creating, amplifying, and sharing disability media and culture. Contact Alice at disabilityvisibil-ityproject@gmail.com.

FIG. 1. Micah Bazant with Sins Invalid. *Justice for Mario Woods*, 2015. Courtesy of Micah Bazant and Sins Invalid.

PART VI. **POETIC WORK**

Now I will crack my sternum

Kristi Carter

unfold my blackened ribs
open them, so I may lift her out.
My mother:
as shriveled
as her voice is loud.

WSQ: Women's Studies Quarterly 46: 1 & 2 (Spring/Summer 2018) © 2018 by Kristi Carter. All rights reserved.

Congratulations:

Kristi Carter

I'm obsessed with my face—
this altar of toxins,
how I gleam in sacrament.
As if the name you gave me
means what it means:
bitter tear of the sea,
virgin whom God deployed for sacrifice.

Congratulations. My galaxy orbits around
a black hole: I'm the pit
into which children roll their dirty pennies
in the science museum they'll never remember
adventuring to, due to the gray matte walls
and the long sighs of their parents,
ashamed to be reminded of laws
that govern the universe, which they too were taught as children
but forgot.—See, I remember more
and thus, I'm awarded a mask that is gnarled
but in high gloss. Once you try it on:
you can't take it off. I wish you told me that
when you knotted the velvet cord
behind my head—pointless—and reminded me,
if anyone saw my smile,
they'd rape me, *Anything that enters you
is violence.*

WSQ: Women's Studies Quarterly 46: 1 & 2 (Spring/Summer 2018) © 2018 by Kristi Carter. All rights reserved.

Congratulations. The technology of voicemail
ensures the smooth capture of your banshee voice
into its ethereal trap, for me to replay later
before the sun comes up.
Me and your voice
in the dark—just like old times! And again,
I'm slain as your voice skins off my dragon skin.
As for my scales,
the bedspread soaks them up oh so politely.

Congratulations. You're still not a grandmother.

This inverse vanity keeps me very busy
contemplating the arrival
of potential fissures in the wall,
once the foundation of my apartment building
sighs just once more.
It's fine,
because the phone never rings
ever since I tore the mask off—on the phone,
you could hear the old flesh rip.

Three years and the flesh has grown back
different: a numb layer of mirror
that keeps the world at bay. Because,
Congratulations, I'm alive.

But for all the fortress under grey firmament
in the gothic myth of childhood you built around me,
I have come out from under the rubble.
Not like a hero aglow with effervescent lumen

who busts out from the rubble with a laugh
or a smug mouth. Nah,
I just scuttle out sideways
in search of a new dark room
with a door that will lock.

Kristi Carter is the author of *Cosmovore*, *Daughter Shaman Sings Blood Anthem*, as well as *Red and Vast*. Her poems have appeared in publications including *So to Speak*, *poemmemoirstory*, *CALYX*, *Hawaii Review*, and *Nimrod*. Her work examines of the intersection of gender and intergenerational trauma in twentieth-century poetics. She holds a PhD from University of Nebraska Lincoln and an MFA from Oklahoma State University. She can be reached at mkristicarter@gmail.com.

To Come Undone

Tanya Grae

My mother used to say lipstick was best
manners, praised the importance of putting on

a good face. Add to the list: the padded bra,
slip & girdle clothes-pinned to the line.

The nakedness of women without makeup
used to shock me, their blemishes & pores.

Be a lady everywhere except the bedroom.

There was the braless summer my aunt didn't
shave armpits, legs, anything, too much skunk

running wild in her appearance. We sang
"American Girl" before she met the Wolfman

who hid her behind dark glasses. Face dolled up
like *Redbook,* how she bent herself in his moods.

Beauty is skin deep, but ugly is to the bone.

My father used to call my mother's name,
& she'd drop everything & go. It startled me,

the urgency of something wrong, misplaced—
his keys, a shoe. But those affairs he had

for years, after she gave up college to marry,
fueled three degrees at choke-down speed.

Make sure you can take care of yourself.

I learned to say no, to outlast the silence.
Tired of hours, contortions to please,

I cut my own hair & let myself go.
Those bare-faced women I used to study,

whose eyes scolded mine, knew one day
I'd shrug at my own face & say, *So?*

If Barbie Had a Brain

Tanya Grae

No, I mean if Barbie could talk,
she would tell you she's starved

for more than an eyeful's attention,
ass clenched tight, kind of holding,

asphyxiated from sucking in, waiting
to stop the tiptoe. She objects

to being posed, back aching, ending
horizontal & naked, because

her clothes are too much of a hassle,
your illusion, undressed. She knows

about the curb, where your things tend
to end & wants you to know

doll patience is painted.

Tanya Grae is the author of *Undoll*, a National Poetry Series finalist, and the chapbook *Lethe*. Her poems have appeared in *AGNI*, *Prairie Schooner*, *New Ohio Review*, *New South*, the *Massachusetts Review*, and elsewhere. She is a PhD candidate at Florida State University and can be reached at tanyagrae@gmail.com.

WSQ: Women's Studies Quarterly **46: 1 & 2 (Spring/Summer 2018)** © 2018 by Tanya Grae. All rights reserved.

On Demand

Linda Flaherty Haltmaier

Come on, honey, give me a smile,
my face slack like a marionette dangling on a nail,
an intricate choreography of a dozen muscles,
a porridge of Latin names,
Zygomaticus major in charge—
a grin in repose,
defiantly blasé.
I don't owe this stranger or this world
my smile,
my pretty,
my perfected body.
Cables that stretch my lips
to placate and fit in,
Lemurs, gorillas, chimpanzees,
furry brethren,
all consider smiling an act of aggression,
a menacing display of dental prowess.
So today, I'll navigate with the ancestors,
glide through city streets
flashing a hint of incisor on my terms—
aware that an unexpected delight
could trip this complex system
of rigs and pulleys,
baring all.

WSQ: *Women's Studies Quarterly* 46: 1 & 2 (Spring/Summer 2018) © 2018 by Linda Flaherty Haltmaier.

Processing Imperfections Over Lunch

Linda Flaherty Haltmaier

I don't need a mirror to study my imperfections,
count my flaws,
catalog my failings,
My friends are here to do it for me
over grilled chicken and Caesar salad—
Not overtly, not with malice aforethought,
we're here to catch up, right?
I love them and they love me
but our tribe is steeped in self-loathing,
reflecting back infinitely upon each of us,
like a carnival fun house.
The ritualistic flagellation,
warped perceptions
of bellies and wrinkles,
the *less-than* status updates,
Light chatter,
self-deprecating banter,
Passing the whip from
person to person,
I'm small and imperfect,
now your turn,
Bonding through bondage,
breaking ourselves down
to connect with the shards,

WSQ: Women's Studies Quarterly 46: 1 & 2 (Spring/Summer 2018) © 2018 by Linda Flaherty Haltmaier.
All rights reserved.

I'll take my salad with a glass of rosé,
its petal-soft pink
the color of blood and water.

Linda Flaherty Haltmaier is an award-winning poet and screenwriter. She is the poet laureate of Andover, Massachusetts, and the winner of the Homebound Publications Poetry Prize for her full-length collection *Rolling up the Sky*. Her debut chapbook, *Catch and Release*, was published by Finishing Line Press, and her new collection of poetry, *To the Left of the Sun*, will be published by Homebound Publications in September 2018. She was named a finalist for the Princemere Poetry Prize and the Tucson Festival of the Book Literary Award. Her poetry has been nominated for a Pushcart Prize and has appeared in journals and anthologies including *Wildness: Voices of the Sacred Landscape*, *Ink & Letters*, *Poetry Breakfast*, and more. She can be reached at lfhaltmaier@comcast.net.

From Underwater

Sarah Janczak

No one is ever able to feel   how far
we swim. How fast knives scrape skin.

Plasma in water is still crimson.
I never knew   what logic was for   anyway.

At 12, I belly-flopped   my stomach raw,
just to learn to dive.

We   chew   slowly.   Savor
dessert, when we glide   to the center

of this table and lie so close
our whispers devour each   other's devotion.

There is no learning
here. I have   already done that.

My mouth commits the felonies   fingers
cannot. We sacrifice   our hands for this.

WSQ: Women's Studies Quarterly 46: 1 & 2 (Spring/Summer 2018) © 2018 by Sarah Janczak. All rights reserved.

After the Illness Came I Went

Sarah Janczak

Skinny as my spine,
a silhouette,
a bare branch.
I don't know

where it came from
only, how it left me
scarred, translucent.
Disease sliced

flanks of flesh
as if hips
were butter
and suddenly

there were thousands
of men to feed.
Invisibility
was a needle,

needles manageable.
A zipped torso
into linen,
into leather. Even

WSQ: Women's Studies Quarterly 46: 1 & 2 (Spring/Summer 2018) © 2018 by Sarah Janczak. All rights reserved.

the afternoon wind
felt like it was
lifting me;
I could lean

into it, and it
would carry me
back to before
steel or cold.

Before I knew
all the ways
that this body
can forsake me.

Congenitus

Sarah Janczak

For Grace

We are called mineral,
gravel. We come heavy
from palms that pound
dough. From the depths

of black water, gills of fish,
marrow. We come from oil.
We are called sunlight
on tennis courts, sweat.

Earth-rising fault lines
that shake, from limbs
like snakes. Carrot seed
and basil, summer,

and all things holy.
Lace tablecloths,
sob stories, salted cod,
an empty field

for a front yard.
We are called broken boots
and floodplains. The bottom
of a well; dark, and damp,
and misty. We stand

***WSQ: Women's Studies Quarterly* 46: 1 & 2 (Spring/Summer 2018)** © 2018 by Sarah Janczak. All rights reserved.

upright in our home.
Sweep the floor,

unlock the doors.
There is already

an open window. It is safe
to let the night breeze in.

Sarah Janczak studied writing and women's history at Sarah Lawrence College. Her poems have recently appeared in *Hayden's Ferry Review*, the *Los Angeles Review*, and *Witness*. She can be reached at sejanczak@gmail.com.

I've Lost My Looks

Elizabeth Johnston

I know you've seen them
just a second ago.
Somewhere around here?

I've looked everywhere,
turned the house upside down.
Crammed fingers into crevices,
flailed arms under beds, rooted
in trash.

For my effort:
uncapped lipstick,
      palmful of sequins,
      Slimfast wrapper,
      three Press-On nails.

Sure, I've always been careless
with things better kept close—
house keys, phone numbers,
certain lovers,
certain truths.

WSQ: Women's Studies Quarterly **46: 1 & 2 (Spring/Summer 2018)** © 2018 by Elizabeth Johnston.
All rights reserved.

Maybe my looks felt neglected,
not paid attention to in years
they ran away.
I mean, I tried:
There was that pricy online lotion,
those Atkins cookbooks,
chia shakes, hot yoga.
But who has time?

I've heard an owner's scent
can coax a stray back home.
So I lay it all out:
miniskirt, thigh-highs, stilettos,
push-up bra, peppermint gloss.
Whole she-bang.

Nothing but tom-cats sniffing around this old cougar.
I begin to suspect something nefarious: Time,
that Robin Hood thief, pilfering my glow,
redistributing the wealth,
slipping my curves into some other
woman's shorts, my perk into her bra.

I keep my eye out,
every passing woman a suspect.
I'm ready to take down
that dollar store clerk,
the cutie pie waitress,
when my daughter ambles in
wearing my jeans
and my smile.

That bitch.
She didn't even ask.

Big Fat Truth

Elizabeth Johnston

Inch by measured inch, she hints:
daughter, you grow fat.

Words she cannot say aloud.
Would be abuse. Unkind. Not motherly.

Instead, she buys her a bike, running shorts, roller skates,
raises eyebrows at the second helping,
frowns at the bikini, stocks
the cupboard with healthy snacks,
rents *Fast Food Nation, Supersize Me.*

She is trying, as mothers do, to stave off meanness:
name left off birthday invites,
seat not saved at lunch,
tight circles of girls she can't squeeze into.
She would not have her daughter starve.

WSQ: Women's Studies Quarterly 46: 1 & 2 (Spring/Summer 2018) © 2018 by Elizabeth Johnston.
All rights reserved.

But when her daughter comes in tears
and asks: *Is it true what they say? Am I fat?*
What else can she do but restate the lie:
　　it's the inside that counts,
　　　not the cover.
Already they both know better:
No one reads the book.
It's about the hook.
The blondest hair. The bluest eye.
The tiny waist to set things right.
　　The big fat truth: it might.

Elizabeth Johnston is a feminist scholar and author whose poems, stories, essays, and plays have appeared widely, most recently in *The Atlantic*, *Feminist Formations*, and *Veils, Halos, and Shackles: International Poetry on the Oppression and Empowerment of Women*. She teaches writing and gender studies in Rochester, New York, and facilitates writing-as-healing workshops. For more information about Elizabeth and her award-winning writer's group, please visit strawmatwriters.weebly.com or email her at ejohnston@monroecc.edu.

Snake Oil

Donna J. Gelagotis Lee

A large fold of skin—I think,
  It's swelling—

but the doctor sees no inflammation—no
  one explained how I'd grow

old—no one told me how the skin's
  loss of elasticity would show

on my fingers, my mons pubis,
  the abdomen, at the bend of the arm—

this thin skin has new meaning
  and soon I can't leave my house

without foundation—every scar, every sun
  spot rises to the surface, the skin

uneven, the face a landmine—I can
  feel the changes, the shift in fat

distribution, the uncertain bones, and could it all be
  hormones?—the doctor says it's normal,

WSQ: *Women's Studies Quarterly* 46: 1 & 2 (Spring/Summer 2018) © 2018 by Donna J. Gelagotis Lee.

but I want my old body back, strong, sleek . . .
    fingers tapered, even if it takes

snake oil.

Donna J. Gelagotis Lee is the author of *On the Altar of Greece*, winner of the seventh annual Gival Press Poetry Award and recipient of a 2007 Eric Hoffer Book Award: Notable for Art category. Her poetry has appeared in journals internationally, including the *Bitter Oleander*, *Feminist Studies*, *Frontiers: A Journal of Women Studies*, the *Massachusetts Review*, and *WSQ*. She can be reached at leedjgel@gmail.com.

PART VII. **ALERTS AND PROVOCATIONS**

On Beauty and Protest

Vanessa Pérez-Rosario

For feminist politics, the question of beauty is a complicated web of no-tions of femininity, desire, sexuality, and power. Beauty has long been used to reinforce hierarchies, sexism, and racism. What is the relationship be-tween beauty and social protest? What are the uses of beauty? On Octo-ber 29, 2017, the contestants of the Miss Peru beauty pageant stunned the audience when rather than giving their measurements as is customary in many beauty pageants, they shared alarming statistics of violence against women in Peru.[1] The women revealed figures such as: *"Mi nombre es Cami-la Canicoba y represento a Lima, mis medidas son 2,202 casos de feminicidio reportado en los últimos nueve años en mi país"; "Mi nombre es Samantha Batallanos, represento a Lima y mis medidas son una niña muere cada diez minutos por producto de la explotación sexual"; "Mi nombre es Juana Aceve-do y mis medidas son, mas del 70 por ciento de las mujeres de nuestro país es victima de acoso callejero"* (My name is Camila Canicoba and I represent Lima, my measurements are 2,202 cases of feminicide reported in the last nine years in my country; My name is Samantha Batallanos, I represent Lima, and my measurements are a girl dies every ten minutes as a result of sexual exploitation; My name is Juana Acevedo and my measurements are more than 70 percent of women in our country are victims of street harass-ment). The hashtag *#mismedidasson* (#mymeasurementsare)[2] trended on social media and the story made news around the world. Beauty pageants have long been trivialized as sites where women's bodies are displayed and consumed by audiences. They are seen as frivolous events that promote dominant ideas of physical beauty where contestants are mostly seen but not heard. This only heightens the impact of the statistics of domestic

WSQ: Women's Studies Quarterly 46: 1 & 2 (Spring/Summer 2018) © 2018 by Vanessa Pérez-Rosario.

abuse and the trafficking of women and children revealed that night. The unexpected focus on ending violence against women in the context of a popular culture spectacle like a beauty pageant that traditionally aims to define the ideal woman was unsettling and disruptive, creating the strange experience of a beauty that has the power to destabilize.

The event organizers had decided that they wanted to host a different kind of Miss Peru pageant that year and turn the event into a protest and a space to promote social change. The master of ceremony, Peruvian actor Cristian Rivero said,

> *No queremos un país con mas violencia. Esta noche no solo se trata de estas veintitres mujeres. Esta noche se trata de todas las mujeres de nuestro país que tienen derecho y merecen respeto. No mas violencia. Este es el mensaje que queremos dar en este Miss Peru.*

> (We do not want a country with more violence. Tonight is not only about these twenty-three women; tonight is about all of the women of our country who have rights and deserve respect. No more violence. This is the message we want to share in this Miss Peru.)

Implied in Rivero's statement is the idea that the twenty-three beautiful contestants representing different regions of the nation, in fact, represent all Peruvian women. Therefore if the country values and celebrates these twenty-three women, it should, by extension, honor and respect all Peruvian women.

During the swimsuit competition, the thirteen finalists walked the stage in gold bikinis while images of newspaper headlines reporting violence against women were projected onto the backdrop of the stage. Including photos of women who were so badly beaten that their eyes were swollen shut and their faces unrecognizable. Some of the headlines read: *Costurero estrangula esposa; Acosador incrusta cuchillo a mujer embarazada y fuga; 63 mujeres violadas a diario; Borracho mata esposa a golpes* (Tailor Strangles Wife; Assailant Stabs Pregnant Woman and Flees; Sixty-Three Women Raped Daily; Drunk Man Beats His Wife to Death). The segment closed with Rivero imploring viewers, "*Que estos títulares no se vuelvan a escribir nunca más. Es hora que nosotros cambiemos. Más importante es hora que las leyes de este país cambien*" ("May headlines like these never be written again. It is time for us to change. More importantly, it's time for the laws in this country to change.") During the interview portion, pageant contestants were asked, "Every day women die at the hand of their partners or ex-partners. What laws would you change in this country to end violence against women?"

The Peru beauty pageant protest is part of larger political movement involving marches and demonstrations against feminicide and violence against women that, in recent years, have erupted in Latin America and around the world. *"Ni una menos"* ("not one less") protests have sprung up in Argentina, Mexico, Bolivia, and Colombia.[3] The 2017 Women's March in the United States was organized in protest of the inauguration of President Donald J. Trump who has been accused by numerous women of sexual assault (The Women's March 2018). The #MeToo Movement went viral as women broke their silence and spoke out against sexual violence and harassment (Me Too Movement 2018). The Miss Peru pageant protest can be understood as part of a watershed moment and global movement to create a world where women are free to live without fear of violence.

As sites of spectacular commodity culture where women's bodies are displayed, exchanged, and consumed, I wonder if a beauty pageant can be a site of protest and a platform for social justice. The beauty pageant industry highlights and reinforces European standards of beauty, encourages women to aspire to unhealthy measurements and weight goals that often lead to eating disorders, low self-esteem, and body modification such as plastic surgery and skin bleaching. In short, the pageant uses beauty as a powerful tool to inscribe racism and sexism. Jessica Newton, crowned Miss Peru in 1987 and one of the pageant organizers, defended the competition in general and the bathing suit segment in particular by noting that all women deserve respect regardless of what they are wearing (Zabludovsky 2017). Newton emphasized that it shouldn't matter if they are wearing a bathing suit. Women deserve to be treated with respect (2017). I think most feminists would agree.

The pageant organizers sought to use their platform to mobilize beauty in the service of justice. Some argue beauty is a powerful distraction that overwhelms our attention and blinds us to injustice by diverting our scrutiny from the things that require it most.[4] Can beauty be used to refocus our attention on social injustice and lead to a more equitable world? Were pageant viewers activated to create a more just society free from violence? Will other nations be motivated to replicate the beauty pageant protest in their countries?

In *On Beauty and Being Just,* Elaine Scarry (1999) explores the relationship between beauty and justice. She is interested in the question of beauty and how it relates to others. Embedded in Western aesthetic philosophy, Scarry posits that when we stand before beauty we are inspired to replicate it in the form of a song, drawing an image, or taking a photo of it. Beauty, she argues, inspires us to create. She advances the argument that the replication, distribution, and symmetry, that beauty demands, lead to equity and justice through teaching perceptual care and radical decentering. She notes that

> the structure of perceiving beauty appears to have a two-part scaffolding: first, one's attention is involuntarily given to the beautiful person or thing; then, this quality of heightened attention is voluntarily extended out to other persons or things. It is as though beautiful things have been placed here and there throughout the world to serve as small wake-up calls to perception, spurring lapsed alertness back to its most acute level. Through its beauty, the world continually recommits us to a rigorous standard of perceptual care: if we do not search it out, it comes and finds us. (Scarry 1999, 81)

She counters the idea that beauty is a distraction by focusing on the distributional power of beauty as a form of justice. The unsettling effects of beauty, she advances, leads to a sense of caring, attention to others, and justice. However, we know that people do not voluntarily give up their positions of privilege in the service of justice. The history of social movements teaches us that rights are only granted after years of long, hard struggle.

The Miss Peru 2017 pageant protest is premised on the idea of beauty's distributional power. Throughout the evening, the pageant impressed upon viewers the notion that "if you touch one woman, you touch all women." As viewers gazed on the beautiful, young, and accomplished women onstage, they were confronted with the reality of the high rates of violence women face. Viewers were directed to make the connection between the horrific headlines projected on the screen, the statistics shared, and the beautiful, young women walking the stage in bikinis. The experience was meant to encourage the audience to imagine these beautiful women befalling a similar fate. And that seems an injustice. The pageant was organized to raise awareness about the pervasiveness of violence against women, and promote the idea that women should be treated with respect. Throughout the competition, emphasis was placed on changing the laws in the country that make it difficult to seek justice for the victims of violence. Viewers were urged to care about the contestant's fate, in hopes that they will be moved to create laws to protect them, and by extension, all women from violence. But we know that the justice of the law is imperfect. It is not applied equally across race, class, and gender. How inclusive is beauty's distributional power?

Beauty pageants are sites where notions of acceptable femininity and national belonging are promoted. These ideas are intertwined with appearance, skin color, and physical features. While the racial ideology of Latin America is one of mixture, or *mestizaje*, where mixture makes the national subject; not all mixtures are deemed the same. Latin American countries have a history of attempting to "improve" Indigenous races through marriages that would result in children with lighter skin and finer features. Does the lateral pressure beauty demands extend beyond and across racial categories? Does the distributional power of beauty extend to certain kinds of others? While we know that women of all races, sizes, body types, and social classes are victims of violence, in Latin America Indigenous and black women are more likely to experience it, and are more likely to be killed as a result of this violence at a rate more than double that of women of other races (ECLAC 2014). In a country where the population is overwhelmingly Amerindian, one cannot help but notice that the contestants of the Miss Peru pageant were of a more desirable mestizaje, with more European features, and fairer skin.[5] Does lateral pressure and perceptual care carry over to the majority of Peruvian women who are Indigenous and the most vulnerable members of the population?

As central sites for ideologies of gendered citizenship and racialized national subjectivity there is still much work for the Miss Peru pageant to do to subvert the ways beauty and race contribute to the reproduction of pervasive forms of racism and sexism that reinforce structures of inequality rather than eradicate them. The Miss Peru pageant protest has sparked conversations around the world about beauty, violence, and justice. It has urged us to create the world we crave, one where women and girls are free to be who they want without the threat of violence. To bring about that world, more needs to be done to complicate and untangle our very idea of beauty, how it is defined, marketed, and manipulated in a beauty pageant such as this one. The Miss Peru pageant mobilized beauty to protest violence against women without questioning the complicated ways that gender, and racialized beauty intersect in Latin America. We need to protest these very ideas of beauty that are tied to power, hierarchy, and race.

284 Vanessa Pérez-Rosario

Vanessa Pérez-Rosario is associate professor of Latino studies at Brooklyn College and affiliate faculty of women and gender studies at Brooklyn College. Her research focuses on transnational Latina feminisms, translation, and poetics. She can be reached at vperezrosario@brooklyn.cuny.edu.

Notes

1. For the full competition see Latina.Pe. 2017.
2. Unless otherwise noted, all translations are my own.
3. See Ni Una Menos 2018. Since the 1990s countries in Latin America have paid special attention to the systematic killing of women given the unprecedented number of women killed and tortured in the town of Juarez on the U.S.-Mexico border, and across South America. See Gaspar de Alba and Guzmán 2010 and González Rodríguez 2012.
4. For an interesting exchange on the question of beauty and social justice, see Ford Foundation and Helicon 2015.
5. For more on the relationship between beauty and racism in Latin America, see Figueroa 2013.

Works Cited

ECLAC (Economic Commission for Latin America and the Caribbean). 2014. *Annual Report 2013–2014. Confronting Violence against women in Latin America and the Caribbean (LC/G.2626)*. Santiago, Chile: United Nations Publications. https://www.cepal.org/mujer/noticias/paginas/9/53409/Annual_Report_2013_2014._C1420458_Web.pdf

Figueroa, Mónica G. Moreno. 2013. "Displaced Looks: The Lived Experience of Beauty and Racism." *Feminist Theory* 14 (2): 137–51.

Ford Foundation and Helicon. 2015. "*On Beauty* Convening." Discussion, Ford Foundation, New York, NY, December 8. Accessed January 20, 2018. http://heliconcollab.net/our_work/beauty/.

Gaspar de Alba, Alicia, ed., with Georgiana Guzmán. 2010. *Making a Killing: Femicide, Free Trade, and La Frontera*. Austin: University of Texas Press.

González Rodríguez, Sergio. 2012. *The Femicide Machine*. Los Angeles: Semiotext(e).

Me Too Movement. 2018. "You Are Not Alone." Accessed January 5, 2018. https://metoomvmt.org.

Latina.Pe. 2017. "Miss Perú 2018 - 29 de octubre del 2017 programa completo." Youtube, November 2. Accessed January 9, 2018. https://youtube/6U9RA713Wic.

Ni Una Menos. 2018. "#NiUnaMenos." Accessed January 5, 2018. http://
s1000050.ferozo.com.

Scarry, Elaine. 1999. *On Beauty and Being Just*. Princeton, NJ: Princeton
University Press.

The Women's March. 2018. "Home Page." Accessed January 5, 2018. https://
www.womensmarch.com.

Zabludovsky, Karla. 2017. "These Beauty Pageant Contestants Gave Out Facts
About Women's Rights as Their Measurements." BuzzFeed, October 30.
Accessed January 8, 2018. https://www.buzzfeed.com/karlazabludovsky/
miss-peru-2018-was-the-most-woke-beauty-pageant-of-all-time?utm_
term=.suO2PyOkl#.joXMbgxGN.

WOLFMAN

NEW LIFE

QUARTERLY

ISSUE TWO

COLUMNS Jordan Karnes *on gender & sports* • Avery Trufelman *reviews every shirt* • *New comics from* @laurencessss • Zoé Samudzi *on photography* • Maya Weeks *on the ocean* • Leila Weefur *interviews Sam Vernon* **REVIEWS CURATED BY** Colin Winnette & Tongo Eisen-Martin *with reviews by* David Brazil, Jennifer Williams, Louise McCune, Claire Stringer, Ali Giordani, Blair Johnson, Ra Malika Imhotep, Pia Cortez & Caleb Beckwith **CONVERSATIONS** Margaret McCarthy & Andrew Evans • Claire Mullen & Raphael Villet • Clara Sankey & E.H. Mann • Tara Marsden & Zoe Donnellycolt • Justin Carder & Sophia Wang • Miranda Tsang & maybe a dog **ESSAYS** Tatiana Luboviski-Acosta *on the feminine divine* • Hannah Kingsley-Ma *on open water swimming* • Amy Langer *on online doll dress up games* **PORTFOLIOS** Jade Ariana Fair, Dionne Lee & Marcela Pardo Ariza **NON-FICTION** Caren Beilin ▬▬▬▬▬ **EDITED BY** Justin Carder, Tara Marsden, Jacob Kahn & Lukaza Branfman-Verissimo **COVER BY** Coco Spencer.

WOLFMAN BOOKS 410 13TH ST. OAKLAND, CA
NEWLIFEQUARTERLY.COM